AMERICAN *in Russia*

AMERICAN

ILLUSTRATED

IN RUSSIA

HARRISON E. SALISBURY

HARPER & BROTHERS *Publishers* NEW YORK

For Michael and Stephan

Contents

Contents

Illustrations

For the Reader

IN THESE pages I have tried to put down something of what I saw in Russia during my years there as Moscow correspondent for *The New York Times*, together with my ideas as to the meaning and significance of what I saw.

I hope my report may help toward better understanding of the great problem of our times—Russia. But I hope, also, that no one will take this as the "last word" on Moscow and Moscow's plans and purposes. I deeply mistrust any man who suggests he has all the answers to a question so complex as Russia and I commend to everyone the wise words of my friend and one-time Moscow colleague, Paul Winterton, who said: "There are no experts on Russia—only varying degrees of ignorance."

This book, like the series of articles for *The New York Times* on which it is, in part, founded, has been written free of the pervasive effects of the Moscow censorship. Naturally, therefore, the impressions recorded here differ somewhat from those given by my dispatches. Moreover, many events in Russia require time for study and the gathering of more complete information.

One word of explanation: Every Russian whom I mention in this book exists. Every conversation which I report actually occurred and these are the words, as nearly as I remember them. But the places, persons and circumstances have been shuffled about in such a manner that, I trust, no one with whom I talked in Russia will ever be questioned by the MVD as a result of what is written here.

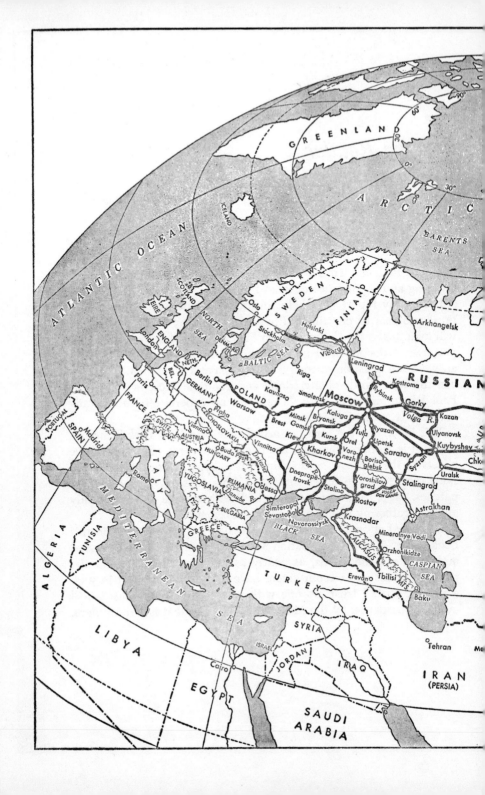

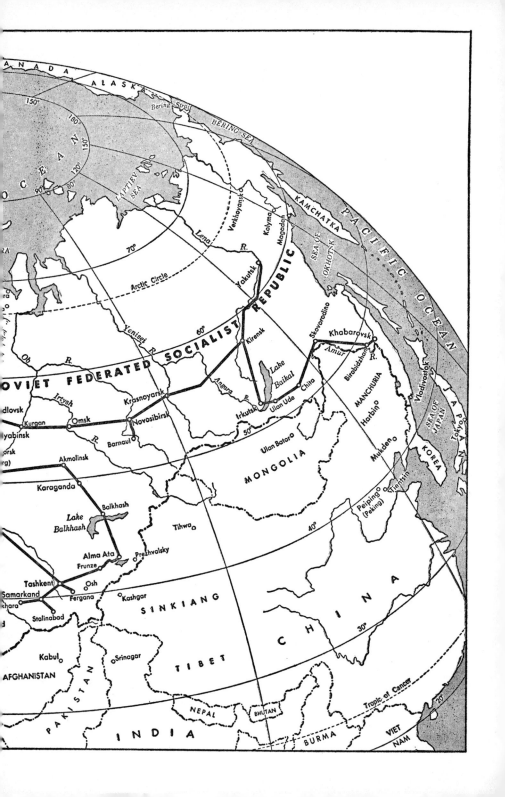

AMERICAN *in Russia*

I

The Red Arrow

THE radio in the corridor outside my compartment suddenly went dead and there was almost half a minute of silence while the train rocked along through the snowy night, and then I heard the familiar sound of the great peal of chimes in the Spassky Tower.

The bronze clamor of the chimes sounded again and again, beating into my ears like the clash of cymbals. Crash . . . crash . . . crash . . . The great bells sounded, drowning the flat-wheeled clatter of the old sleeping car in a shimmering cone of reverberation. Twelve times the chimes clanged and then the voice of the announcer cut in while the air was still vibrating: *"Govorit Moskva! Vremya Dvenatzit Chasov Nochy!"* Moscow speaking! The time is twelve o'clock midnight!

As I listened there came the full-throated chords of the Soviet national anthem. I waited until the last notes of the music had died away. Then I opened the scarred mahogany door of the compartment and looked up and down the train corridor. It was empty except for a Red Army colonel who stood idly watching out the window. Reaching up to the loudspeaker I yanked out the connecting plug, went back into my compartment and sank down in the red plush seat.

It was quiet now and there was nothing but the dead sound of the flat wheel as it turned over and over again, spanking the rail with each revolution. The train was moving steadily along at thirty miles an hour. We were somewhere south of Leningrad, Moscow-bound. The date was March 8, 1949, and the time was just after

midnight. Seldom had I felt less like sleeping. The sound of the
Spassky chimes stirred feelings deep inside me and strong memories as well. It had been five years since I had heard those chimes
—five full years, five years of welling bitterness, five years from the
seeming warmth of wartime comradeship to the chill of cold war.
Five years is a long time, time enough for friends to turn to enemies,
time for loves to cool and hatreds to burgeon. Long enough to win
a war . . . Or lose a peace.

I wondered what I might find this time in Moscow and I wondered, too, what Fate, which had with so light a fancy sent me for a
second time whirling off toward this Muscovy which I had promised
myself never again to visit, might hold in store. There was no person
in Moscow whom I looked forward to seeing, save possibly one,
and the chances of such a meeting I reckoned roughly at a million
to one. Moscow was the capital of a system of government, a scheme
of philosophy and a way of life which my possibly anarchistic and
certainly individualistic personality detested. It seemed doubtful,
indeed, that any special purpose, great or small, was going to be
served by my return to Moscow. Of course, Stalin might die and
great changes might come. But, to be more realistic, if I read the
latest signs correctly I probably should consider myself fortunate if
I just managed to stay out of serious trouble.

The optimist in me could not help hoping for something better
than mere survival. But it was a rather blind hope and I found it
hard to justify logically although, of course, the picture was not
entirely negative. For instance, there was the mere fact that I was
here, sitting in this old plush-and-mahogany compartment of the
Krasnaya Strela, the Red Arrow Express, running from Leningrad
to Moscow. That was something.

The mere fact of being in Russia, of having gotten a visa to return
to Moscow. That was a real hard fact. Just as this old Wagons-Lits
car was a hard fact. The first thing I had done when I was shown
to my compartment in the Moscow station in Leningrad was to
peek into the lavatory which I shared with the Red Army general
in the next compartment (all the passengers on the International
car were Red Army and Navy officers except a young secretary of
the Greek Embassy in Moscow and myself).

I had wanted to assure myself that the International car was of the same vintage as that on which I had made my first journey from Moscow to Leningrad, in wartime. The evidence I was seeking was there, the little brass plate which was a monument to the days before 1917 when this car was the property of and operated by the Compagnie Internationale des Wagons-Lits. Here at least was one enduring feature in an otherwise ever-changing world. It had its origin at the dawn of the century in those peaceful days when "sinful and wicked capitalists" ruled all the world. It had survived the storm and thunder of World War I. And it had come unchanged and unmarked through the fire and flame of Bolshevik Revolution. Year after year it was polished and shined. . . . Through the years of Lenin . . . of NEP . . . Trotsky . . . Stalin . . . the First Five Year Plan . . . collectivization of agriculture . . . famine . . . starvation . . . purges . . . hysteria . . . executions . . . and, finally, War again.

I had first seen it during World War II. It had survived that war and here it was tonight, burnished and clean for all to read, the little brass plate, inscribed in French with its simple but tasteful message: *Sous le lavabo se trouve une tasse.*

I chuckled to myself at my joke—an old joke, one I had laughed at in 1944, too. It was good to be laughing as we clicked off the snowy kilometers toward Moscow. It was good to be laughing in Russia. But I wondered how long it would be before I stopped laughing, before I lost my sense of proportion and no longer could see what was funny and pompous and ridiculous. That was a problem, a real one for me, as I knew from wartime. Then, my temper had worn paper thin with only eight months in Russia and during the war as well, when, as everyone insisted, relations between Americans and Russians had never been better. "The golden era" the old Russian hands among the correspondents and diplomats called it. But, even in those conditions, the red tape, the obstructions, the stupidity, the half-concealed hostility, the perennial suspicions, the spying, the surveillance, the clash of Slav and Saxon temperaments, the collision of the American spirit of "Let's get going!" with the Russian, "*Zaftra, budyet* . . . Tomorrow . . ." had been more than I could take. Not to mention the clamor and the persistence of Communist propaganda and Marxian ideology. It was like an unceasing rain that permeated everything. A child's toothbrush became a symbol of Soviet culture. A haircut was a capitalist survival (unless your neck was razor-shaved and the hair cut short and bristly). A peasant couldn't plant his sunflower seeds in springtime without scoring a victory for Socialist agriculture. On and on it went until your ears hurt and your head ached and you longed for a jackplug to yank out as I had snapped off the radio on this Red Arrow Express. But there was no jackplug and all you could do was to try to shut off your ears as some people did to commercials on the radio at home and try to avoid getting into political arguments with Party hacks and red hots.

But so long as you were in Russia there was no escaping the ideology, the propaganda, the bureaucracy and the suspicion. The only escape was to get out of the country. I could remember as clearly as yesterday my own departure from wartime Russia . . . the Russian DC-3, touching down from Moscow in the shimmering heat of a Tehran afternoon . . . stepping out on the dusty ground . . . breathing deep the crystal mountain air and saying to myself: Never again. Never will I touch foot on Soviet soil again. Never . . . never . . . never . . .

Yet, here I was sitting in the compartment of the Red Arrow, almost surrounded by baggage and boxes, headed for Moscow to reopen the bureau of *The New York Times*. There was nothing in the news to suggest that conditions were going to be better in Moscow. In fact, the latest reports were enough to make any correspondent, particularly an American, think a long time before crossing the Soviet frontier.

It was a curious situation, indeed, and it had come about in that freakish manner which so often seems to determine whether this person or that shall go to Moscow. For some months past I had been dropping in at regular intervals to talk with the late Mr. Edwin L. James, the managing editor of *The New York Times*. I was trying to persuade him to send me abroad as a correspondent for the *Times* for I was fed up with my desk work as Foreign Editor of the United Press.

Mr. James was a very remarkable executive for such a vast enterprise as *The New York Times.* No matter how much work cluttered his desk nor how many urgent matters needed attention he always had time for a chat with a foreign correspondent, either actual or potential. Thus it was that I had had a good many pleasant conversations with Mr. James without actually advancing my personal plans to any material extent. The plain truth was that the *Times* had no vacancies in its foreign staff at that particular time. One day, however, Mr. James made an offhand remark which was to have very unexpected results. He knew that I had been in Moscow during the war and now he said: "You know, Salisbury, we have been trying for eighteen months to get a correspondent into Moscow. We have kept our bureau open, hoping the Russians would give us a visa but it looks as though there's no hope."

I agreed that the chances certainly seemed very slim. I knew that the Russians had refused to give Drew Middleton a return visa when he went out on leave from Moscow and that three or four applications had been made since that time without results.

"We are going to close up the Moscow bureau this month," Mr. James said. "There doesn't seem anything else to do. You used to be in Moscow. Is there any chance the Russians would give you a visa to go back?"

I hadn't the faintest idea whether they would or not and told Mr. James this. I also told him that of all the places in the world where a foreign correspondent might work Moscow was the place in which I was least interested.

Mr. James had smiled a quizzical grin at this.

"We don't have any openings in the foreign staff," he said. "I've told you that before. But, of course, if the Russians would give us a visa for you to go to Moscow that would be quite a different matter."

So the whole thing had started. At the time it seemed like very nearly a hopeless proposition. The Russians were giving no visas to correspondents, American or otherwise and, obviously, they were nursing some very strong grievance against the *Times.* Moreover, my prejudice against going back to Moscow was so strong I could hardly bring myself even to consider the matter. However, it was apparent that it was Moscow or nothing so far as the *Times* was concerned so, after consulting a few persons whose opinions I respected, I promised Mr. James I would investigate the visa situation and report back to him.

I found the Russians pleasant-mannered and polite. They saw no reason for any objection. Of course, it was a question which only Moscow could decide.

It was all pretty vague but Mr. James decided to go ahead and a formal application was made by the *Times* for my visa. Then Mr. James had an inspiration. In the column which he always contributed to the editorial section of the Sunday *Times* he wrote an "open letter" to Generalissimo Stalin. Citing an appeal which had been made by a Russian journalist named Boris Isakov for better understanding between Russia and the United States, Mr. James said that sentiment was fine but practical steps were better. He pointed out that *The New York Times* for more than a year and a half had been trying to get a correspondent into Moscow and intimated that Moscow might give concrete evidence of its desire for better understanding by approving my visa request.

Mr. James's "open letter" appeared the day after Christmas, 1948. Toward the end of the first week in January a call came through from the Russian Embassy in Washington. Mr. Salisbury's visa was ready. When could he come and pick it up? I don't know who was more surprised, Mr. James or myself.

So it was that I sat here tonight, coming back to Moscow. Filled with plenty of doubts. Receiving the visa had not dispelled my doubts at all. In fact, they had increased. I expressed them very frankly to Mr. James. I did not know the Russian language and, despite my months in wartime Russia, I was no specialist in Russian or Soviet affairs. From all I knew of it I hated the stupidity of the Party-line approach, the blind subservience to what was called Party discipline and the immorality of Communist tactics. Communist ideology simply bored me. I had never read Marx or Lenin and hoped I never had to. I did not believe that any man or group of men had or ever would invent a perfectionist way of life or a Book of All the Answers. And if he pretended he had I disagreed with him on basic principle. I was and am an individualistic product of an individualistic society. By chance of geography I happen to come from Minnesota, which is a part of the United States where citizens do not permit anyone to dictate political or social opinions to them. Possibly by tradition but perhaps, as we like to think, because we have free and inquiring minds we Minnesotans are very likely to be "agin-ers." We vote against candidates rather than for them, against the party in power rather than for the party out of power. And the quickest way to insure our opposition is to tell us that we should, or ought or must vote or believe in a particular man or a particular philosophy. Thus, any absolute doctrine was quite incompatible with my personal character. I might manage to live for a time among Communists or Moslems but I could never become a John Reed or a T. E. Lawrence.

The fact was that on the doctrinaire side I simply knew very little about communism. I knew it was not the same as socialism but it had been a surprise to me when I had been in Moscow before to learn that the system of economics and government which was supposed to be in force in Russia at the present time was called by the Party "socialism" rather than "communism."

I had, to be sure, read a little more Russian history than most Americans because my interest had been stimulated by my war experience. I had a real interest in Russia, as opposed to communism, and still do. And I certainly knew something about Communist and Russian ways of doing business from the time I was there in 1944. But beyond this I could bring to the Russian assignment only the general qualifications of an all-around newspaperman, the product of years of hard agency training—reporting in the Midwest, in Minneapolis and Chicago, more reporting and more desk work in Washington and New York that gradually led to specialization in foreign news. I had covered Al Capone's trial in Chicago and Huey Long's assassination in Louisiana and I thought I knew newspapering inside out. And I certainly knew too much about Moscow to take on this assignment with any illusions. Even in the easier prewar days Moscow had whipped bigger and tougher correspondents than I and now the steel barrier that Mr. Churchill had christened the iron curtain had slammed down. Things were really grim and if I read the news of the past two weeks correctly they were getting grimmer fast. I had even wondered whether the green-capped frontier guards might not tell me that my visa was no longer valid.

I smiled to myself bitterly. Fine thoughts with which to enter Russia. I had been inside the iron curtain now for about fourteen hours and so far everything fitted the pattern. . . . The little argument over my books in the baggage car on the Helsinki-Leningrad train. I was bringing in half a trunk full of them. Why does the *gospodin* have so many books? That was the question of one suspicious customs examiner. And then there was the other examiner, a grimy-faced tough little Leningrad woman who spoke a smattering of English, quickly replying: "But he's a correspondent. He is a writer. Writers need many books." And, turning to me, she said: "You'll write the truth about Russia, won't you? You'll write that we don't want war. We people of Leningrad know what war is. We don't want it again."

She was earnest and intense and she touched my heart, which is soft and easily touched where Leningraders are concerned. Leningrad was the first of Russia's war-torn cities which I had seen in the winter of 1944. So long as I might live I would never forget the young girl in the Putilov Steel Works, telling of the days of the siege in the winter of 1941–42 when a million people, more or less, died in Leningrad; telling how each afternoon two or three of the strongest went out of the plant with sleds to make the rounds of apartments where their families were living, to see who was still alive and to pick up the bodies; telling how she came back one evening and glanced quickly around the room to see if all her friends were still there, and how pleased she was when she saw them all sitting, just as she had left them, and how it was not for some little time that she realized that two of those, sitting so quietly, would never move again—dead of cold and hunger in the huddled circle of the living.

And in this little customs woman there was something of the same spirit of that girl at the Putilov plant, and so I felt that while the words she spoke might be the very same words of the peace propaganda, the same words voiced on the radio and in *Pravda* so often that they had turned to meaningless clichés, when they were in her mouth I respected them. She was a Leningrader and she had earned the right to speak of war and peace and to be listened to with respect.

But, if the little customs woman had warmed my heart another experience was quickly to follow to bring back to me another side of Russia, a side I hated and detested—ox-dumb bureaucracy, blind, callous, stupid, infuriating and very nearly all-powerful.

I had hoped to stop two or three days in Leningrad, en route to Moscow, to see again what had been for me one of the most gallant and romantic cities in the world—a city like an empress dethroned, living from hand-to-mouth, condemned to shabby finery and mended gloves, but gracious still with an imperial air which no parvenu could hope to imitate. A capital without a kingdom, filled with people who walked a little straighter, who stood a little taller, who spoke a little more clearly and softly than anyone else in Russia. People who looked you in the eye when they talked.

Many people have fallen in love with Paris, and when I finally got to see it I did too. But Leningrad was my first love and now I hoped to spend a few days renewing the old romance.

It was a measure of how far I had gotten away from Russia in five years that I should even have thought that such a thing might be possible. When I told the sullen, black-haired young Intourist girl at the Astoria Hotel that I wished to spend a few days in Leningrad before going on to Moscow she looked at me as a tired kindergarten supervisor sometimes looks at a hyperactive five-year-old at the end of a long and trying day.

"You will take the train for Moscow tonight," she said, wearily. "You have a ticket on the Red Arrow Express. You will leave at 11 P.M. You will pay for the ticket, now? Yes?"

No, I said, I will not take the train. I do not want a ticket on the Red Arrow. I will not pay for the ticket, now? No! I will stay in Leningrad for two or three days. You will make the arrangements.

Of course my talk was nonsense. It was a way of wasting my breath. It was nonsense to talk about calling Moscow and asking the Press Department of the Foreign Office to arrange for me to stay. (But I did talk about that.) It was nonsense to fumble through my notebook for the name of the Mayor of Leningrad and propose to telephone him. (But I did just that.) The Intourist girl knew that nothing would come of all this. I could talk as much as I wanted to. I might rave and curse. But she knew what I would do. I would take the train for Moscow . . . tonight. I would accept the ticket . . . on the Red Arrow Express. I would leave . . . at 11 P.M. I would pay for the ticket . . . now.

She was right and here I was on the train to prove that bureaucracy is always right and that only someone who had been away from Russia for a long time or who didn't know Russia at all would talk as I talked.

Russia hadn't changed too much in five years, cold war or no cold war. Like the little brass plate on the *lavabo* the bureaucrats survived any turnover. I thought of the story they told about Vertinsky, the famous singer who spent a good many years in exile in Paris before returning to Moscow during the war. When he got off the train in Moscow he looked around him. "All the new buildings!" he exclaimed. "The new streets! There's nothing I recognize. I can't believe I'm in Moscow!"

Then he looked down at his feet where he had put his bags while he was admiring the new Moscow. The luggage had disappeared. Vertinsky breathed a sigh of relief and said to his friend: "I feel better now. They've stolen my luggage. The buildings have changed and the streets have changed. But it's still Moscow!"

I rose from my seat, switched off the light and pulled back the curtain. For a few moments, my eyes still blinded by the light, I could not see out the window but gradually it became possible to see, dimly and imperfectly. A light snow was still falling and the moving train swirled it up in small clouds along the track. Snow lay deep on the countryside and I could make out that we were passing through a not too heavily forested region of birches mixed with pine. The birches stood virginal and lovely against the snow even in the dim light. I remembered the first time I had seen these great forests of mixed birch and pine on this same train from a window of a similar compartment going to Leningrad from Moscow in wartime and how much the countryside reminded me of the north woods in my native Minnesota. The same kind of country and the same kind of trees but how different the people and how easy it was to be misled by the similarities, to give them an emphasis that was really naïve. I remembered making that mistake myself quite frequently on my first visit to Russia. It was a common mistake for Americans but just as dangerous as the complementary mistake of overemphasizing the differences in ways of life and mores.

The truth was that, even with the best of conditions, Russia was an extraordinarily difficult country to report. I thought of the plain and simple editorial statement which the *Times* had published after the Russians had given me the visa: "Mr. Salisbury's instructions . . . to get and present the news fully, accurately and without bias. He will be subject to the restrictions imposed by the Russian Government. . . . We do not expect him to have the same access to information and the same freedom. . . . He will do the best he can to give our readers a truthful and impartial picture. . . . We hope he can contribute to a better and more friendly understanding. . . ."

Straightforward, honest, sincere words. But what value would the Russians put on them?

"Everything in the Soviet Union is political." The advice had been given me by a very shrewd observer of Russia some years before and I had never seen any evidence to challenge that conclusion. Obviously, the decision to give the *Times* a visa for a correspondent was a political decision. Therefore, in itself, it should be a favorable augury for my mission. But Russian policy never followed a simple straight line. That was what so often confused people who tried to study it. Basically, Russian policy followed two lines, dialectically expressed as thesis and antithesis. On the one hand they were friendly with a given country. But behind that country's back they tried to be friendly with their "friend's" enemies, too. So, if ever the time came when Russia wanted to change her policy and stop being friends the lines were already laid for the switch. The friend, overnight, could become an enemy. The enemy, overnight, could become a friend.

This basic feature of Russian diplomatic policy (by no means unique to Moscow since Machiavelli had advised his Prince to follow it some centuries before) had been emphasized to me by the man in whose judgment on things Russian I had up to this point placed my greatest reliance, a small, very old, but still sprightly and intellectually alert Englishman named Sir Bernard Pares.

Pares was a brilliant product of the late Victorian epoch, the era
in which a certain number of the sons of upper-middle-class English
families were consciously and deliberately prepared in order that
they and their lives might be dedicated to certain countries whose
importance was paramount to Empire. It was the era which brought
forth England's most brilliant Sinologists, her amazing students of
India, her Egyptologists and Persian scholars and a few men like
Pares whose lives were tribute to Russia, its language, its history,
its culture and its people.

There was almost nothing which Pares did not know about Russia.
If he did not seem to know a certain fact it almost certainly was
because, being an old man, he had forgotten it. He had been a page
in the old Imperial Duma during the days after 1905 when Stolypin
with his land reforms tried vainly to lash the Russian troika into the
twentieth century at almost any cost. He had been a friend of Prince
Yusupov in whose palace Rasputin was murdered. He spoke of the
late Czar as "Nicky" and it was no affectation. He had addressed
mass meetings up and down Siberia, trying to rally the people
against the Bolsheviks and to stay in the World War. And he had
leaped to his feet in a box at the Bolshoi Theater in Moscow, where
he was supposedly observing a Communist Party meeting, and made
a violent speech denouncing Lenin's policy.

It was to Pares I had gone with my doubts about taking this
Moscow assignment and it was his enthusiastic moral support which
helped to make up my mind to come to Moscow.

"You must go to Moscow," he insisted. "It's a great opportunity.
They are not offering the visa just for fun. It has some meaning.
Everything in Russia has a meaning. You must go and find out what
it is."

Besides, he went on, he was sure that the "hard" policy which
Russia had followed since the end of the war was not going on
indefinitely. Sooner or later, he insisted, there would be a turn and
I should be on the spot to take advantage of it.

"They will follow this policy just so long as it appears to advantage them," he said. "Then they will change. The change can
come overnight because there is no moral basis to Russian foreign
policy, only practical considerations."

"You go to Russia," he said. "See the people. Talk to them. Your time will never be wasted."

He brushed aside my objections that I did not know the language and that, even if I did, it was no longer possible to talk to Russians, to live with a Russian family as he had done in the years just after 1900. He would have none of these arguments.

"You can learn the language while you shave in the morning," he said. "That's what I did."

And Pares, an elderly and distinguished English scholar, picked up an old piece of gray cardboard from a candy box and proceeded to rule off squares, which he filled in with Russian verb and case endings.

"There," he said. "Prop that up beside your mirror and go over it every morning when you shave. In no time you'll have the language down. Meantime, go to Russia and see what they're up to."

I wondered idly, as I prepared to take my first night's sleep in Russia in the berth of a Red Arrow compartment, what kind of reception I was going to get in Moscow.

If there had been, as I half suspected, a slight easing of tensions in the New Year's period in which my visa had been granted—a temporary fumbling about by Moscow, trying out a few moves (antithesis) designed to relieve some of the bad feelings created by the Kosenkina case and the subsequent recriminations between Moscow and Washington—the rudder of Soviet policy had apparently in the past fortnight or so been sharply swung back to the former "hard" course again (thesis).

In the time between my sailing from New York and my arrival at the Finnish-Soviet frontier at Vainikkala two events had occurred in Moscow, neither of which seemed to be a very pleasant harbinger of what might lie in store for me in the Soviet capital. The first was the arrest and expulsion from Moscow of a thoroughly disagreeable but quite fascinating American woman, Anna Louise Strong, who had spent most of her life as an active propagandist, apologist and enthusiast for the Soviet cause. Often enough, of course, Moscow had turned on its own supporters but there was something particularly ominous and foreboding about the Strong case. She was charged with trying to act as a go-between between Tito and Mao (the Russian break with Tito having occurred in the previous year) and her presence in the Soviet Union was blamed upon security lapses, occurring in the Foreign Office. The Foreign Office, it was said, had been careless in issuing visas to correspondents who turned out to be nothing more than spies and saboteurs.

This had a familiar and most unpleasant sound to my ears. I, as it happened, was the first correspondent to receive a visa from the Foreign Office after Miss Strong. Not a very good omen. And the other item of news from Moscow which I had heard on shipboard was equally disturbing. It was the announcement that a book had just been published in Moscow "exposing" the spying, war-mongering and black-marketing activities which were alleged to be taking place in the American Embassy in Moscow. The book was written by a woman named Annabelle Bucar, who had worked in the United States Information Offices in Moscow for some time and who had dramatically quit the Embassy and, presumably, her American citizenship in order to marry a rather good-looking tenor named Lapshin, who was singing in the Moscow Operetta Theater.

I had heard, previously, about Miss Bucar's defection. The book, it would appear, was the price she had to pay, perhaps quite willingly, for her romance with the star of *Silva*. It was, I gathered, a typical exposé, full of dire revelations about nefarious activities said to have been indulged in by a long list of prominent Americans, headed by the American Ambassador, General Smith.

Between the "sensations" of the Strong case and the "revelations" of the Bucar case it didn't seem as though a very hospitable atmosphere awaited me. But I would see soon enough for myself. Tomorrow I would be in Moscow. Back, once again, to the Metropole Hotel. The very thought made a shudder go up and down my back. But I felt a pang of nostalgia, too. There had been good times as well as bad in Moscow but there was not much to look forward to now, except the blank stares of men and women whose only interest and only concern was to keep their tiny bureaucratic jobs and not attract unnecessary attention.

It looked as if Moscow spelled trouble. And quite possibly danger. It was with such thoughts in my mind that I finally dropped off to sleep on the Red Arrow, my nerves finally lulled to drowsiness by the monotonous iteration of the flat wheel as it slapped again and again on the light rails of the October division of the Soviet railroad system, that first and most prized link of the Imperial Railroads between St. Petersburg and Moscow which until October 26, 1917, Old Style, was known as the "Nicholas line."

II

End in Siberia

I HAD hardly gotten settled in my room at the Hotel Metropole in March, 1949, than I heard about the arrest of Michael Borodin. It was to be several years before I would be able to piece together a fairly coherent picture of what happened to Borodin but one fact was immediately clear. The arrest of this old Bolshevik was one of the central facts of the *petite terreur* or "little terror" which I found slinking through the Moscow streets when I came back to the Metropole.

The premonition of evil which had come to me on the Red Arrow as I thought about the news of Anna Louise Strong's arrest and the publication of the Annabelle Bucar book proved more than justified. In fact the situation in Moscow was worse than I had imagined.

I had been worried about anti-American agitation and the cold war. But what I found in Moscow was something more chilling—a revival of an old and raddling Russian scourge, xenophobia, and its cousin of Polish and Czarist origin which both Hitler and Stalin used when it suited their purpose, anti-Semitism.

If the outbreak was not as bad as that of the thirties nor so terrible as what threatened later in the winter of '53 it was bad enough. It was a "little terror" and, if you study the documents which the Kremlin employed at that time, you may reach the same tentative conclusion which I ultimately came to, that, for example, the pen which wrote the indictment of Anna Louise Strong and the hand which ordered the arrest of Michael Borodin was the same which

16

four years later was to scrawl out the fantastic charges of the "Doctors' Plot."

And if I could not yet fully understand the Borodin case the implications for the future seemed ominous. The fog of suspicion and fear hung over Moscow like evening mist over a tamarack swamp. Nor was it confined to the Russians. Everyone, Russian and foreign alike, was infected to a greater or lesser degree. Even the smallest things which ordinarily would be ascribed to chance aroused suspicion in this fetid atmosphere. For example, I was given Room 393 at the Hotel Metropole, a gloomy cavernous chamber with a sagging balcony that overlooked a dark interior courtyard. To me it was just another Metropole Hotel room—dismal and depressing but somewhat cleaner and better furnished, like the hotel itself, than I would have expected in 1944. But my newspaper colleagues lifted their eyebrows when I told them. "Hummm . . ." one of them said. "Alec Werth's old room." (Werth was an English correspondent who spent some years in Russia.) "Very interesting."

"Why in heaven's name is that interesting?" I asked.

My colleague whispered in my ear. "It's all set up. . . . Saves them the trouble of putting the microphones into a new room."

Freshly arrived from the United States I snorted at this. I was determined not to be infected by the familiar Moscow phobia of seeing "little men" following me wherever I went and of worrying myself sick over microphones and dictaphones. But, long before I left Moscow I found myself remembering this incident. Because when I finally moved out of the Metropole and vacated Room 393 it was given, in succession, to three other newspaper correspondents and I couldn't help thinking that my colleague in 1949 had been more right than myself.

However, I was determined not to allow myself to fall into the state of one otherwise fairly normal American who, after undressing and going to bed each night, indulged in a five- or ten-minute monologue, largely profane. He explained to friends who questioned him about this curious custom that he delivered the nightly speech for the benefit of the men whose headphones he was certain were connected with the microphone which he believed to be installed in the wall over his bed. Nor did I desire to emulate a good-looking stenographer from Chicago who never went out on the Moscow streets alone, during a period of two years, for fear she would be "compromised." Very few Americans ever went anywhere in Moscow, even to the theater or to the stores, except in pairs, and many of them had only the vaguest idea of what the city was like. I remember giving a dinner party at the famous Georgian restaurant, the Arogvy, a couple of years after coming back to Moscow and my astonishment at learning that of the eight Americans I had invited only two had ever dined before in a Russian restaurant. An experienced diplomat who should have known better took me aside about this time and warned me that I should not trust any of my American newspaper colleagues because "we don't know which of them may be Russian agents." He took my colleagues aside and gave them similar warnings about me. The fact was that there had been a series of defections from all the major Western embassies, the American, the British and the French, which left everyone in a state of jitters.

In at least one instance this nervousness and the precautions to which it gave birth directly caused another of the defections which these extraordinary measures were supposed to prevent. And I knew other cases of individuals almost driven into the enemy camp by hysterical security precautions.

There was at this time no American Ambassador in Moscow, General Smith having gone home, preparatory to giving up his post, and no successor having been appointed. There was a great deal of talk, also, in certain American circles about leaving the ambassadorship unfilled and placing the embassy, more or less permanently, in the hands of a chargé d'affaires. Exactly what this was supposed to accomplish even its sponsors found it difficult to explain beyond, in some way, showing our resentment against the Russians. During this interim our embassy was in the hands of Foy Kohler, a very able and hard-headed career officer, but he was almost powerless to effect any improvement because the atmosphere, despite the invisible wall that had arisen between the foreign community and the Russian community, was constantly being reinfected by the tensions and suspicions which prevailed in Russia's Moscow.

Because, if foreigners were behaving in a strange and neurotic manner in Moscow, Russians were behaving in a manner even more strange and even more neurotic. We have come to regard rather neurotic behavior as more or less normal in Russia but in 1949 even I was shocked and surprised when Russians whom I had met and known quite well in 1944 looked right through me when they happened to see me on the street.

I wrote a letter to Boris Isakov, the journalist whose plea for better understanding between the United States and Russia had, it would seem, touched off the chain of events which led to my return to Moscow. He had spent some years in the United States, covering the United Nations meetings, and I had seen a good bit of him at Lake Success. He was a quiet little man who walked with a slight limp as a result of wounds received in the war. He had a couple of young sons and he knew that I did as well, and he used to say that we fathers must see to it that our sons were spared the horror of another war.

Now that I was back in Moscow, I thought certainly he is one Russian with whom I can have lunch. But I never had a reply to my letter and after I had been back in Moscow two or three weeks I understood that I had been naïve to write him. As it turned out it was five years before I ever saw Isakov, not until after Stalin was dead. We didn't have much to say to each other when the meeting finally occurred but I think we each understood what was in the other's mind pretty well. Isakov had written some pretty nasty things about America and Americans during those five years but I couldn't find it in my heart to blame him very much. After all war wasn't the only horror against which he must strive to protect his sons.

I wrote letters to other Russians, too, in the first few days after getting back to Moscow. To Ilya Ehrenbourg, the novelist, and Konstantin Simonov, the playwright, for both of whom I had done some small favors when they had been in America three years before. Actually, from the time I first met him during the war days Ilya Ehrenbourg had always seemed to me to be one of the most disagreeable personalities I had ever encountered. Simonov was almost equally objectionable. He had as inflated an idea of his own importance as any Hollywood actor and he had written a particularly obnoxious play about American newspapermen as a result of his trip to the U.S.A. However, both of them were important in their way and both owed me a little small change and I saw no reason why I shouldn't collect it. Of course, I never had any answers to my letters and both the gentlemen cut me dead on such rare occasions as I saw them. My only satisfaction was to hope that receipt of letters from an American correspondent might have caused them a few moments' unpleasantness with the security agencies.

Actually, in the nearly six years I was in Russia I received only one letter from a Soviet citizen outside of a few business communications which the telegraph authorities simply had to write.

This was a letter from the late Maxim Litvinov which he sent me in April, 1950, in reply to my suggestion that he might write for *The New York Times* a brief memoir of the late President Roosevelt, based on the conversations they had at the time U.S. recognition of the Soviet regime was negotiated.

Not knowing where Litvinov was—in fact, not knowing, for certain, whether he was alive or dead—I sent my letter to him through the Soviet Foreign Office with a request that it be forwarded. Three days later the reply, by ordinary Russian mail, rather poorly typed in English on a sheet of plain notepaper, was in my hands. Mr. Litvinov thanked me for the proposal and regretted that his poor health prevented him from doing any writing.

It was obvious that he had dictated his reply to his wife, an Englishwoman whose name was Ivy Low before she married Litvinov. And it was typical of the Westernized mind and manners of Litvinov that he alone of all the Russians to whom I sent notes in my nearly six years in Moscow had the courtesy and grace to send me a reply.

And it was equally typical of the Stalin regime that when two years later Litvinov died this man who had fought with skill and courage for the Soviet regime and, after all, for Stalin, on many a vital diplomatic battleground and who, perhaps, had done more than any other single individual to win confidence and friends for Soviet Russia in the West was given a third-class funeral, attended by not a single Soviet official or personage of any consequence except Gromyko, who was assigned by his chiefs to represent the Foreign Office.

MOSCOW.

9th April,1950.

Mr.Harrison Salisbury ,
Hotel Metropole,Moscow.

My dear Mr.Salisbury ,

    I have received your letter of
April 6th, transmitted to me by the Ministry of
Foreign Affairs, in which you suggest that I write
a memoir of the late President Roosevelt , on the
occasion of the fifth anniversary of his death.

    I regret being prevented
by indisposition from complying with this request,
which otherwise I should be glad to do.

    Yours truly,

Letter from Maxim Litvinov, April 9, 1950

Anticipating this churlish conduct I suggested to a number of Western diplomats, including the Americans, that the occasion provided a unique opportunity to teach these iron-faced Stalinists a lesson in manners and morals and, in a quiet way, to show that it was possible to respect a man for his service to his country without agreeing, for a moment, with that nation's policy or principles. I proposed that the Western diplomats attend the Litvinov funeral and send the appropriate wreaths, just as they would attend the funeral and send the appropriate wreaths if, in Paris or London or Washington, a senior statesman and former secretary of foreign affairs should die.

Unfortunately, my diplomatic friends proved incapable of rising very much above the level of manners of the country to which they were accredited. Several thought it was a good idea. But they couldn't get together quickly enough to do anything. The Americans were coolest of all and horrified at the thought of doing anything so extraordinary as going to a man's funeral without first getting instructions from Washington.

So, as it turned out, Max Litvinov's body was carted down the staircase of the dingy old Russian Foreign Office by some clerks and a few strong-backed soldiers. There was Gromyko present, looking pained and uncomfortable. Ivy Low and her son and daughter, looking grieved and a little too firm-lipped. There were half a dozen wreaths, including one from the Swedish Ambassador. But no diplomats. And no foreigners except myself. *Sic transit* . . . Russian-style, 1950.

Why was the atmosphere so grim and fear-ridden in Moscow during 1948 and 1949? I sought in vain for the full answer in the weeks after I got back to the Russian capital. One correspondent who had spent more than ten years in Russia believed that the essential cause was the shock of Tito's defection. "Nothing like that has happened before," he said. "It has given the Kremlin the jitters." But what had that to do with the revival of anti-Semitism which, under the guise of a campaign against "cosmopolitanism" among literary critics, was cutting a fresh swath through the Moscow intelligentsia? In the weeks just before my return one blow after another had been struck at the Jews. The Jewish theater and the

Jewish newspaper in Moscow were closed down. The Jewish publishing house was shut. The Jewish anti-Fascist committee was
dissolved. Jewish cultural institutions, newspapers and theaters in
Minsk, a great center of Jewish population, had been shut. There
were reports of Jews being shipped east from Odessa and other
Black Sea regions—reports which I was later able, partially, to verify
when I visited Odessa, but reports which, like so many things in
rumor-ridden Moscow, had been badly exaggerated. Jewish professors were quietly being dropped from their university posts.
Many Jewish writers, including a number who long since had
adopted Russian names, found that editors no longer desired their
contributions, and critical articles appeared in the press, attacking
persons who hid their true identity under pen names and giving
lists of such Jewish writers.

The correspondents in Moscow had been almost completely defeated by the censorship in their efforts to make plain that "anti-
cosmopolitan" was virtually a synonym for "anti-Semitic." But if
the listing of names in the papers was not enough to make the point
clear the satirical weekly *Krokodil* came out with a savage cartoon
against the "homeless cosmopolite," who was depicted with the
traditional hooked nose classically associated with Semites.

One Jewish acquaintance who was desperately trying to convince
himself that these phenomena really were not anti-Semitic blamed
the whole thing on Mrs. Golda Myerson, the first Israeli Minister to
Russia. Her arrival in the Metropole Hotel had touched off unprecedented manifestations. Hundreds if not thousands of Jews, not
only from Moscow but from other Russian cities, came to the
Metropole to pay their respects. Many came, actually, to inquire
about emigrating to Israel. Some days there were long queues of
people outside the temporary Israeli offices, in a Metropole Hotel
suite.

"Mrs. Myerson should not have permitted it," this man said. "Naturally, the Soviet government could not allow such a thing, especially in the heart of Moscow. And it was bound to frighten the
Kremlin—the sight of such open sympathy for a foreign state. It is
all Mrs. Myerson's fault. If she had been more tactful nothing would
have happened."

While there was a germ of common sense in what this man said, since anyone who knew Russia could hardly have failed to foresee that the government would not put up with such manifestations on the part of any minority group, this was a dubious excuse indeed for the wholesale drive against Jews which was now in progress. About all one could say in extenuation was that it was not so bad as Hitler's campaigns. Jews were not being shot or executed. They were being deprived of jobs, important and prominent jobs, but they were free to work in less rewarding capacities. They were in some regions being uprooted in considerable numbers and shipped off to other areas but no more brutality was being shown them than was usual in such population transfers, and if they starved or died of cold or disease it was not due to design but simply to graft, stupidity, inefficiency or indifference, born in the fact that they were people and not some valuable state property such as cattle.

And the Jews could not say they were the only minority race against which special measures were being taken, because in a methodical, bureaucratic way all kinds of small population groups which were judged, for one reason or another, to present some security problem were being chivvied and harried and, in many cases, being resettled out in Siberia, the Far East and Central Asia.

It was some years before I was able to make a first-hand inquiry into the results of all this chivvying. But eventually I was to do so. The picture was not a pleasant one, but not perhaps, by the everyday standards of Russian life, quite as bad as some of the more imaginative propaganda had by that time caused people to suppose.

When you considered the intensity of xenophobia in Moscow in the winter of 1949, the force of the campaign against the Jews, the heightened security precautions against any elements suspected to be in the slightest way unstable, the obvious concern in the Kremlin at Tito's defection and the growing anti-Americanism, it does not seem too surprising that Soviet security agents finally moved in on Michael Borodin, on the Moscow *Daily News,* on Anna Louise Strong, and not a few other individuals.

I don't think that anyone who was brought up on Vincent Sheean's *Personal History* and the stories of Rayna and Bill Prohme and the

Chinese Revolution of 1923–25 could ever forget Michael Borodin. He was the very figure of Revolution incarnate—a fiery orator capable of stirring crowds to storm the barricades, a midnight plotter of assassinations, a genius of disguise.

Certainly I never forgot the picture Sheean painted and I remember gawking like a schoolboy when a tall, gaunt, rather seedy man was pointed out to me, going into the press gallery at the Great Kremlin Palace in 1944 for a meeting of the Supreme Soviet. "That's Borodin," a Russian whispered. "Do you want to meet him?"

I did. Lenin and Stalin might have been greater revolutionists but, knowing my Sheean, I doubted it.

I did not for a moment believe that this man was guilty of treachery to the Communist cause. But as I studied the case I came to realize that, implausible as it might seem that Borodin or Miss Strong or the others could have been linked with Tito, or with any attempt to subvert Mao, or with any kind of maneuver or plot directed against Stalin or the Soviet regime, these people did have certain internal contacts which were of just such a kind as to arouse the suspicions of any persecution-deluded mind.

Miss Strong, by this time a rather elderly and highly opinionated American woman who once had been a starry-eyed I.W.W. supporter from Seattle, was actually the founder of the Moscow *Daily News*. She was an old and close friend of Borodin who, having failed to pull off the Chinese Revolution, was at the time the *News* was founded in 1930 occupying a sort of job-on-the-shelf, running the Soviet paper-pulp industry.

Later, Miss Strong, who, for all her Communist sympathies and left-wing enthusiasms, was much too apt to go off at tangents ever really to fit into the bureaucracy which Soviet communism had become, found herself eased out of the Moscow *News* editorship and Borodin took it over.

Although Borodin never returned to China after he had to flee when Chiang turned turtle on his Communist sponsors he continued to follow developments in the Far East with close interest and attention. He was supposed to be one of the main hands, in the strategy field, for the old Comintern so far as the Far East was concerned. I have heard, and I am inclined to believe it, that

Borodin privately was sometimes at odds with Stalin on Far Eastern questions but there was no evidence Borodin had ever sought to press his position. He was too disciplined a Bolshevik for that. (Stalin virtually abandoned revolution in the Far East after the fiasco of the twenties and, following a purely empirical policy, supported the Kuomintang nationalists.)

Miss Strong, whose enthusiasms in the thirties had begun to shift from Russia to the Communist China of the Long March, of Mao and of Chou, had spent a great deal of time with the Chinese Communists. She had actually devoted herself much more in recent years to China than to Russia, and she was on intimate personal terms with the Chinese Communist leaders. She had a son and a daughter in Moscow, born in her Moscow *News* days when she was married to a Russian, and it was her custom, en route to and from China, to stop off in Moscow and spend some time with them and also with Borodin.

There was, it should be emphasized, nothing secret about this. In fact it is most difficult to imagine anything being secret in connection with Miss Strong because she insisted on talking about nothing but her own affairs and usually at the top of a voice that was not only loud but peculiarly penetrating.

On this visit to Moscow, which proved to be her last and which may well have spelled Borodin's downfall and the wrecking of what remained of Moscow *News* as well, Miss Strong was, as usual, en route to the Far East. She wanted to accompany Mao and Chou in the final phase of taking over all of China and, as usual, she paused in Moscow to see Borodin and her other old friends and to arrange for her plane flight east across Siberia. All might still have been well, although in Moscow's mood of that time even this seems dubious, had not Miss Strong sometime previously paid a visit to Tito, who was in the process of the famous break with Moscow.

If one adds to this concatenation of forces the fact that Borodin was a Jew and that both Borodin and Miss Strong really represented a survival of these international revolutionary elements which Stalin had almost completely managed to exterminate during the thirties, what happened in February, 1949, becomes quite explainable.

Miss Strong was arrested one night at the home of her daughter and carted off to the Lubiyanka. After a cursory examination which lasted only two or three days she was ordered expelled from the U.S.S.R. and a statement was issued, denouncing her as a long-term agent of the United States intelligence services, a Titoite spy, a wrecker, diversionist, and all the other things which are customary to say in Moscow on such occasions. How sudden, unexpected and unfounded were these accusations may be deduced from the fact that the American Communist newspaper, the New York *Daily Worker*, was serializing some articles of Miss Strong's, one of which appeared the very morning of Moscow's announcement that she was a spy, wrecker, etc.

At the same time, with no fanfare and no publicity but with an accompaniment of rumor which sent a chill through that small demi-colony of Muscovites who still had some kind of association, usually through the nature of their work, with foreigners, the security forces moved in on Moscow *News*. Borodin and some of the principal editors were arrested. The paper was closed without a word. The staff was dismissed after undergoing questioning which, in some cases, went on intermittently for months. Some of the paper's writers found themselves unable to get jobs, even a year or two after being given a clean slate, so fearful were the editors of other newspapers, publishing houses and the like to give employment to anyone who had been associated with so dangerous a case.

If one liked to daydream he might conjure up a kind of Alfred Hitchcock scenario about Borodin. . . . About a spare, dry, lanky-framed man who worked, year after year, doing the dullest party-hack writing—but only as a cover for a painfully intricate plot . . . a scenario about a man who hated Stalin with a deadly hatred born in the days when China's Revolution was betrayed . . . a story of a man who swore vengeance in those bloody days of Hankow and who plotted, year after year, against the Kremlin . . . a story in which the vocative Miss Strong was cast in the role of a pawn in machinations which reached from Belgrade, Tel Aviv and Washington all the way east to Peiping. . . .

A fascinating plot for a movie . . . But what is far more fascinating is the fact that there is good reason to believe that this story, or something very much like it, is exactly what the Kremlin charged Borodin with doing.

Did Stalin really believe that the old revolutionary Borodin, the man who had joined the Bolshevik party in 1903, who had been treasurer of the Society for Aid to Russian Political Prisoners before World War I, a man whom Lenin had called back to Russia in the summer of 1917 from Chicago, who had tried to foment revolution in Scotland during the early twenties and had succeeded in bringing on revolution in China a few years later—did Stalin really believe that this veteran Bolshevik was plotting against him?

I can't say for certain. Stalin, in his completely cynical way, may merely have been taking out a bit more insurance for the internal stability of the regime; carrying out one more object lesson to demonstrate to his subjects the danger of any kind of contacts with foreigners. The object-lesson theory would seem to be supported by some facts. Miss Strong was arrested but she was quickly released and expelled from the country. She was not, like most persons who are accused in Russia of espionage for a foreign power, condemned to death or given a long prison sentence.

Exactly what happened to Borodin I did not learn for some time. There was never any public announcement of his arrest or sentence, but some years later I was told that Mao Tse-tung, himself, intervened with a plea for mercy for Borodin. Perhaps this is why Stalin ordered him sent to prison exile in eastern Siberia to face the prospect of a lingering death instead of giving him a quick pistol shot in the back of the head. Perhaps this was Stalin's idea of "mercy." I do not know and it was not until early fall, 1953, that I heard anything more about the case.

I had happened to encounter one of the few individuals whom I know who has succeeded over the past decade in precariously maintaining one foot in the Russian camp and at least a tiny toehold in the Western. We stopped as we usually did for a few minutes' small talk and he said: "Don't you think Michael Borodin deserves an obituary in *The New York Times?*"

Indeed he does, I replied, but I hadn't heard of his death. Well, said my acquaintance, he's dead all right. He died out in Siberia a few months ago . . . just a little too soon.

Just a little too soon . . . How true that was. For there was hardly any doubt that if Michael Borodin had lived a little longer he would have lived much longer. A paradox, but like so many Russian paradoxes a perfectly true one.

A little too soon . . . And yet it seemed to me there was something of the perfection of classic tragedy about Borodin's death in Siberia. When had it happened? No one knew precisely. But it must have been late 1952 or early 1953.

How amazing, I thought, is Russian life in its ability to imitate art. No one who has read Dostoievsky or Tolstoy or Chekhov is ever lost for long in Russia because very quickly you will see something or something will happen which comes right out of the pages of *The Brothers Karamazov, Anna Karenina* or *The Cherry Orchard.*

But what I had always been reluctant to admit was that Soviet life also had an uncanny way of presenting itself in terms even more melodramatic than those used by Koestler or Kafka or even Orwell. I had always found Koestler a little too adolescent and Kafka too mystic and Orwell's work rather more tours de force than genuine social criticism.

Yet, the fact was that Soviet life had an uncanny tendency to imitate the more maudlin passages of Koestler, the cloudiest flights of Kafka and the more obscene parodies of Orwell.

And here was Borodin's life to provide one more example.

He had been, perhaps, a little too soon, a little too early with his revolutionary plans and devices for China, but his failure there was not of his own making; it was the product of natural forces, possibly assisted by Stalin's own blunders which, doubtless, grew out of the exigencies of his quarrel with Trotsky. Yet, whatever the cause, Borodin had served the Revolution and its Russian masters to the best of his ability. When failure had come he had once more obeyed orders and returned to Moscow. Whatever he may have felt personally he had gone on serving the Kremlin, his feet plodding the dull treadmill, day after day and year after year.

Then, finally, as he approached the age when any man may begin to look forward to honorable retirement and possibly even a nook in an Old Bolshevik's Home, came the bolt from the blue, the mid-

night rap on the door, the hurried trip to the Lubiyanka, the inter-
rogations . . . Siberia.

But still he was tough, this Old Bolshevik. He managed to survive
one year of life in the camp. He survived a second year. What did
he think of in those years? How did he sustain his life? In what did
he believe and in what did he hope? I don't know. I've seen the
country of the camps, the abomination on the earth's surface that
is called eastern Siberia. I know what kind of a life Michael Borodin
endured that first year and the second year as well. I don't know
where hope comes from in such a life, and yet certainly without
hope you cannot live very long in eastern Siberia. There were his
memories, I suppose. And surely his pride, for you had only to see
him to know that he was a tough and stubborn man. He lived
through '51, as well. By now he was sixty-eight or sixty-nine and
sometime, possibly late in '52, possibly early in '53 the end came
to Michael Borodin. It is hard to say what may have happened.
Possibly word reached the camp of the curious events of the Nineteenth Party Congress and he saw in them the extinction of
any possibility of reprieve. Or he may have lived long enough to
hear of the Doctors' Plot and to have understood from its macabre
terms that there was no hope. No one will ever know exactly what
killed Borodin, but one thing is very certain. Had he lived past the
date of March 5, 1953, he would in all probability be alive today.
Because one of the first things which the men who succeeded Stalin
decided to do was to comb through the camps and the prisons and
release the Old Bolsheviks who were still to be found moldering
there.

If Michael Borodin had still been alive on March 5, 1953, he would
have paid a visit to the Kremlin sometime in the course of 1954 to
be decorated with the Order of Lenin by President Voroshilov, his
old friend. Because in 1954 Borodin would have celebrated his
seventieth birthday and the new rulers of the Kremlin have established the custom of giving to such Old Bolsheviks as survive a
medal, a visit to the Kremlin and a paragraph or two in *Pravda* on
whatever quintenary birthday happens to remain to them—their
seventieth, their seventy-fifth or eightieth.

III

A Chance Meeting

IT WAS one of those sun-drenched afternoons of mid-May in Moscow when suddenly you look out the window and everything is golden and blue and green and the grim, gray ugliness of winter seems to have vanished by the conjuring trick of a great magician only half an hour before.

Every day since I had arrived in Moscow in March, 1949, I had looked out of my office window into Sverdlov Square and watched a gang of women who were half-heartedly tearing up the asphalt and building a new park just outside the Metropole Hotel. It was an unlovely and rather depressing sight to see them shovel and dig while two or three male bosses stood by.

Two months had passed and today when I looked down at the square all was changed. The women had thrown off their heavy cotton-padded gray jackets and their clumsy *valenki* or felt boots. Today they wore bright pink calico prints with clean white kerchiefs on their heads. Their hips and shanks moved rhythmically as they spaded the earth and their great breasts swelled and burst against stout brassières. No longer were they gray, faceless animals of work. At a stroke they had become women, full of the juice and taste of life, with rosy cheeks and sparkling eyes. Like the Russian soil which each year is born again after the long Russian winter so had these worker women suddenly come alive. When I opened my window I could hear their chaffing and shouting as they laughed and joked and I could hardly count the number of "supervisors" who had suddenly appeared on the scene and who made no secret of their admiration for these newly revealed feminine charms.

In a word, it was the day that spring had arrived in Moscow— the short, hot, panting Moscow spring which is more of a mood and a moment than a season—something like a vivid exclamation point which seems to be slipped in, almost by accident, between the nearly nine long months of winter and the three brief months of summer.

With the hot sun drenching the office it was quite impossible to struggle through any more paragraphs of the *Literary Gazette*'s dreary effort to define again the nature of "Soviet man" and the duties and obligations of the Soviet writer, the "architect of human souls." Not even a new diatribe against the "homeless men without passports," critics and writers named Finklestein and Cohen and Goldenberg whose sins of "cosmopolitanism" had just come to light, was able to hold my nose to the grindstone. Comforting myself with the thought that every word which the *Literary Gazette* was saying had been said, not just once but many times before, I decided to abandon myself to the mood of spring.

I left the hotel and walked through the hot sunshine around the periphery of Sverdlov Square under the old wall which once sur- rounded the miscalled Kitai Gorod (Chinese City) and into the statue-strewn Revolutionary Place subway station. I paid my fifty kopeks for a ticket and, my eyes dreamy, took a place on the long escalator and rode down to the train level. I had no very clear idea in my mind as to where I would go but I knew I wanted to get a long way from the Metropole Hotel. As far as possible, in fact.

As I stood waiting for a train, my eyes idly resting on the bowed backs of the sculptured figures of soldiers and workers which had always struck me as so symbolic, it occurred to me that there actu- ally was a place where I wanted to go—Sokolniki Park, one of the old imperial parks on the northeast outskirts of the city. It was a big, largely undeveloped piece of countryside, quite unspoiled and barren of the Soviet monuments of "rest" or "culture" which cluttered the landscape of most Moscow parks.

Walking through the underpass to the adjacent Hunters' Row subway station I boarded my train and began to think about the last time I had been in Sokolniki. It had been five years back—in the summer of 1944, during my wartime months in Moscow—and I had gone there with Galya, a tall, beautiful and rather sad-faced Russian girl. We thought we were in love and possibly we were too, in the sudden, hasty, snatching way of wartime romance. In any event it had been a warm and pleasant time, heavy with the bitter-sweet feelings of two people who really want, very much, to believe that they are in love and who know, very well, that they are quickly to be separated.

That was the way it had been on one summer's day when we had come out to Sokolniki. We had come early and the grass was still damp from a very heavy dew but it grew hot as we walked and walked, endlessly and with very few words, across the open fields and the small forested hills of the park. Finally, we had found a spot in the shade on a hillside and sat there awhile, looking into each other's eyes and holding hands.

Thinking of those times as the subway clattered endlessly forward I easily understood how, on the first hot day of Moscow spring, the vague stirrings inside me had brought to the surface, first, the sudden urge to go to Sokolniki and, now, these reminiscences. The excursion to Sokolniki had been the last free time Galya and I had had together—free that is, of tragedy and grief. Almost immediately afterward I had received instructions from my office to leave Moscow and return to America. Then, in the very same week there had been another and more serious blow. Galya's brother, a brilliant and merry youngster on whom all her mother's love and aspirations had centered since the death of her husband in the purge years of the thirties, was killed at the front. It was a blow of incredible sharpness since the boy had actually been home on leave (a very great rarity in Russia) only a few weeks previously and his mother and sister had taken this as a sure sign that he would, after all, survive the war. Moreover, he had been told that soon he was to return to Moscow to enter a special training school. And now the worst had happened. Galya's mother simply lost her mind when she read the plain buff postcard on which the government notice was written—simply and completely. Galya, herself, was not much better although the necessity of holding together in order to care for her mother helped a bit. I remembered one of the worst moments.

Since I had been leaving I had given Galya my good winter boots
for her brother. But, of course, there had not been time to send
them off. One evening she came to me and gave me back the boots,
saying: "You can have back your old boots. We won't be needing
them now. Perhaps, you can sell them in the market." Then she
started to cry with the silent almost tearless crying of grief in which
there is no hope and no remorse, the grief which is beyond words
and beyond comfort.

With such thoughts in my head I finally arrived at Sokolniki and
clambered up the steps and out into the hot almost cloying air of
spring. My heart was heavy as I paid the one ruble admission fee
and entered the cracking concrete archway of the Park. After walking some distance down the main *allée* I struck off across an open hill,
trying vaguely to recall just where I had walked with Galya. Not
that I cared particularly, but I wanted to shift my thoughts from sad
and painful emotions to the simple recall of landmarks. It was a
futile struggle and finally I gave in to the mood of sentimental melancholy and sat down on a lonely park bench that overlooked a
small glade of white birches.

The longer I sat and thought the more sharply I began to question my wisdom in returning to Moscow, so cold and unfriendly
seemed the mood of the city. Perhaps it was not quite so dangerous
as it first appeared when I arrived, but the Strong, the Bucar, the
Borodin incidents; the creeping anti-Semitism; and certain other
symptoms which even now I think it more discreet not to record
here were not calculated to build confidence.

I thought of the vast difference between my life in Moscow in
1944 and my life in 1949. I had now been here more than three
months. I had made no Russian friends. I had met some of my old
Russian friends in the streets. But not one had spoken with me.
Such impressions and pictures as I had of Russian life were almost
entirely secondhand. True, I walked the streets of Moscow. I went
to the shops, to the restaurants, to the theaters and to the movies. I
knew, as everyone knew, that Russian life, in a material way, had
improved a great deal since wartime days. When I had been here
during the war there were practically no shops, of any kind, operating in Moscow. Public restaurants, the first two or three, reopened

only in the summer of 1944. Food was still so short, even in Moscow, that correspondents saved every scrap of bread, butter, cheese or other leftovers to give to their friends and employees who only had second-class ration cards (correspondents and diplomats were among the privileged first-class card holders).

Today, there were almost as many restaurants as before the war. Rationing was a thing of the past. The menus were still expensive but nourishing, if dull. There were plenty of shortages still in consumers goods, as the queues four blocks long around the Mostorg Department Store for oilcloth or enamel teapots attested. But oilcloth and teapots were to be had.

I only had to look at the people to see that they were much better dressed, even if they still looked drab and colorless by Western standards. And it was easy to judge by the quality of old clothes and shoes offered for sale in the market that a vast improvement from the wartime days had occurred.

While it seemed equally obvious that Moscow citizens were more crowded than ever in the slum quarters that passed for housing, I really had no firsthand evidence of this because I had not been inside a Russian home or even a Russian apartment house.

Yet, in general, I could testify that materially the Russians were much better off than five years before. But, spiritually, what was there to say? The pages of that ledger were largely blank, which was in itself a striking commentary on the changed times.

How vastly different it had been in 1944. Then there was not enough food for anyone. Russian girls frankly gave themselves to foreign men for a bar of soap. Soap was a precious article. A warm bath was a luxury beyond dreams. A pair of shoes cost a whole *sumka* (handbag) full of rubles. Old copies of *Pravda* sold for ten rubles a copy in the market, to be used for rolling cigarettes or a dozen other purposes. People were often cold, oftener hungry and many times miserable. The suffering was real and it was general.

But there was something which made up for the hardships, or went a long way toward making up for them. There were friendship and comradeship and warmth of spirit, which are qualities which no Celsius thermometer yet made can accurately measure. (If I now wondered at times about the sincerity and depth of some of those friendships at least at the time they had seemed most genuine.)

I thought about my first weeks in the Metropole Hotel in 1944 as contrasted with the first weeks in 1949. In wartime the grim and gloomy old hostelry had bulged with roistering and friendly newspapermen. There were twenty or thirty Americans and Englishmen alone and many other foreigners too. It was a poor night, indeed, when a party was not in progress in someone's rooms and usually there were several to choose from. And the guests were not just foreigners. There were as many Russians as foreigners and often more. And not just party girls, attracted by the excitement of meeting foreigners, the chance of food and drink, a bath or a warm bed to sleep in. While I had, it is true, heard in those times a Russian say that no respectable Soviet citizen would permit himself to enter the Metropole, that was obviously pure snobbery. Because the day did not pass when well-known Russian artists and writers and singers, famous Party propagandists, proud holders of the Order of Lenin or the Order of the Red Banner of Labor, Red Army colonels and generals, scientists and publicists, playwrights and ballerinas, did not enter the Metropole. And not only did they enter the hotel, they visited the foreign correspondents in their rooms and sat around drinking vodka or, sometimes, "American wine" as they fancifully called bourbon whisky, arguing about the war, the second front or the latest Deanna Durbin movie.

Within a month of arriving in Moscow in 1944 I knew a great many more Russians than I could remember the names of. Galya and I had met at a party given by another American within the first week of my arrival in Russia. Before a month was out we were in love, or thought we were, and my great problem was not meeting more Russians but avoiding such meetings so that I would have more time free with Galya.

How completely different I found life in Russia now. Then I had awakened every morning with a sense of excitement and thrill, wondering what the new day would bring in this strange and fascinating Russian world—a quick trip to the south where Red Army troops had just liberated the Crimea from the Germans; a long walk through the pine forests with Galya; an excursion to an old monastery on Moscow's outskirts—with Galya; a visit to a little gypsy restaurant across the Moscow river—with Galya.

I laughed a little to myself. How often those sentences ended with the words "with Galya." In this particular mood of sentiment or sentimentality it seemed as though the chief difference between the Russia of 1944 and the Russia of 1949 was Galya, or rather the absence of Galya. And, of course, it was quite true that from the moment I had known I was returning to Russia the thought of her crept into my mind, and particularly the thought that somehow, somewhere, sometime we might meet again.

It was, of course, a romantic and unsensible thought. And if we were to meet it would probably be one more bitter and rude occasion. I could see her walking down the street toward me and me starting to greet her and her walking on past me with a fixed stare and unseeing eyes and only the faintest tremor of her long upper lip to show that she had noticed me. She, naturally, was the one person in all of Russia whom I really wanted to see again and she, I somehow knew as I sat there in the golden sunshine of the spring afternoon, watching the light catch the pure white of the birches and sparkle on the incredibly tender green of the first leaves, was the one person of all whom I had known before in Russia whom I would never meet again. If I lived on in Moscow, God forbid, for fifty years I would not see her. Not that I had any feeling that she was dead. To the contrary she seemed most alive to me. I did not even have to close my eyes to see her walking with her long, lean, somehow un-Russian gait down the path in front of me. She was not there and she never would be there but I could imagine one missed meeting after another, year upon year. She walking down one street and I, pace by pace, walking down the next one, neither of us knowing that the other was only a hundred steps away but each perhaps feeling a passing agitation, the source of which we could not imagine. I could see her on this very afternoon, sitting in the sunshine on a park bench, in another park, miles away from Sokolniki, and thinking about our times together. I could see her on a railroad train whirling past a small suburban station where I stood on the platform and each of us getting a sudden quick glimpse of the other, but so sudden and so quick that to the end of our days we never could quite

be sure whether we had seen each other or whether it was a trick
of false recognition.

So it was, I thought, and so it would be. And while it might gratify
some deep melancholic impulse within me to spend this spring afternoon with gloomy and bitter thoughts of the past I was simply
twisting the whole picture of Moscow out of context if I pretended,
even for a moment, that the big difference between the two times
and the two cities was in Galya's presence or absence.

At best it merely symbolized a whole complex of changes which
had occurred and which foreigners in Moscow were beginning to
call the "deep freeze"—the complete severance of any kind of
ordinary human relations between Russians and foreigners which,
in turn, simply reflected the impressive xenophobia of the Soviet
government and the degree to which they had made it plain to all
Russians that the most certain, if not the quickest, way to obtain a
one-way ticket to Siberia or places even more distant lay in having
anything to do with a foreigner.

There were some apparent exceptions to this rule—but a little
study showed that they were more apparent than real. For instance,
there were still three or four Russian women working as secretaries
and translators for foreign correspondents. And there were a handful
of chauffeurs and other workers employed by the correspondents,
just as there were a small number working for the foreign embassies.
But a week did not pass in which some member of this little group
did not slip away—either quitting his or her job, often because of
open intimidation by the police, or suddenly being arrested for some
obscure cause but actually of course, simply because of working for
a foreigner.

In place of the twenty or thirty Western correspondents of the
wartime period there were now only seven representing American
and British papers and agencies. And two of these, I knew, were soon
to leave Moscow. They and the newspapers they represented were
completely discouraged by the handicaps and hardships of attempt-
ing to cover Moscow under "deep freeze" conditions—the absence
of both casual and official contact with Russians (a new State Secrets
Act had recently been imposed which was so strict that it could be
interpreted as forbidding a telephone operator from giving the cor-

rect time to an inquiring foreigner), the harsh and erratic censorship which often killed even dispatches which did little more than quote from a *Pravda* article, the deep atmosphere of suspicion and surveillance which inevitably had affected foreigners as well as Russians—small wonder that, when these circumstances were coupled with sharply rising costs due to an artificial and prestige-seeking exchange rate, such sound newspapers as the *Christian Science Monitor* and the New York *Herald Tribune* began to question the desirability of further maintaining their bureaus in Moscow.

I had been, I knew, extremely fortunate in persuading the Russian wife of one of my newspaper colleagues to work for me as a secretary-translator. Even at this time it was quite apparent that this was a dying profession and I recognized that eventually and probably sooner rather than later I had better place myself in a position to read the Russian press myself since the time was sure to come when, unless things radically changed, it would be impossible to persuade any Russian to work for a foreigner, and particularly for an American correspondent.

Acting on the basis of this analysis—reinforced by my very deep conviction that in Russia of all countries it is only possible to do an adequate and objective and reliable job of coverage if the correspondent, himself, is able to read the original news sources; to understand the language well enough to carry on at least simple conversations with the people; and to gain, at first hand, some knowledge of Russian life and literature and history—I had already started to learn Russian. Although it was to be nearly three years before my rough and ready efforts—concentrated initially on one task, to instruct myself well enough to read *Pravda*—bore sufficient fruit so that I felt I could trust myself to operate without Russian secretarial assistance, it was undoubtedly one of the soundest decisions of my nearly six years in Russia.

For, as I had anticipated, the time did come in the year or so before Stalin's death when not a single Russian secretary-translator remained to work with the five (at one time four) Western correspondents who stood by their posts in the very worst years of the cold war.

If, indeed, sitting on the park bench at Sokolniki, I had been able to envisage the full coldness and the full loneliness and the accompanying deep but constant feeling of fear which was to become the ordinary condition of life and work in Moscow, it is truly doubtful that, for all the Welsh stubbornness in my blood, I myself would have stuck it out. There are times when blindness or inability fully to see the future is a most fortunate thing.

I suppose that I must have sat for an hour or two on that bench in the park, so lost in my thoughts that I was hardly aware of my surroundings. I was not, of course, alone in the park. There were, some distance away, a few old *babushki*, looking after their children, and occasionally a pair of youngsters, holding hands, would stroll by. But of this I was largely oblivious. In fact, it was not until the sun was suddenly cut off by the hill and long dark shadows started back over the meadow toward me that, feeling the quick chill in the air, I roused from my reverie. It has been almost six when I got to the park and now it was time that I ran along.

Walking slowly back along the powdered red-brick surface of the path I felt a deep melancholy. I was lonely and frankly depressed. As I strolled back toward the Metro station I noticed, off to the right, a big, old dilapidated cathedral and what appeared to be a long queue of people waiting to enter it. The queue ran all the way around the church and doubled back to the street. This struck me as strange and I went over to investigate. I found a rather curious sight. The queue was not lined up at the entrance of the church and when I followed it around to the rear I discovered that a low, one-story building attached to the cathedral and, possibly, at one time its priory had been turned into a Government Milk Store, Milk Store No. 52, in fact. The queue of several hundred old *babushki*, young girls and even family men who stood holding tin cans, old bottles and pots and pans, was waiting for the distribution of the evening milk quota.

I was immediately struck by a difference between this queue and the queues so often to be seen around Moscow in front of vegetable stores, grocery stores, meat stores and other food establishments. I was thoroughly familiar with queues, which were an entirely normal aspect of the Russian consumer distribution system as they still are. Eric Johnston once mildly reproached Stalin on the subject of queues, pointing out the enormous waste of man (or more properly woman) hours, involved in a system which forced millions of people to wait in line every day for so many articles of ordinary consumption. Johnston proposed (this was during the war) that Stalin invite in some American distributive experts, men from the chain stores, the mail-order houses and the big department stores, to help Russia organize her retail business. Stalin, rather sarcastically, rejected this well-meant offer, asserting that before the system of distribution could be improved you had to have something to distribute.

That Stalin's objection was not entirely valid was evident in the Moscow of 1949, where, despite the fact that there were no real shortages of basic foods (although there were continuing short supplies of this item or that), queues such as this for milk continued to exist.

But what struck me as curious about the milk queue was not that it existed but that it seemed to be rather too fluid. There was a great deal of coming and going among the women, even though the passing out of milk had not yet started. Puzzling a bit over this I wandered around to the front of the cathedral and, seeing that there were many people inside, passed within its gloomy depths myself. Like all Orthodox cathedrals it had no pews or places to sit. There were a good many large, central columns painted with religious drawings whose nature could only be guessed at in the fading light, and along one side there were several shrines around which were clustered little groups of believers, many of whom had sunk to their knees in devout prayer. Other believers were purchasing small pink and yellow candles from an old hag whose rough wooden stall was almost hidden in a murky corner and lighting them before the shrines in memory of their beloved ones who had passed away.

When my eyes became more accustomed to the gloom and shadows I saw that in the church, just as in the milk queue, there was a great deal of bustle, of women coming and women leaving, and when I saw that most of the women in the church clutched bottles or pails in their hands it became clear to me what was transpiring.

Possibly back in the days of the first decade of the Revolution when the Communists were carrying out their active campaign of repression and terror against the Church some commissar had decided, as a mark of contempt and, perhaps, reprisal, to commandeer the back quarters of the Cathedral for Government purposes. The buildings probably were not originally used as a milk station. They may have been used as offices or, as often happened, as small shops for shoe-repair men or tinsmiths. The use was not too important. It was merely a kind of symbolic way in which the Bolsheviks sought to strip the Church of its aura of faith and mystery, a Communist way, if you will, of figuratively wiping their feet on the Church altar cloth.

But somewhere along the line this particular piece of nastiness had collided with that practical, earthy quality which so distinguishes the Russian peasant and which so often succeeds in distorting or diverting some high-flown Party purpose. At some time the shoe shop or the tinsmiths' quarters had, in turn, been requisitioned for Milk Shop No. 52. If the Government had deliberately set out to make things easy and convenient for the Church believers it could have done no more. Because every *babushka* and every woman taking care of a child for blocks around came every day to the milk queue and, instead of standing for an hour or more idly gossiping with her neighbor, the women had organized the queue so that each of them who wished could go to the church and make her prayers without losing her place in the milk line. Thus, thanks to the Government's having taken away the church's rear buildings, the Cathedral at Sokolniki probably now had more regular worshipers than ever before in its history.

This little lesson in pragmatic Russianism made me chuckle and helped, a bit, to relieve my moody feelings as I again entered the Metro to return to the Metropole Hotel. The Sokolniki station is the end of that particular Metro line and the car I sat down in was practically empty, but at the next stop a few people got on, including a rather buxom young woman who sat down directly opposite me. Under the influence of my spring mood I gave her somewhat more than a passing glance and saw that she had wide, straight shoulders and a frank, open, if not particularly pretty face. She saw me looking her over and smiled. I smiled back and then looked away, a little surprised to find my pulse beating faster.

How strange it is, I thought to myself. Here is this plain, honest-looking girl, attractive only in the most general sense of the word, a girl to whom I would ordinarily never give a second glance or a first thought, and yet she only smiles a bit and my heart starts to twitter. The reason was simple, of course. She was the first ordinary Russian girl to smile at me in three months in Moscow and, although I did not know this at the time, one of two or three Russians who would show such friendliness while I was in Russia. For the moment I basked a little in the pleasant feeling of that smile and then let my eyes wander back to her. Her clothes were almost the plainest possible. She had on a very short knee-length skirt (the Moscow mode of the moment) of light-blue rayon, a dark-colored blouse of some light material, a dark-blue pullover sweater with a conventionalized reindeer pattern across the chest and a dark blue or black spring coat of some very sleazy-looking material. Her shoes were little better than cardboard. She was wearing bunchy, tan rayon stockings and a head scarf of cotton print, apparently of roses on a black background.

She was, in other words, a conventionally dressed Moscow girl of that period—no better and no worse than her neighbors. I guessed immediately that she worked in a factory and that she was an average, unskilled piece worker, earning five or six hundred rubles a month, and, probably, living in a workers' barracks or "communal housing establishment" as the Soviet euphemism would have it.

Seeing me again looking at her she caught my eye with a frank straightforward look and again smiled. I smiled back and all the way in to the Hunters' Row Metro Station we traded smiles and I carefully selected from my small store of Russian words the ones it would be necessary to use to invite her to have dinner with me if, as I hoped, it turned out that she, like myself, was headed for the center of town.

We both got up at the Hunters' Row stop and walked to the escalator side by side. I had already canvassed in my mind the ever-present thought that she might be a provocateur or MVD agent but decided that this was of very little consequence since I only proposed, if possible, to have dinner with the young lady. Moreover, it seemed unlikely since she had boarded the subway at a station beyond mine and since it was a matter of sheer chance that I had happened to take that particular train.

In my halting Russian I managed to ask the girl if she was busy and, if not, whether she wouldn't join me at supper. To this she shrugged her shoulders noncommittally and replied in the peasant way: "Why not?" Her name proved to be Nadja and there was little doubt that she was precisely what she appeared—an ordinary working-class Moscow girl who liked to have an occasional fling with a man and was not very particular about who he was provided he could take her to a restaurant, buy her a few drinks, a good meal, and dance with her a bit. Her language, in so far as I could understand it, was pretty rough and ready. Unfortunately, she had studied German as her required language in school, and, remembering a smattering of it, attempted to speak German to me, apparently on the theory that any foreigner would find another foreign language easier to understand than Russian. This did not prove to be true in my case. Nor was she able to make much of my fumbling and very limited Russian. So our communication tended to be limited to the most simple subjects.

I had taken her to the Moskva Hotel restaurant rather than the Metropole, thinking that she was less likely in that more Russian background to get into trouble with the MVD than at the Metropole, where there were always agents sitting in the lobby to watch everyone who went in and out. I ordered vodka for her, which she called "the white" (wine in her slang, was "the red") and she insisted on washing it down with a beer chaser which, like her slang, was a certain sign of genuine proletarian, or Moscow worker background. After Nadja had downed a shot or two of vodka I began to have considerable doubts as to the wisdom of this little adventure (I kept telling myself that it was a wonderful opportunity to learn something about how ordinary folks in Moscow lived and felt— which it was—but I knew very well that it was really the product of my spring mood, my loneliness and the most primitive and fundamental kind of man-meets-woman attraction).

She announced in a firm voice that she was a member of a Physical Culture Society and that she was a very strong girl. In case I doubted it I could feel her muscles. In fact, I had better feel her muscles anyway because, perhaps, I thought she was telling a lie.

From Nadya's generally robust appearance, her square shoulders and straight back I felt certain she was no more than telling the truth. My conviction was strengthened when, at her insistence, I did feel her muscles and found them, literally, as hard as iron. After this demonstration she proposed that we dance. I objected mildly but as this seemed to disturb her I hastily agreed only to find myself quickly encircled by arms like steel pinions that pressed me to a body that had the solidity and firmness of a sack of cement which has been left out in the rain.

Nadja, it was evident, was quite a woman. She was as proud as a child of her strength. She deliberately bent me backward as we were dancing and laughed with uproarious glee at my look of surprise and concern, quickly reassuring me that she would do me no hurt. She was literally strong as an ox but surprisingly tender. She worked in the Serp and Molot (Hammer and Sickle) works, doing heavy manual labor and enjoying it. She was not married and that also seemed to be her preference. My guess that she lived in a barracks was not correct. She had managed to get a bed of her own in the corner of a room belonging to a friend which she warmly suggested that I might like to share except for the fact that I, being a foreigner, might not think it "right" to come to an ordinary worker's room.

My romantic inclinations having been squashed in the iron clutch of Nadja's embrace I quickly seconded her thought that it would not be quite "right," adding that, since I was a foreigner, it might get her and her friend into trouble. This appeared to puzzle her. Trouble with whom? What kind of trouble? Trouble with the police, I said. Why? Because I am a foreigner, I explained. That didn't make sense to her. Hadn't the Soviet Government given me permission to come to Moscow? Yes. Well, then, why could any trouble come?

I wasn't certain whether this was naïveté or something else but it sounded like naïveté. However, my then practically nonexistent Russian didn't enable me to explain. Nor, I found, did I really feel like explaining such things to Nadja. It didn't seem to make much

difference. Just a petty detail. Because as I listened to her talk and
looked at her broad plain Slavic face the conviction deepened
within me that I had, by chance, stumbled upon the real heart
strength of the Russian state—the Soviet state, as it now happened
to be. But the Russian state as it was before and as it might be again.

Here was this woman—strong, honest and naïve. There was absolutely nothing wrong with her as a human animal. She could work
and she could suffer and she could bear children who would be, like
her, as strong as oxen. She was plain and simple and robust and it
was obvious as the nose on my face that she knew nothing about
any ideology and cared nothing about any ideology. There was an
ideology—that she knew. But it existed and she accepted it. There
was a Communist state which existed and which she accepted. I
was morally certain that, along with this, she accepted the Orthodox
Church, just as it was, unquestioning and in full faith. I was sure
that her mother had accepted the Czar, unquestioning and in full
faith, and that her grandmother had been a serf and had accepted
serfdom with the same open, honest blue eyes. Here was Mother
Russia, the great maternal Slavic force which flows on regardless of
Czar or Commissar, regardless of Church or communism, living and
breeding and nourishing one stronger and bigger generation after
another, making good the ravages, human and material, of war after
countless war, of famine after famine, of one male folly after another.

True, I was in an impressionable mood. But I could see this
woman with her sinews of iron and her good-natured rough manners,
marching on and on and on, her shoulders squared to one great
weight after another—enduring and eternal and as irresistible as the
flood. Where had I seen her before? But, of course. I had seen her
or her blood sisters earlier that afternoon, with their picks and
shovels in the park outside the Metropole Hotel, with their bright
cotton dresses and their great breasts, and the men clustering and
neighing around them.

I laughed to myself. How often I and other foreigners, seeing
Russian women do this rough work of the streets or the factories or
the fields, had expressed our horror at permitting the "weaker sex"
to handle these manual chores. We made jokes about the "equality
of the sexes" in Russia—equal rights to dig ditches and plow fields.

So we said, with a sneer. But, looking across at Nadja and watching the play of her strong sinews under the flimsy blouse and skirt, I wasn't so sure that we Westerners had anything to sneer about.

Not that all Russian women were like Nadja. There was Galya, for instance. But as the thought of Galya came back in this curious moment, I saw suddenly for the first time one basic reason why we had been so much attracted to each other. It was not because Galya was Russian but because she was Russian in a sense that was not important in these cold, harsh days of the final years of the Stalin epoch in Russian history. Galya was sensitive, intense, brooding, emotional, introspective, gay. She knew English, French and German. She knew all the classics of these languages and those of Russia best of all. She could quote Pushkin and Lermontov and Shakespeare and Byron and Goethe. Once there had been a Russia in which women like Galya had lived lives that sometimes were as beautiful as roses in a summer garden. But that Russia, at least for a time, was dead. And the Russia of the Nadjas endured—as it had in the past, as it would in the future.

Clumsily I called for the waiter and paid our check and somehow I managed to steer Nadja out of the Moskva and into a taxicab.

As I walked down the street toward Sverdlov Square and the Metropole Hotel I thought that I really should have thanked Nadja for the brief insight she had given me into this fundamental of the great Slav world.

IV

What Is Your Truth?

THE early months of my return to Moscow were filled with many doubts and worries but I tried my best not to let them divert me from my basic job of making as accurate an evaluation of Russia and the Russians as possible. What I was seeking was a very simple yet a very complicated thing. I was trying to find out the truth about Russia.

I needed to know more about the economy of the country and how fast it was recovering from the war wounds. I could see in the improvement of living conditions in Moscow that industry was steadily expanding, but how broad and how deep was it? I knew that Moscow would get the best of what there was but how much was there?

I wondered, too, what effect the constant emphasis on the military was having on the people, whether they were much affected by propaganda and if the Kremlin's apparent fears of attack from abroad, particularly by the United States, were shared by ordinary citizens. My own guess was that behind all the bluster the Kremlin was concealing some very real fears, probably founded in the knowledge of how weak World War II had left Russia and the distance she still must travel to make good those weaknesses.

But my opinions were founded on Moscow—on Moscow conditions, Moscow talk, Moscow gossip. And Moscow is not Russia any more than Washington is America. Nor were secondhand reports any good. You never knew whether a diplomat was basing his story on fact or on some preconceived notion of what ought to be true or what might serve to justify his country's policy.

Ordinarily, correspondents are able to trade back and forth a good bit of information about the country in which they are stationed. But by this time, outside of myself, only news agency men were left in Russia and the exigencies of their work did not permit them to leave Moscow.

It was perfectly plain what I had to do. The truth about any foreign country is never easy to come by and it certainly was particularly difficult to get at in Russia. However, whatever the handicaps there is no substitute for getting out and around a country. You may not find out the truth, which frequently, after all, may prove to be a relative and even a subjective thing. But at least you can get a little closer to the people and the ordinary way of their life. Even with the restrictions on travel and my own great ignorance of the Russian language at that time I must try to find out what the Russian people were thinking about, what they thought about their government, what they dreamed about and what they feared. I must learn, if possible, what they felt about America and whether the vast storehouse of good will which we had amassed in wartime had entirely melted away in the hot flame of *Pravda* editorials and Party slogans.

I decided to visit two Russian cities, each of which in its own way I regarded as having particular significance so far as the country as a whole was concerned. The first was Stalingrad and the second was Leningrad. One of the special virtues of both cities was the fact that I had seen them during the war days and therefore was in a better position to detect what changes might have occurred.

Stalingrad, of course, was most famous as a historic battleground but I thought it would, also, serve as a fairly accurate barometer of the rate at which Russia was recovering from wartime devastation. This rate of recovery was a vital factor in estimating Soviet military potency and the extent to which the Kremlin was likely to back up the hard words of its foreign policy with acts of force.

I had seen Stalingrad in the deep winter of 1944. It had been, before June, 1941, a medium-sized industrial city with a population of about 500,000, located on the right bank of the middle Volga where that river most closely approaches the Don. Around the city is an open and usually arid steppe.

A full year had transpired since the famous encirclement of Von

Paulus and defeat of the Nazis, but when I first saw Stalingrad it was still a city of death, destruction and almost complete devastation.

In fact, the only activity in Stalingrad in January, 1944, was a little smoke coming from the chimney of the snow-covered sod hut which served as an airport station and a switch engine, puffing aimlessly in a still wrecked and tangled freight yard. I deduced that there might also be a few citizens living in bunkers or sod huts, but I saw nothing to justify the Soviet propaganda claims that the famous tractor factory had already been put back into production.

Thus, whatever I might find in Stalingrad now it would be wholly and completely a postwar reconstruction effort. With these thoughts in mind I applied to the Press Department of the Foreign Office for permission to make the trip. All travel in Russia by correspondents was (and is) controlled by the Foreign Office and the Ministry of Internal Affairs or MVD, which of course has an absolute veto in such matters.

It worked like this. I was accredited to the Press Department of the Foreign Office, which gave me a press card. In addition, I had to obtain from the Visa Department of the Ministry of Interal Affairs, called OVIR, a Soviet residence permit or *Vid Na Zhitelstva*, allowing me to live and work in Moscow and its immediate environs. But if I wished to go to any other city I had to get a visa from OVIR, just as if I was visiting a foreign country. In theory I could travel anywhere but in practice I knew that it was impossible to get a visa except to points listed in a circular of the Foreign Office to the diplomatic corps as approved for travel by diplomats.

Moreover, it often turned out that I was refused a visa to cities which were listed as open to diplomats. After the death of Stalin when the government opened large areas to free travel the visa rule became a serious matter. It prevented me from visiting several areas in Central Asia where British diplomats went and it barred me from two or three Siberian places which were open to diplomats but which the diplomats didn't bother to visit because they knew conditions there would be very rugged. The visa rule even prevented me from motoring to Kiev in the summer of 1954 although by that time practically every military attaché in Moscow had driven there.

However, in the summer of 1949 I simply wanted to go to Stalingrad and with no more than the customary bureaucratic delay the permission was forthcoming. At about the same time the new American Ambassador, Admiral Alan Kirk, arrived in Moscow. Kirk was a very common-sense kind of man with a sizable bump of curiosity and no illusions about achieving any diplomatic coups during his tour of duty in Moscow. (In this he differed sharply from his predecessor, General Smith, who came to Russia with very high hopes indeed, and, as so often has happened, left the Soviet capital a sadder, wiser and rather embittered man.)

Kirk proposed to do a good bit of traveling in Russia and decided that his initial excursion would be to Stalingrad. So we agreed to join forces and one pleasant September evening we went to the Kazan station and embarked for the south. We were accompanied by the Ambassador's son, Roger, who was specializing in Russian language studies, and an embassy attaché named Morgan who also had some knowledge of Russian. Our party occupied two compartments of an ordinary "soft" car (that is, one in which mattresses, bedding and blankets are supplied) and two more compartments were assigned to the four-man MVD bodyguard who traveled with the Ambassador wherever he went. At all times when the Ambassador was outside the embassy these Russian policemen stayed even closer to his side than Secret Service guards stay beside a U.S. President. When, in the following year, Kirk achieved a lifelong ambition and made a trip out to the famous Lake Baikal in eastern Siberia he was not allowed even to row a boat on the lake except with his "boys" as oarsmen. These guard details had been assigned by the MVD to the principal foreign ambassadors in Moscow ever since the assassination in early revolutionary days of the German Ambassador, Count Von Mirbach. Their duty, ostensibly, was to protect from harm ambassadors whose death might complicate Soviet foreign relations. Actually, in recent years the bodyguards had acted to isolate, almost completely, the leading ambassadors from any ordinary Russsian citizens, except for housemaids, cooks, chauffeurs and the like—all of whom, of course, had to have a security clearance before they could work for the foreign envoys. After Stalin's death such guards were abolished in a move to improve relations with the ambassadors.

This was my first close-hand experience of an ambassador's plain-

clothes detail and I soon resolved that, in future, I would forgo
the pleasure of the Ambassador's company for the sake of freedom
from his policemen. Not that the MVD men were obnoxious in any
way. They were polite and even tried, in little ways, to be helpful.
But they did provide an almost complete barrier between our party
and the ordinary Russians in whose sentiments and opinions I was
so deeply interested.

Nevertheless, the Stalingrad trip was not without value and it
did have its humorous moments. One of Kirk's desires was to take
a ride on the Volga and to visit the caviar fisheries. He proposed
that we hire a launch and go out on the river. This simple and ordinary request was turned into a major operation by the Russians, who
finally came up, not with a launch but with a good-sized excursion
steamer. Apparently, in view of the Ambassador's exalted naval rank,
an ordinary river launch was not regarded as suitable to the occasion.

With appropriate exclamations of awe we (and, of course, the four
little men) embarked on the handsome craft and headed out into
the river. True, we felt a little lost—eight people, including the four
policemen, aboard a boat built for five hundred—but it was a good
sunshiny day. We sailed down river a way and inspected the sturgeon
fisheries from a distance, this not being the season of active caviar
fishing, and then headed majestically back upstream toward the city.

It had been a pleasant experience and almost as impressive as our
Russian hosts hoped it might be. The captain of the steamboat who
had been serious looking and somewhat apprehensive when we had
boarded this Volga River luxury liner now had relaxed and was
smiling and affable on the bridge of his craft.

But pride, as it is so correctly said, goeth before a fall. As we
came up opposite the Stalingrad landing and turned to head in to
the wharf our boat gave a shudder and then slowed to a halt. We
were lodged, solidly and completely as it turned out, on a sandbar!

Consternation and horrors! You could almost see the thoughts
racing through the mind of our proud river-boat captain. What ig-
nominy! With an American admiral aboard as an honored guest the
steamer runs aground. What a disgrace for Soviet seamanship! And
not only were we aground but we were firmly aground. Our steam-

boat huffed. It puffed. The captain ordered full steam ahead. He ordered the engines reversed. He tried to let the boat swing sideways into the Volga current. Nothing helped. Great brown puddles were stirred up in the chocolate water by our whirling engines. Seamen with long poles tried to shove us off the bar. But fast we stuck.

Through it all Admiral Kirk displayed a true seaman's gallantry. He firmly turned his back on the hectic activity and cautioned us not to smile or laugh. "This is a serious matter," he said. "The least we can do is to pretend we don't notice what is happening."

So, with only an occasional glimpse at the red-faced captain and the sweating crew, we admired the distant shores and discussed the state of the caviar industry. Not until we felt, by the movement of the boat, that we had finally slipped off the sandbar did we turn about and gaze toward Stalingrad again.

"Ah," said Kirk, "I see we are approaching the city."

I do not suppose that the captain of our steamboat understood English but I am sure that he understood the admiral's tact and I thought I saw a grateful crinkle in his eye as we finally debarked. From that time forward I had no doubt that regardless of how barren Kirk's stay in Moscow might be we were being represented by a man who understood the true essence of diplomacy.

One more detail of that Volga River grounding comes to mind, a vagrant happening with a faintly nightmarish quality. While we were lodged on the sandbar a small motor-driven barge passed very close to us—an ordinary unremarkable barge except that its sole cargo appeared to be a single mangy camel, which stood on knobby legs, solemnly gazing out over the Volga and occasionally baring its greenish teeth in a kind of camel leer.

I could not imagine then, nor can I now, what that camel was doing, riding in lonely splendor down the center of the Volga.

Despite our guards, despite ill-conceived attempts to impress us and the natural protocol surrounding a visit of the American Ambassador, the trip to Stalingrad did show me some things which I needed to know. Enormous strides had been made to get the city operating again and I was most interested to see that the restoration of industry had been given first priority. This was followed by restoration of communications—particularly streetcars, buses and trucks to bring workers to the factories; a minimum rehabilitation of consumer services, stores and the like; a fairly impressive start on the creation of a heroic ensemble of public buildings in the heart of what had been the Stalingrad battlefield and, finally, very much at the tag end, a slow and most haphazard approach to the housing problem.

While we did not get into the famous tractor plant or the equally famous Red October Plant (both of which were key points in the Stalingrad fighting) it was obvious that they were working at something like the prewar level. Most of the visible war damage had been repaired; smoke poured from giant stacks and in the railroad yards train after train of flatcars was loaded with gray-painted tractors and machinery turned out by these factories. The Government claimed that Stalingrad industrial production now exceeded the prewar level and I was inclined to accept that claim. If Stalingrad's industrial recovery was typical, and this seemed quite probable, it meant that the government's general claims that prewar industrial levels were now being achieved or surpassed probably were true.

This had important implications for Soviet policy in general since it should mean that the Russian industrial plant, once more, was able to support very large-scale military operations.

On the other hand the shabby and almost pitiful state of civilian conveniences and creature comforts showed, more plainly than anything else, that the Russians needed a good deal more time to fully make good the horrible damages of war.

Moreover my impression was that Stalingrad had by no means regained its prewar population. My guess was that only as many persons as were needed to man the industrial plants and the essential services were being permitted to live there.

Much construction was going on, of course, and a start was being made in the areas near the Red October and tractor plants at building new workers' flats. A great deal of this work was being done by German prisoners of war who were then still in Russia by the hundreds of thousands. I saw them working on buildings, clearing rubble sites and being marched, or sometimes trucked, to and fro about the city. I even saw an occasional German, easily recognizable by his forage cap, walking with apparent freedom in the central city park.

Considering the fantastic destruction in Stalingrad great strides had been made. But, as I viewed the city, panoramically, from the heights of Mameyev Kurgan where the Nazis, too, had looked it over I was more impressed with the tasks that lay ahead than with those which had been accomplished. There was a vast rubble area not far from the apartment house where a certain Sergeant Pavlov with a squad of Russian soldiers had held off Nazi attackers for nearly two months. Pavlov's apartment house had been restored and I saw washing hanging out the windows, but when I walked across the rubble field I had a very strange experience. One part of the field had been smoothed down and cleared and here two bands of youngsters were playing football. But, as I strolled across the field, I suddenly realized that I was walking right over one of Stalingrad's big residential areas. Spotted all over this huge field were tin pipes and occasional brick chimneys protruding a bit from the ground. Under the rubble thousands of people were living in the basements and cellars of destroyed buildings. Even the youngsters' football field covered a living area.

Then, watching more closely as I wandered about the town (having temporarily separated from the admiral and his bodyguard), I saw that the majority of Stalingrad citizens must be still living in such temporary quarters or other improvised places in half-ruined buildings.

Later, when I wrote about my Stalingrad trip, the censorship permitted me to describe the rehabilitation of industry and transport. I could describe the new workers' apartments, the new Pobeda movie theater, the new Children's Theater and the plans for the vast Stalin *embarcadero*. But nothing about the underground cellars of the workers. That was deleted by the censors. I could describe the newly reopened Stalingrad department store in whose basement Von Paulus had his final headquarters, but not the beggars in their ragged Red Army uniforms and their maimed or missing arms and legs who cried for alms beside the one-story shacks in which Stalingrad's "shopping center" was housed. Nor was I allowed to tell how I watched women, young and old, shrieking and struggling to get into

the new department store when it opened at eleven o'clock in order
to buy before the meager stocks were exhausted, and how the dozen
militiamen on duty at the scene casually and callously shoved the
women sprawling into the street in order to clear the doors.

I was, however, allowed to report what I believed were the completely sincere and honest words of one Stalingrad woman who had
been in the city during the opening weeks of the German assault
and who had been one of the first to return after Von Paulus' sur-
render. She said: "No one who has suffered as we have would ever
want to inflict such suffering on another people."

These words, or words much like them, I was to hear over and
over in every part of Russia so long as I stayed there. I believe they
are true and that they represent the conviction of most Russians who
went through the hellish suffering of World War II. It is a deep
and vital sentiment and one which any government, including
the present Russian government, must take account of. I am afraid,
however, that the sentiments of the people are not necessarily
decisive.

We were told by the city authorities of Stalingrad, who showed us
the truly grandiose plans for the reconstruction of the city, that this
was a ten-year project and that it should be completed about 1954.
I confess that when I turned from the neat plaster-of-Paris mock-ups
of the architects to the enormous rubble fields and crazily twisted
wreckage which still was everywhere in Stalingrad I felt more than
a little skeptical.

But to my very genuine amazement when I returned to Stalingrad
in the summer of 1954 I found that the predictions of the city authorities had been very largely fulfilled.

Stalingrad was not only restored. It had been beautified beyond
plan and beyond, I am sure, the hopes of any of its prewar residents.
I could hardly recognize the center of the city, which now was a
place of enormous prospects, beautiful theaters, promenades, statues
(including the inevitable one of Stalin), a railroad station that
looked like a miniature Kremlin, gardens, flowers and a grand staircase down to the Volga River landing stages.

Nor was this all. Workers' apartments had sprung up like weeds
all over the city. They didn't seem well planned and many of them

were not well built but, at least in a quick survey, I was unable to find anyone still living in basements or dugouts. The stores were full of merchandise, possibly not quite so full as Moscow's but much fuller than in many other cities of this size. The famous department store which had been virtually the only restored building in the center of the city five years before was now literally hidden by great new and taller government structures.

Of course, rubble was still to be seen in many places but there was hardly a sign of war damage in the center. I did, however, recognize the old city market, which was as dusty and fly-clustered as ever although there was improvement in the quality and variety of food on sale.

New industrial establishments have been built in Stalingrad, as well, and it seemed apparent to me that someone, somewhere along the line—most probably Stalin before his death—decided to give a special priority to Stalingrad, possibly because it is the focus of so many foreign visitors. There is a Peace Street in Stalingrad at one end of which is a new planetarium which is the gift of the East German government, and along the new streets and avenues peace posters are to be seen. I must say that in this setting calls for peace make a certain impression.

My second journey in search of greater understanding of what was happening in Russia was to Leningrad, the one and only city in Russia for which I have a real affection. I set out alone this time, hoping that I might have a little more luck in talking to people than in Stalingrad.

It was early winter before I got there although according to the calendar it was only October. Winter comes early and stays late in this northern city and, I should say, winter really becomes the great metropolis which Peter built in these Baltic marshes in order to give his empire its famous "window on the West." The massive buildings of gray stone stand firm against the sleet and blizzards and the mantle of snow is kind to them and hides the scars of war and the less forgiveable marks of neglect and disdain.

When I first saw Leningrad during the war I was so impressed by its imperial grandeur and so carried away by the romance of its traditions that it seemed to me impossible that, once the war was over, the Russians would not remove their capital from stodgy, ugly Moscow to this handsome setting by the northern sea. I even remember writing a story along those lines.

By this time, however, I knew better. I knew that considerations of romance or history or glamour would play no role whatsoever in the grimly realistic calculations of the Kremlin. And one had only to see the state of Leningrad, the shabbiness of the public buildings, the way in which beautiful structures like the Hermitage Art Gallery had been allowed to deteriorate, and the general absence of any new construction to realize that not only did the government have no intention of moving its headquarters back to Leningrad but that it was, by calculation and intention, allowing the city to decay.

I do not mean to suggest that nothing had been done to Leningrad since wartime. Far from it. The citizens of Leningrad are the most energetic and talented in Russia. In so far as they were able they had repaired war's damages, but what balked them was, obviously, the refusal of the government to appropriate funds in any substantial quantities.

For instance, in 1944 the city architects had shown us the plans for a great new subway system which was badly needed in the sprawling city. Moscow's subway had been started nearly fifteen years before but nothing had been done about Leningrad's although the population of the two places had until the decade of the thirties been just about equal. In the thirties as a result of a deliberate policy of discrimination Moscow began to forge ahead.

However, the Leningrad architects said they had been assured that construction of the new subway would start even before the war ended. Now five years later hardly any progress had been made beyond sinking a pair of exploratory shafts, although, in the same time, great new sections of subway were being built in Moscow. And even five years later, after the Malenkov government had begun to spend a little more money in Leningrad, the first section of the Leningrad Metro had not yet been opened.

In the face of this kind of treatment the Leningraders were doing the best they could. I went out to the great Putilov Steel Works, or Kirov works as the Communists called them, where in 1944 we had heard the stories of the Leningrad siege. Here there was change enough. I could hardly recognize the area which had been in the front lines during the German siege. The Putilov works were booming. New shops had been put up and only one building showed outward signs of damage. Around the works where I had last seen the desert of battle there were now many new apartment houses and some new factories. This, however, was the only place where much had been done in the way of construction. In the old Viborg section of the city, the working-class area which had been a hotbed of bolshevism in the Revolution of 1917, the buildings looked so shabby and forlorn that it was difficult to believe that it had been any more of a slum under the Czars than it was under the Commissars.

True, when I made a snowy trip by electric train out to Peterhof, the fabulous palace which Peter built as a rival to Versailles, I found that great progress had been made in repairing the utter destruction wrought by the Germans. Here in the reconstruction of this most grandiose jewel of the imperial past, Stalin apparently was willing to spend an infinite amount of money. I had not believed the Leningrad architects when they told me in 1944 that Peterhof would be rebuilt down to the last detail. Although the cost, quite obviously, would run into hundreds of millions of rubles and the effort would require perhaps twenty years, it now seemed to be true that this incredible job was going to be done.

The sight of the acres of Peter's golden statuary, now restored to pristine gilt, standing amid the snowdrifts at Peterhof, while all the way back into Leningrad the electric train rumbled through one desolate and half-ruined industrial suburb after another, left me with a very bad taste in my mouth and I was glad to find when I got to the Hotel Astoria that Intourist had managed to get me a seat at the ballet that night at the Mariinsky Theater. I do not now remember what ballet I saw performed although the other details of the evening are indelibly etched in my memory. I remember, for instance, that my seat was in the second row and was the second seat in from the left center aisle.

I had arrived at the opera house early because I wanted to see if the damage which had been done by German artillery fire had been repaired. It had been. The Mariinsky is the old Imperial Opera

House, probably the finest in Russia although the Bolshoi in Moscow now out-glitters it. It has, I believe, been rechristened the Kirov Theater (many landmarks in Leningrad have been given this name, in honor of a Party leader and friend of Stalin whose assassination in the early thirties set in motion the events which culminated in the great purges), although everyone in Leningrad, except for the Intourist guides, continues to call it the Mariinsky.

Taking my seat I squeezed past a tall, thin, rather intellectual-looking man of forty or forty-five who was occupying the seat on the aisle. I gave him no more than a second glance and set about studying the program which I could barely make out with my limited Russian. I suppose my companion may have noticed my difficulty, or perhaps, as so often was the case, it was my clothes. In any event, speaking in a soft cultured voice, he asked me politely in Russian if I were not a foreigner.

"Yes," I replied. "I am an American."

My neighbor beamed and said in halting but almost perfect English: "How very fortunate to meet you! As you see I speak English but it is most seldom that I have an opportunity."

I smiled and expressed my pleasure also, explaining that I spoke Russian most poorly indeed. At this point the orchestra struck up the overture and it was not until intermission time that we were able to continue the conversation. He told me that he was an architect and that a friend of his, an artist connected with the Mariinsky, had given him a ticket for the performance. He asked me if I had ever been in New York and when he learned that I had worked there for many years he was in raptures.

"Oh, your skyscrapers!" he said. "They are so beautiful. What I would not give to see them. Of course, we all have studied the pictures but it is not the same. Is it really true that your Empire State Building has more than one hundred stories?"

I assured him that it was true and could not help adding that, apparently, his government did not share his enthusiasm since I had recently been reading in the press that American skyscrapers were horrible creations which swayed so much in the wind that people became seasick. Moreover, the government would not even permit the word "skyscraper" to be used in describing Russian buildings, which were said to have nothing in common with these American abominations.

My friend sadly shook his head. "Unfortunately," he said, "what you say is true. My friends and I, however, sincerely admire your fine skyscrapers." He came closer to me and whispered, conspiratorially, into my ear. "I'll tell you a secret," he said. "We have drawn plans for skyscrapers, too. To be built right here in Leningrad. If the day ever comes . . ."

I asked him about my impression that the government was spending little money in Leningrad. Again he came up close to me. "It's true," he said. "The government has no interest in Leningrad. Every year they take another of our scientific institutes, one of our cultural organizations or a precision-instrument shop and move it away—to Moscow, to the Urals. Anywhere so long as it is not in Leningrad."

He said this was not because of the military danger of Leningrad's exposed position. "It is because they do not like us in Moscow," he said. "We are the window on the West, yes? That is what Peter said. Peter wanted a window on the West. But, perhaps, now a window is not wanted. Sometimes things can be seen from a window which it is better not to see."

This was frank talk, indeed. Perhaps too frank. I was a little worried for my friend as we went back to our seats and I thought the least I could do was to give him a gentle warning.

"You know," I said, "perhaps it is not so good for us to talk. Sometimes people who talk to foreigners get into trouble."

His face quivered as though I had slapped him.

"Oh, no," he said. "You don't know what this means to me. To actually talk with a person from the outside, to talk to a man from New York. It is what I dream about for years. Please do not be afraid. For my part I am not afraid. No one will ask me and if they should—poof. It is nothing."

At the second intermission our talk continued. He had been one of those who had lived through the siege of Leningrad, the most terrible months of late 1941 and early 1942 before the ice road over Lake Ladoga was opened and when it seemed almost certain the Nazis would take the city.

"But still the city did not fall," he said. "It was terrible, yes. But we lived together and we died together. No one who went through those days could ever be afraid again. Nothing so horrible could ever happen. Even in the worst times we worked. I was an architect so I drew plans for the city which we would build after the war. Good plans. Many good plans were drawn in those days. Now they gather dust."

I remembered then that I had heard in 1944 of how Leningrad's architects with freezing fingers had drawn plans for new buildings while the Nazi bombs and Nazi artillery slowly crumbled the existing buildings into rubble and dust.

After the performance we walked down the dark street together, our heels crunching on the hard-packed snow. It was cold, fifteen or twenty below zero Fahrenheit, and crystal clear. Stars sparkled in the northern sky and the great Leningrad buildings loomed handsome, black and majestic in the shadows.

When he found that I was staying at the Astoria my friend said he would walk with me, since he lived in the next street. Despite the cold we walked slowly and he peppered me with questions, many of which I could not answer, about American art, American music, American writers (Was it true that Hemingway had written a great novel about the Spanish Civil War which had some unpleasant things to say about Russian commissars? Why hadn't Steinbeck written anything worth while since *The Grapes of Wrath*? Or had he written some good novels which were no longer being translated into Russian? Had any American written a good novel about the war or were the American war books just as poor as the Russian ones?), American movies (What pictures had Charlie Chaplin made lately? Why didn't they see any more pictures by Shirley Temple or Deanna Durbin in Russia?), American automobiles, American engineering. . . . His curiosity was irresistible and unlimited but I noticed one thing, he made no remarks about foreign policy, foreign relations, President Truman, the atom bomb or anything of the like.

Finally, we reached the architect's apartment house and he invited me to come in and meet his wife, and have a drop to drink. I thought we had tempted fate and the MVD far enough and gently but firmly declined the invitation, so we stood on the sidewalk, still

talking. What, I asked, did the people of Leningrad think abou
Americans? Did they still remember the days of the war?

My friend smiled, sadly. "Of course we remember," he said.
"American Spam . . . we still make jokes about it but we were glad
to eat it at the time. American butter . . . American sugar . . .
We haven't forgotten that America helped us. We Leningraders
never forget a friend."

"Well, then," I said, "do you or your friends ever listen to the
American radio, *Golos Amerika* [the Voice of America]?"

For a moment he hesitated and I could see that he was making
up his mind how to answer this question.

"I'll speak frankly," he said, "because there is no use in speaking
otherwise. My friends and I never used to listen to the American
radio. It simply never occurred to us. Then, not so long ago, something happened. Our Government started a big campaign against
the Voice of America. There were articles in the paper denouncing
it, and special stations were set up to interfere with the broadcasts
from America and make it impossible to hear them."

He said that when the Soviet jamming program was begun he
and his friends became interested in the American programs.

"We thought that there must be something to hear, an American
truth which was important. Otherwise, our Government would not
have taken such measures to keep us from listening. So we started
to experiment to see if we could hear the American stations because
we all wanted to know what it was, this new American truth. It was
not easy. The jamming stations were very powerful and it was not
good to let the neighbors know that you were trying to hear the
American station. So we had to work quietly and diligently."

At last, he said, a friend of his succeeded in evolving a technique
of tuning through the jamming in such a way that with great care
and delicacy it was possible to hear the Voice of America.

"It was a great moment," he said solemnly. "I listened. My friend
listened. We looked at each other. We could not believe it and we
listened a little more. Then we knew and we turned off the radio.
We had heard the new American truth. But it wasn't a truth. It
wasn't a truth at all. It was propaganda. American propaganda."

He did not have to tell me of his disappointment and his disillu-

all there in his voice as we stood talking in the
grad evening.
said, "we were sick to death of propaganda. All our
e heard propaganda, propaganda, propaganda. That
e were so thrilled and so excited when we heard about
truth of the Americans."

pologized a little, explaining that, perhaps, this was just the
R ian way, the way of seeking and hunting for a new "truth"
which would make the world understandable. And perhaps, he said,
he and his friends had been a little naïve to suppose that the "truth"
would be found on an American radio broadcast. After all America
was a long way off and how were the Americans to know what it
was that Russians were longing to hear?

"Anyway," he said, "that is what we told ourselves after we got
over the first disappointment. That is why it was such an event for
me to meet you tonight, a real American. I couldn't help thinking
that maybe if I met and really talked with an American I might after
all be able to find out what is your truth."

We shook hands then and I went on down the street and around
the corner by St. Isaac's great towering bulk to my snug, warm room
at the Astoria Hotel with its flossy French bed and its neat English
hunting prints. I am afraid that I hadn't dared ask my friend at that
point whether I had been able to help him to learn the American
"truth" but I knew very well that he had helped me far more than
he might ever imagine to learn a Russian, or at least a Leningrad,
"truth."

V

Bereft of Grace

I FIND, as I write about my years in Russia, that a curious thing has happened. While the events which began with 1952 are recorded with camera clarity in my mind much of the period of 1949 through 1951 remains murky and frequently lacking in chronological sequence until I consult my notes.

I remember, for instance, going to what now seems like dozens of anti-American plays with my Russian teacher, Nina. But without refreshing my memory it is hard for me to tell one of these plays from another. Yet the stories Nina told me at that time about life in Moscow remain fresh in my mind.

The reason for this is not hard to discover. When I reread the record of that period it impresses me as so formless, so sterile, so lacking in human qualities, so faceless, that I quite understand why it appears in my memory as a barren and endless wasteland, illumined by some half light which surely does not emanate from the sun, a land over which few living mortals wander, gray and dusty. It is a landscape remarkable only for its occasional grotesqueries.

And surely there was nothing in the Soviet life of which Nina told me to suggest spiritual life or vigor. It was an existence singularly bereft of grace. Nor was much, except lip service, left to remind one of the Revolution. Moscow, like Stalin, was gray and old and conservative and a little pale from being too much indoors, not getting enough sleep and poring too long hours over the endless masses of paper.

It had seemed to me when I was in Russia during the war that very little revolutionary fire remained in Russia and five years of postwar life had quenched even those tiny sparks. Of course, the "cause" of the Revolution was kept technically alive because the Kremlin found it a useful adjunct to foreign policy.

But one had only to look at Stalin's cynical pact with the Nazis or his years of complacent support of Chiang Kai-shek against the Chinese Communists (only to cite two of the more spectacular among many examples) to realize that revolutionary principles in his lexicon had no more value than a streetcar transfer which enabled him to shift from one line to another. Stalin had little enough trust in anyone at any time but it sometimes appeared as though of all people he trusted his foreign "comrades" least of all.

Thus, I was not much impressed by Communist slogans, like "Workers of the World, Unite," nor by the raucous activities of the foreign Communist parties which, frequently, produced such vocative counter-reactions that in the ensuing smoke and fire, the silhouette of the real threat to world stability—Russian power and Russian policy—was sometimes lost sight of.

I was never—nor am I now—very much afraid of the possibility that William Z. Foster would succeed in overthrowing the United States Government. Nor did it seem likely to me that Harry Pollit would manage to win a majority in the British House of Commons. Naturally the lower levels of economic and social development in Asia and certain parts of Europe give the Communist menace more reality in those areas. But I have never been addicted to the type of science fiction which postulates that someday the flea may replace man as the dominant form of life on this globe.

I was, and still am, seriously concerned lest the stentorian tones of the sideshow barkers distract our attention from the main tent which, of course, is Moscow and Russia and whoever happens to be in control of the Goliath at the given moment, be he Romanov Czar, or Georgian Commissar or Three-Man Committee.

I do not think *all* our troubles would vanish if the Communists could, somehow, be whisked off the world stage. Nor do I think that all would be apple pie if the Communists should be driven from the Kremlin and a new batch of guaranteed, triple-plated, honest Injun, "democratic" Russians were put in their place. Such comforting calculations unfortunately run headlong into certain hard rocks of economics, geography, industry and resources, not to mention that most impressive figure of all, Russian woman with her infinite capacity for producing new and ever larger and stronger generations of Russian children, Russian men, Russian women, Russian workers, Russian peasants, Russian soldiers.

I do not wish to minimize the Communist element in what we have come to know as the "Communist conspiracy." Far from it. Living as I did within the Kremlin's very shadow, Communists, Communist rule and the "Communist conspiracy" were not mere words to me. They were the tough and inescapable facts of daily life. The man who ran Russia was a Communist and a dictator. All the men of his government were Communists. They had fashioned of the international Communist movement one of the most useful and deadly instruments for the support of a national foreign policy which the ingenious mind of man had ever invented. They had their spies and agents in every country of the world; their allies; their dupes; and their claques. Communism liked to advertise itself as "the wave of the future." It pretended to be a holy doctrine, like a religion, and it sought to inspire in its followers a fanaticism like that of some of the early militant Western sects. A useful camouflage, indeed, for a mechanism which, regardless of its origin in the flush of Russian revolutionary ardor, had long since become little more than a kind of human telegraph apparatus for clattering out the current gyrations of Soviet foreign policy. Moscow weighed the value of each foreign Communist carefully—but only in *poods*, never in pounds.*

If I read contemporary history correctly, it was yet to be proved that the international Communists could endanger a nation unless it was already honeycombed by social ills which the existing social structure had failed to cope with. I knew of no revolution which had been successfully exported by Moscow—except at the point of a bayonet in Eastern Europe. It was an army and not a conspiracy which came close to taking over Korea, and to me the strategic mili-

---

* A pood is a Russian measurement of weight equal to about thirty-six pounds.

tary expansionism of the two great Communist powers, and not the
Third International, was the prime danger.

In all these considerations I placed China, rightly or wrongly, in
a special category. In any event, with the notable exception of
China, I interpreted the activities of the foreign Communists in this
period as primarily in the nature of a diversion, a kind of global
smoke screen designed to distract our attention and preoccupy our
interests while Russia recouped her wartime losses.

I attributed Soviet bluster, Soviet harshness and Soviet stubbornness in diplomacy largely to Soviet weakness and, essentially,
to a desire to postpone decisions until the Russian position was
stronger and Stalin could come to the conference table with more of
a feeling of security.

What vitally interested me in this time was the extent to which
Stalin in his effort to mobilize the productive force of the country
and to unify it under the crushing stamp of his personality, had,
literally, pulverized the nation's spirit. Only such people as Nadja
could pass through the iron press of the Stalin era relatively unmarked. I could understand my architect in Leningrad and his
friends, looking for a new "truth" and I hoped they would survive
to find it. As I had hope for the future, I also hoped that persons
like Galya, for whom the spirit was everything, would find the
strength for survival in that spirit.

What did Stalin offer these people? Nothing.

Basically, Stalin had no use for people of spirit. They disturbed
him. He was, I think, afraid of them. They were an upsetting influence. They did not produce. I felt this was one reason why he didn't
like Leningrad. He didn't trust it, was afraid of it—particularly after
his friend Kirov had been assassinated up there.

Of course, he posed as a patron of art. He read every novel before
it was published. His opinions on poetry were sacred. Plays pros-
pered or withered at the flick of his hand. Russia had, perhaps by
accident, the finest musicians, the greatest composers in the world,
but he set them topsy-turvy trying to get them to compose operas
that would remind him of the tunes from Verdi he used to hum as a
boy in the cafés of Tiflis.

As for art—it was simply unbelievable. Even I who saw it can't quite believe it today. I have preserved a list which I made at this time of the paintings placed on exhibition at the famous Tretyakov Art Gallery in Moscow. These were the best works of the year of the best artists in all Russia, ninety-five works in all. Thirty-eight of those ninety-five paintings and sculptures were devoted to Stalin and another thirty-eight showed other Soviet leaders or Party ideological themes. The remaining nineteen works showed life on collective farms, railroad engine depots, fishermen hauling in their catch and a ship construction scene.

Stalin was depicted reviewing the parade in the Red Square, 1941; standing under a big fir tree on the Black Sea coast with members of the Politburo; with Lenin in Smolny Institute during the Revolution Days in 1917; being expelled from Batumi as a young radical agitator; addressing workers in Baku; leading a demonstration at Batumi; leading a "circle" of revolutionary workers in Tiflis; offering a toast to the Russian people at the end of the war in June, 1945; at a meeting of the State Defense Council with members of the Politburo; visiting the cruiser *Molotov*; as a schoolboy with his books; with the famous flyer Chkalov, beside a big globe of the world; in the print shop of the Georgian newspaper *Borba*; reading the newspaper *Iskra*; reading a letter from Lenin; in Siberian exile, et cetera, et cetera ad nauseam.

You might suppose that the number of paintings of Stalin would have been somewhat limited by the relative paucity of striking events in his life. No such thing. Any decree which he signed, any meeting which he presided over would do as a subject. And there was no limit to the number of paintings which might be executed on a particular theme, especially a subject like Lenin and Stalin. An artist could easily keep busy, year around, merely painting and repainting Stalin visiting Lenin at his *datcha* outside Moscow with slight variations of perspective or distance.

I wonder what has become of all those "works of art"?

One of the first things the new government did after Stalin's death was to pack up these masterpieces and take them away. They did not remove paintings which were already hung in public buildings (as was the case when Beriya was arrested) but no more were put up. In the summer of 1954 I visited the Tretyakov again, just before leaving Moscow. Once again the "best" work of the year was on exhibition. I can't say that it exactly suited my own artistic taste since it ran, largely, to pictures which "told a story" or drew a moral. But in one respect it marked a great advance. There was not a single portrait of Stalin on view. Not one. And not a single portrait of the present government leaders. No pictures of Khrushchev presenting the new Decree on Agriculture, nor of Malenkov addressing the Supreme Soviet.

Moreover, the famous collection of birthday gifts to Stalin was packed up and carted off, God knows where. If it wasn't dumped into the Black Sea it should at least have been sent, like the famous bell of the Uglich cathedral, into exile in Siberia for three hundred years. However, knowing the Russian penchant for saving and preserving every last knick-knack of state property, I have no doubt that this agglomeration has been placed in some warehouse where armed guards faithfully protect it against the depredations of enemies of the state.

This collection was assembled to mark the occasion of Stalin's seventieth birthday, which occurred in December, 1949. It filled one whole museum, the Pushkin, whose collection of classic ancient and European art was put into mothballs until the summer of 1953 in order to provide space for the display of Stalin's gifts. And it filled, in addition, rather more than half of the Museum of the Revolution on upper Gorky Street. I have no doubt that the Kremlin received enough gimcracks to fill a dozen more museums and I suppose Stalin felt he was exercising considerable restraint at not taking over the Tretyakov and the Lenin museums as well.

It must be admitted that the Stalin gifts were enormously popular. Peasants and workers flocked to see them by the hundreds of thousands. Not merely in organized excursions. When they came to town they wanted to see the *podarki,* the gifts, because they had heard about how wonderful they were from their neighbors.

And this, I think, is the true indictment of the Stalin regime and the extent to which it debased, or allowed to sink to its natural level, the taste of the Russian masses. For if the artistic level of the Tretyakov art exhibition was low the level of the exhibit of Stalin gifts could only be measured with a casting lead.

If you try to imagine the worst collection of horrors which might be assembled by combing the secondhand stores of Third Avenue for Victorian goucheries and adding in a few Coney Island souvenirs of 1910 vintage it will give you a faint idea. I have in my possession a carefully compiled description of several hundreds of these "objects of art." Here are a few samples: a photograph album done in pale blue and purple mosaic by the workers of Azerbaijan; an embroidered picture of the White Sea Ship Canal, done by thirty-three Ukrainian peasant women (I wonder whether, by any chance, they were among the slave laborers who "rehabilitated" themselves by working on that notorious project); a silk embroidered tobacco pouch in purple, yellow and orange, the gift of wives of members of the Moscow Military Air Academy; a "decorative" engraving on stainless steel of a bridge being blown up during the civil war, the gift of Chelyabinsk steel workers; an inlaid wood mandolin from the toy artisans of Vinnitsa; a hand-engraved tommygun, bearing the greetings of the Moscow City Party Committee and the legend that it was the two-millionth which had been turned out.

I spare you the rest.

This junk was really popular. You only had to stand in the museum five minutes, listening to the ohs and ahs and watching the jaws of the good citizenry as they gawked at such wonders as a pipe made of stainless steel with a malachite bowl (gift of the Urals machinists) to realize that Stalin shared a common taste in culture with the muzhiks, or booboisie as Mencken used to call it.

If Russia's art was debased what might be said of her literature, which even more faithfully should reflect the life and spirit of the country?

In the winter of 1949–50 I was actively working on the Russian language. I tried working alone, at first, but made very little progress. After several false starts I began to take lessons from a young woman named Nina who was doing some translating for one of the embassies.

Nina was not a great teacher but she was an enthusiastic theatergoer and in the course of the next year or so I saw many, many plays, including every single one of the plays used for anti-American propaganda which was showing in Moscow, from *Uncle Tom's*

Cabin to *Another Part of the Forest.* This was supposed to serve two purposes—to improve my Russian vocabulary and to keep my finger on the pulse of Russian "creative" ideology.

Once again, it is only by rereading the notes I made at the time that I am able to recapture the tawdriness of the Soviet theater in the years 1949, 1950 and 1951. It was never possible in that time to convey through the Soviet censorship the full depth of the slander and vituperation which was being spewed out against the United States and against Americans by the Kremlin's favored playwrights. Literally, dozens of examples of this could be cited.

When I went to an anti-American play such as *Missouri Waltz, The Conspiracy of the Doomed* or *The House on the Lane* I was usually able to report, in guarded terms, the general plot line. But, invariably, the more vicious samples of dialogue were simply deleted by the censorship. In the case of one particularly slanderous play, called *The Mad Haberdasher,* which dealt with the then President Truman, the censorship refused for months even to permit the transmission of dispatches mentioning its name. Not until after copies of it had found their way to the United States and excerpts had been published there was I permitted to send an article to *The New York Times* about this scurrility, and even then the worst passages about Mr. Truman were cut out by the censors.

In addition to encouraging me to go to plays Nina was valuable in another way. She gave me glimpses, often clouded or distorted, into what was going on inside the great gaunt courtyards of Moscow where half or two-thirds of the people still live, even now with the thousands of new apartments which have been built in the postwar years.

Nina was a perfectly cynical girl, a fairly typical product, I should say, of the Stalin era. She had gone to the languages institute and had first studied Chinese but, finding that very difficult, switched over to English after several years of Mandarin. Since graduating from the language school she had worked for two or three foreign embassies as a secretary or translator. She was, of course, in the employ of the MVD. I was perfectly aware of this and she was perfectly aware that I was aware of it. But we never mentioned the matter. Her police connections made little difference to me. In the first place I had nothing to hide from the Russians. In the second place I operated on the assumption that any Russian who worked with foreigners had, at a minimum, to report regularly to the MVD.

I suppose the MVD may caution people like Nina with regard to their conversation with foreigners but I suspect such cautioning probably has more to do with security matters than anything else. In any event Nina was a chatterbox and I don't think any power on earth could have kept her from gossiping.

The stories I heard from Nina fitted perfectly into the picture I was forming of a city and a country whose ideals and spiritual aspirations were steadily being ground to dust by the pragmatic and materialistic bureaucracy created by Stalin.

Take Nina, herself, for example. She regarded herself as a member of the "intelligentsia" although she had nothing in common with such persons as the Leningrad architect whom I have described (she would have spit, quite literally, on his views and quickly and competently turned him in to the police). Or with Galya, whom she would have hated and envied (and really, feared) and whom she also would have denounced to the MVD.

Nina had many friends in what she called the "intelligentsia." These mostly seemed to be singers in the musical-comedy theater, dancers in the Stanislavsky theater or writers of skits for the *estradny* (vaudeville) stage.

Not infrequently Nina would turn up with a terrible hangover.

"Oh, what a head I've got," she would complain.

"What's the trouble?" I would ask.

"Last night we had a wedding," she would say. "Volodiya and Natasha got married. What a party!"

Volodiya, she would explain, was a dancer at the Stanislavsky and Natasha was his girl friend. Both were members of the "intelligentsia."

Or another time she would call up and cancel a Russian lesson because she was "sick." Later, it would develop that the "sickness" was caused by having to stay up all night drinking with a friend. Who was it? I would ask.

"Volodiya," Nina would reply. "He felt so bad I had to stay with him."

"What about his wife?"

"That's just the trouble," she would reply. "Natasha has left him."

The "weddings" and "separations" followed one another much too rapidly for me to keep track of. It was, obviously, very seldom that the "marriages" were registered. Usually, they simply constituted a public statement by two young people that they, henceforth, were living together.

Not that living together was necessarily such an easy matter. Frequently it presented great problems because one or both members of the couple would already be "married" or at least living with someone else and while it might be easy enough to break up an unregistered marriage it was quite another matter when it came to getting the third party to give up his or her quarters so that the new spouse could move in.

The sad case of Volodiya illustrated the results of such a situation. He already had a "wife" when he "married" Natasha. The "wife" refused to relinquish her rights in the room she shared with Volodiya and since Natasha had been living in a single room with her parents the newlyweds were without a place to set up housekeeping. Volodiya kept trying to bribe or threaten his first "wife" to leave the communal chamber but she wouldn't budge. Natasha upbraided him for being a mollycoddle and before they got through quarreling she flounced out and that was the end of the "marriage." After a suitable period of grief and anguish, marked by much drinking of vodka and comforting by Nina, Volodiya returned to his first "wife" and everything was ready for the pattern to repeat itself.

Nina had other worries in addition to those over the kaleidoscopic affairs of her fellow members of the "intelligentsia." Most of these worries originated in the apartment where she lived. She was very proud of the fact that she had a room of her own and that it was in a building very close to the center of town—only two or three blocks from the Kremlin. That this building was half in ruins, from lack of maintenance; that she had to walk up five flights of crumbling marble stairs (never lighted at night); that her room gave on an interior courtyard filled with toilet and cooking smells in summer and eternally dark in winter; that the room was one of seven in a communal flat, sharing a tiny kitchen equipped only with electric hot

plates and in which the water tap had long since ceased to function—
none of these facts even occurred to Nina as being anything worthy
of notice.

What was important to her was that she actually had her own
room in a building just off Pushkin Street, and she was so proud of
this that once when I made some sarcastic remark about housing
conditions in Moscow she actually took me to see her quarters, in
order to refute, once and for all, any allegation that Moscow was ill
or inadequately housed.

I was very grateful to Nina for this and never disclosed to her
that she had proved, much better than I ever could have done, the
exact reverse of what she thought she was proving. Her room had
somewhat less than the theoretical nine meters square of floor space
to which each Muscovite was supposed to be entitled. It was a
chamber about twelve feet long and possibly six feet wide. There
was one narrow window, looking on the courtyard, so dirty that
there was no practical need for curtains or drapes which was just as
well since there were none. A single iron bed, blue-painted, an old
straight-backed chair, a tiny table and a mirror made up the furnishings. Nina had no *shkaf* or wardrobe for her clothes and had merely
curtained off a few hooks with a piece of green rep. The rest of her
belongings, apparently, were packed in a cardboard suitcase which
protruded from under the bed. On the wall were several photographs, including one of her brother who was killed in the war
and others, obviously of various tenors and dancers, members no
doubt of the "intelligentsia," and probably including one or two of
the "husbands" whom she claimed to have left for good and sufficient cause.

How Nina had come to acquire this jewel among rooms she never
explained to me and since such reticence was unusual I deduced
that perhaps the MVD had helped her out.

The worries which bothered Nina arose from the nature of life
in a communal apartment. There were six other households in the
flat and seldom a dull moment.

One day Nina told me: "I just don't know what I'm going to do
about Masha."

"What's the trouble?" I asked.

"She took fifty rubles out of my purse again."

"You mean she stole it?"

"No, no. She just took it and then told me about it. I don't mind because I can ask Volodiya for some money but this is the third time this month and I think it is time she went to work."

"You mean Masha hasn't got a job?"

"That's right. You remember I told you she got married and she quit work. But now she has left her husband and she hasn't gone back to work."

I said I didn't see how Masha could live.

"Well," said Nina, "it isn't a good situation. As a matter of fact she is really just a prostitute."

I observed that if Masha was getting money from men she ought to be able to support herself.

"Oh," said Nina. "You don't understand at all. She isn't getting money from men. As a matter of fact that is what she took the fifty rubles for. So she could buy vodka and caviar for her boy friend."

Nina explained that Masha was entertaining a succession of boy friends, "a different one every night," and that it was giving the flat a bad name.

I continued to hear at intervals about Masha over a period of a couple of years but as far as I could tell she never did go back to work. Half the time she was being supported by "loans" from Nina and other residents of the flat and half the time by various boy friends. This was not according to the Socialist rule book but it appeared to be very much in the actual pattern life in Moscow.

Once I went with Nina to see a play called *The Law of Lycurgus,* a poor and distorted dramatization of Dreiser's *American Tragedy,* which was playing at the Red Army theater.

I was pretty scornful of this effort and I found that Nina was too.

"There's a lot better murder case going on right now in Moscow," she said. "Everybody's talking about it."

Needless to say nothing about any murder case had appeared in the press. What had happened, Nina said, was that there had been a graduation party of young people attending one of the institutes of Moscow.

"They were all from good families, too," Nina said. I gathered that good families in her definition meant families of persons prominent in the party or government.

After a great deal of drinking two of the youngsters began to quarrel about a girl. The girl was a coquette and she encouraged the rivals. Finally, one youngster had run out of the apartment where the party was being held. He was gone an hour or so but returned just as the party was breaking up and, drawing a long-bladed "Finnish" knife, stabbed his rival in the chest. The boy died of the wound and now his assailant was on trial for murder.

"His family have hired the best lawyer in Moscow," Nina said. "They say that if anyone can get him off this man will. The defense is that the boy was under eighteen and that he was drunk and didn't know what he was doing."

The trial lasted several days and each day Nina gave me a report on it. She said that the courtroom was mobbed with people. In some apartment houses individuals had been designated to go to the trial in order to give a firsthand report to their neighbors in the evening.

In the end the boy was convicted but his sentence was very light—three years in the "corrective labor" camps.

"At that the lawyer did pretty well," Nina said. "What stopped him from getting the boy off completely was the fact that he ran home for the knife. Everybody agreed the boy was drinking too much but, still, he knew enough to go and get his knife."

I suggested that three years in the labor camp might be hard on the boy. But Nina scoffed.

"What's hard about it?" she said. "It's different if you're old. But for a youngster like that he'll never know the difference."

She then proceeded to tell me about the son of one of the neighbors in her apartment who had just come back from seven years in the camps.

"Naturally," she said, "he isn't supposed to be in Moscow but what can his mother do? She wants to see him. But the worst part is he has brought a friend with him."

The boys, I learned, had been members of one of the many gangs which prowled about Moscow toward the end of the war, directed in most probability by an older criminal, some recently discharged

Red Army man. The youngsters (but not, apparently, the Fagin) were arrested and given seven-year sentences in the camps. Young and hardy, they had not suffered physically and said that life in camp was no worse than life in the Army, which is where they otherwise would have been.

Now released, they were supposed to be forbidden to approach within one hundred kilometers of Moscow. But they had come into town anyway, and were living in Nina's apartment. All of the neighbors knew the facts but no one, apparently, thought to inform the police. Despite Nina's connection with the MVD it was quite clear that she had no intention of telling on the boys. On the contrary, she seemed to have a kind of fellow feeling for them. My guess was that there was a strong social or class bias to Nina's attitude with regard to informing. I knew she had no compunction about reporting on me or any foreigner, and I was sure she would have no compunction about informing on any person of superior talent, mentality or, if the phrase can be used, social origin. But, so far as petty crime was concerned—theft, prostitution and the like— Nina and her ilk obviously regarded these as venial sins, at worst.

Regardless of the neighbors the two boys were speedily in the clutches of the police again because they resumed their connection with the same or another gang of thieves and were arrested as they tried to sell a stolen watch in the market. Once again they were sent off to Siberia for seven-year terms but, according to Nina, this did not dampen their spirits. "After all," she quoted the boys as saying, "we have to work somewhere. So why not Siberia?"

Nina had a boy friend who was a cameraman in one of the big Moscow film studios, and one evening after we had gone to a play which dealt with the efforts of a group of American spies to undermine a people's regime in one of the satellite countries, which obviously was Hungary, she began to giggle. The play was supposed to show the unquenchable faith and loyalty of the Hungarians for their elder brothers, the Russians. On the rock of this mutual confidence of Hungarians and Russians the nefarious Americans came to grief.

"What is so funny?" I asked. "I thought it was a pretty dreary play."

"I'm not laughing at that," she said. "The play just reminded me of something."

At first she wouldn't tell me what it was but finally she said that recently a group of Hungarians had come to Moscow to visit the film studio where her boy friend worked.

"Everybody worked overtime for a week in advance," Nina said. "They cleaned up the whole studio for just about the first time since the war. And on the day the Hungarians came everyone was told to wear his best clothes."

Moreover, Nina said, everyone was warned that there was to be no conversation with the Hungarians except through the official interpreter. Two persons in the studio who understood Hungarian were specially cautioned not to reveal that they could talk the language. It was not believed that any of the visitors spoke Russian, but if unhappily this proved to be the case and questions were asked of any random workers they were to refer the inquiries to the director.

This last precaution was said to be most important because "you can't trust these people." And that's right, too, Nina informed me solemnly. The Hungarians are a very untrustworthy people, as she well knew, because she once had had a Hungarian boy friend.

Came the great day at the studio. The Hungarians arrived. Everything was swept and clean. The studio was decorated with flowers. There were flowers for the guests, as well. Everyone had on his best clothes and best manners. And the visit was going splendidly.

Then, suddenly the worst happened. It was right in the middle of the tour. One of the Hungarians asked a young studio worker a question in French. To the director's consternation the girl happened to know French well and replied with a fluent stream of words which most of the Hungarians appeared to understand but which neither the director nor the party secretary could make head nor tail of.

The official interpreter interrupted and tried to break off the conversation but by this time several Hungarians had clustered around the young girl and the conversation was going too strong to stop. It was nearly five minutes before the situation was brought under control.

"You know what happened?" Nina said. "The director called the girl in as soon as the Hungarians left. He denounced her as a saboteur and said he would do all kinds of terrible things to her. But in the end he had to let her go because it was all his fault."

"Why?" I asked.

"She was home sick the day the instructions were passed out and nobody told her that she wasn't supposed to talk to the Hungarians. It was the director's responsibility to see that everyone knew and so, in the end, it was he who got the reprimand. He nearly lost his job."

"Well," I said. "What was it all about? What difference did it make anyway? What did the girl tell them about?"

"Oh," said Nina. "She didn't tell them about anything. It was simply a matter of principle. Everyone knows you can't trust the Hungarians. That's why the play made me laugh so much."

I didn't say anything but I didn't think Nina's bosses would have liked this conversation very much.

Not long after this I was fortunate enough to go back to the United States on leave. I was gone from Russia for several months and this proved to be a very valuable respite. In fact, without that breather I do not believe I could have stood many more months of a Moscow compounded of the sort of life and incidents and people which seemed entirely normal to Nina. Moreover, the situation was to grow worse—much worse.

Thus, I was out of Russia when the Korean War broke out and did not return until the early fall of 1950.

The question which was worrying the people in the United States the most that summer was whether Korea was going to be the curtain raiser of a world war with Russia. Many people felt certain that before the year was out the Big Show would be on. No one was more worried than I. After all I was heading back to Moscow and many a night I was kept awake thinking about what might happen if war should start after I had returned to Russia. I didn't think the chance for survival in such circumstances would be great. With atom bombs falling on Moscow and Washington the fate of a handful of Americans in Moscow would hardly arouse much concern.

Yet, despite the threatening situation my own guess, based largely on the picture of Russia which I have drawn here, was that the war in Korea probably would remain isolated. But, of course, I could not be sure. So with a view to checking as well as I could on whether Russia was displaying any signs of increased military preparations in the West I arranged to return to Moscow through Prague and Warsaw and by train through Brest-Litovsk and Minsk.

If Russia was preparing for general war I did not think it possible for her to conceal the concentrations of troops and war material which would be necessary in the west. And I was positive that if Russia planned war or expected war she would want to strike before the autumn rains turned Eastern Europe into a quagmire.

My guess as to the reality of the situation was fully supported by what I saw coming back into Russia. I stopped over in Warsaw for several days and conferred with the handful of Western newspapermen who were still at that time there and with the American and other diplomats in the Polish capital. None of them felt that war was in the making. They had seen no unusual preparations and had heard of none through their Polish contacts which, while gradually growing more and more limited, were still numerous as compared with my Russian contacts in Moscow. My train stopped over a full day at the border junction point of Brest-Litovsk. I spent the time poking about the city, which is a great railroad center (but little else). I found, as I expected, many, many Russian troops and officers, moving in and out of Germany, but no signs of any special or unusual activity along Russia's western marches.

Unless I was being completely fooled nothing but routine troop movements were under way. There were no shipments of guns or tanks (visible to me, at least); no special security precautions; no sign of congestion in any of the freight yards. On the other hand, civilian construction programs continued to be pushed all along the Brest-Moscow route, which ran through an area of very great German devastation.

What I heard in Moscow supported this analysis and I wrote several articles for the *Times*, outlining the situation as I saw it.

Unfortunately, I was unable at that time to cite two very strong and very revealing bits of evidence supporting my belief that Russia did not intend or expect the Far Eastern war to widen.

The first of these I had heard about before I left Moscow. It concerned what happened earlier in the year at the time of the so-called Baltic plane incident when the Russians shot down a U.S. naval reconnaissance plane off the Baltic coast. Since then plane incidents have become common. But this was the first, and when the Soviet communiqué was published it created a minor but very real panic in Moscow. The Russian people thought it meant war. Some thought the plane had been headed for Moscow with an atom bomb and that other planes were sure to follow.

So serious was this public nervousness that party agitators had to go into the factories and shops and deliver talks, reassuring the people and promising them that war would not come—at least not at this time.

I had felt this was a most revealing indication both of the mood of the public and of the Soviet Government and this was deepened when I heard that very much the same thing had happened when the news of the outbreak of war in Korea was published.

The Soviet communiqué blamed the outbreak, of course, on the United States. But, I learned, this was not believed by the Moscow public. The Moscow public believed the war was started by the Russian side and it feared that general war would follow. The panic and alarm, I was told, were much deeper than at the time of the Baltic incident.

Once again the party agitators had to make the rounds, speaking to workers and employees, assuring them that Korea did not mean general war and that the United States was not going to attack Russia. Here, surely, was a strange and striking anomaly. The Communists who had been shouting from the rooftops that America was preparing to assault the Soviet Union had to send their workers out to convince the Russians that there was not to be any attack— at least for the present.

The fact that the Party and Government itself twice in the course of one year had given direct assurances to its public that there would not be war and, particularly, that the United States would not attack Russia seemed to me very strongly to support the correctness of my analysis.

Naturally, the censorship struck out of my dispatches all references to these events. I was hardly surprised. For with increasing tension the censorship like everything else in Russia had grown more harsh and more rigid. It was more difficult than ever to construct a dispatch which after being subject to censorship cuts still gave an objective, even if limited, picture. Yet, this was what I must strive unceasingly to do.

Everything from now on was going to make my task and my life more difficult. For, if it now seemed fairly certain that there would not for the time being be any hot war, I could feel the temperature of the cold war dropping and dropping toward absolute zero.

In fact, from now on, in Moscow my real problem would be the direct and simple one of survival; a fight for sheer existence; for maintaining my vitality and will power, my intellectual integrity and curiosity, in this moral and spiritual desert, this Stalinized land so bereft of grace.

VI

A Performance of Othello

I DID not know when I boarded a train for Tiflis toward the end of May, 1951, and headed south for the Caucasus that this was to be virtually the last time that I would leave Moscow for well over two years and that, for all practical purposes, I was becoming a prisoner of the Soviet capital and its immediate environs.

Nor did I know as I settled back in the compartment which I shared with three Soviet Army officers that this trip down to Georgia was to give me a very great insight into the origins of the strange and terrifying events which before too long a time had passed were to shake Russia and the world.

When I traveled down to Georgia I traveled back into the pages of the past, into a mountain kingdom with a history like a storybook. Georgia's only affinity for Russia was purely and entirely that of geography, and yet here by a fateful and not entirely accidental chance had been born the youth Josef Djugashvili, who was to become Stalin. And one of his chief lieutenants, Lavrenti Beriya, as well.

Georgia, I was to discover, was a land with a way of life and a point of view toward the world which had survived from medieval times almost unchanged into our day. Within an hour's walk of Gori, Stalin's birthplace, there were stone cities which had been founded twenty-five hundred years before Christ and endured with hardly a change.

Seldom has so small, so remote and so obscure a land had so great an effect on history. For, as I soon found, if Stalin had made post-Revolution Russia what it was today, surely Georgia had made Stalin what he was.

My curiosity about this kingdom of Iberia had long been simmering, because I was certain that only there could I discover the answer to many questions about Russia and about Stalin and the reign of steel, terror and mystery which he had imposed upon 200,000,000 people. It was a long, long way from the mountain village of Gori to the pinnacle of the Kremlin and I thought it was worth trying to retrace as much of the early part of the route as possible.

With that idea in mind I had been working for months, trying to get the stone-brained bureaucrats of the Press Department to arrange some facilities for this Georgian trip. But, as usual, after promises and fair words it had come to nothing, and now, seething with resentment and frustration, I had set off on my own with small hopes of being able to accomplish very much once I got to Tiflis.

In that I was rather mistaken, principally because an almost Oriental hospitality is one of the deepest and most pleasant of Georgian traits. A Georgian mountaineer would murder a stranger without turning a hair for the sake of stealing his horse—if they met alone on a high trail. But if the same stranger knocked at the Georgian's hut and begged for aid he would be treated like a member of the family.

Two of my three Red Army companions were Georgians and the third was a Ukrainian. Their friendliness and hospitality were almost oppressive. If they were not trying to persuade me to drink a water tumbler of vodka they were pressing beer and wine on me by the bottle. There were many Georgians on the train and not a few of them traveled with small wooden wine kegs to which wooden or leather handles were affixed for ease in carrying. When they went visiting—even as far distant as Moscow—they took their own wine, made of their own grapes and pressed by their own women. Foreign wine—meaning any wine not grown in Georgia—was not, in their opinion, fit to drink. In Georgia itself I encountered men who would drink only the wine of their own little district. Or sometimes only the wine of their own vines.

Once the train got south of Rostov-on-Don it took on much of the atmosphere of a holiday excursion. At every stop there were Georgians getting on and off, most of them carrying their little wine kegs. They gathered in the corridors and compartments, trading drinks, flirting with all the girls on the train and singing songs. In wartime days I sometimes had been with Russians when they were drinking, flirting and making merry. But it was nothing like this. The Georgians were full of warmth and color, flashing white teeth and swarthy complexions, hot temper and sparkling eyes. But there was a somber side as well which probably reflected the Georgian heritage. Georgia once had been a great and proud kingdom but now she had been suffering for centuries. Only Georgian pride had managed to survive the centuries of defeat, of torture, of poverty and oppression. And it was the fierce, savage pride of the narrow world of the high Caucasus. The songs the Georgians sang were of great tragedies of love, of knighthood duels, of suicide leaps from mountain crags, of clannish feuds and purple passions . . . of kidnaped brides . . . blood quarrels . . . murderous revenge . . . ambushes . . . poison . . . anger . . . jealousy.

There were many Russians on the train but the further south we went the more inconspicuous they became. They seemed to shrink into the corners of the compartments and lose their voices as the Georgians took over the stage.

Looking out the train window at the blue of the sea, the snow-topped mountains, the red-tiled cottage roofs, the tall Lombardy poplars and palms in the white resort cities I felt that I was no longer in Russia but in some distant Mediterranean land. Italy, perhaps. Or Sicily. Or Greece. On reflection I realized that this was natural enough since Iberia's coast in the misty past had been colonized by Greek soldiers and traders and it was culturally bound far more closely to the sapphire Aegean than to the great land mass of Russia to which, as it happened, this earth bridge to Asia and the south was attached.

One of the first discoveries which I made about Georgia was that in the home country Beriya was, in some ways, more of a figure than Stalin. Perhaps it was because Stalin had been gone so long from his homeland. (He had hardly been in the Caucasus since the Revolution and had not been to Tiflis since the funeral of his mother in 1937.) There were not, actually, many Georgians who personally knew or remembered Stalin. He was to them, as he was to so much of Russia, a great godlike figure, mounted on a pedestal much too high for ordinary mortals to reach.

Beriya, on the other hand, seemed to be closer to the ordinary Georgian. The principal square in the city of Tiflis was named for Beriya (the name of this square provides a capsule history of the times. Before the Revolution it was plain Erivan Square, named for the highway that led south to Erivan, capital of Armenia. After the Revolution it was called Svobodna, or Freedom Square. It was named after Beriya in the late thirties. After his arrest and disgrace in 1953 the name was changed once more, this time to Soviet Square). Many other Georgian places and institutions also bore Beriya's name and his picture was more often seen in the streets and in offices and factories than that of Stalin himself.

Before I went to Georgia I had sometimes heard that Beriya was more of a patron saint than Stalin, but the first confirmation of this came as the train rolled south from Sochi, the great Black Sea resort. One of the Georgians was showing off the sights.

"There is Generalissimo Stalin's datcha," he said, pointing to a great white palace, almost surrounded by palms on the side of a hill well back from the sea. I had hardly fixed my eyes on Stalin's villa when the Georgian grabbed my arm in excitement. "Look," he exclaimed. "That house there. That's Comrade Beriya's datcha."

Beriya's resort home appeared at a distance to be just as big as Stalin's and it was obvious that Beriya produced considerably more emotional response in my Georgian friend than Stalin.

"What sort of a man is Beriya?" I asked this Georgian.

"Comrade Beriya is a fine man," the Georgian said. "We call him Beriya the Builder because he did so much for Georgia. Everywhere you go in Georgia if you see a new factory, a new power station, a new mine, or a new building—usually it was built by Comrade Beriya."

Many times in Georgia I heard that characterization of Beriya— Beriya the Builder—repeated. I am sure that Beriya was guilty of great crimes and cruelties to his own people in Georgia. He was, after all, the chief of secret police in Georgia for a number of years before becoming chief of the Georgian Communist Party in 1931, a post he held until he was called to Moscow by Stalin to take over the national direction of the Police and Internal Affairs departments toward the end of the great purges in 1938.

I suppose that the passage of twenty years since he had been the local police boss may have served to dim the recollection of his Georgian oppressions. Or, perhaps, it was deemed untactful to talk of "Comrade Beriya" in any terms other than ones of praise. Not infrequently, however, I think the Georgians were speaking quite sincerely. It was perfectly obvious that since he had achieved so much power in Moscow Beriya had turned Georgia into a kind of personal satrapy and had procured for "his" people many favors, not the least of which was a fairly stabilized and relaxed life in which the customary repressions of the police and the state were much diluted by home-town and family links and influence.

Everyone in Georgia seemed to be related to everyone else and I quickly became convinced that nepotism, operating through the structure of party, police and state, served to ameliorate many of the worst abuses of the Soviet system. If you knew how to wangle things properly you could do almost anything you wanted to in Georgia, even to the point of running a small business.

When, almost a year later, a purge was launched in Georgia as, or so it turned out, a blow at Beriya, there was hardly a crime on the calendar which was not charged against Georgian officials and individuals. Judges were said to take bribes to let thieves off. Police took protection money from gangs of robbers and fences. Factory directors padded the payrolls and divided the profits with crooked bookkeepers and investigators of the State Finance Ministry. Directors of small artisans' co-operatives turned them into private profit-making concerns. State and party jobs were bought and sold. Many collective farmers devoted themselves entirely to their private vineyards or sheep herds and worked not a day in the whole year to the collective farm account. Most of the charges, I suspected, were true.

The reason life seemed more free and relaxed in Georgia was simply that it actually was more free and relaxed. Not because of principle. Just because of corruption. And favoritism and nepotism.

It is probably important to emphasize that no great principle was involved in this relatively free and easy environment in Georgia, because later on after the death of Stalin and Beriya's arrest some foreigners professed to believe that Beriya was a great liberal and that he had followed a very liberal policy on the question of treatment of national minorities in the Soviet.

Beriya's treatment of his Georgian countrymen is cited as one support for this argument but, as I have noted, unless a man is deserving of praise for corruption and favoritism it is doubtful that Beriya should win any plaudits on this account.

The other argument cited in Beriya's behalf is that he was more humane toward the Jews than the Soviet regime as a whole. Since Beriya, as police chief, actually carried out a series of highly anti-Semitic measures, involving the arrest of some thousands or tens of thousands of Jews and their forcible deportation to some of the worst forced residence areas of the Soviet state, I find little grounds in his actual conduct to support this argument, either.

The only possible substantiation for portraying Beriya as less anti-Semitic than some of the other chief Soviet leaders lies in certain things Beriya did down in Georgia. It also has been said that Beriya, who was born in Mingrelia, a tiny mountain area close to the Turkish frontier, was half Jewish and that his mother was a member of the extremely ancient and tiny sect of Mingrelian Jews. While I have been told this both in Tiflis and Moscow by both Georgians and Russians, other Georgians indignantly deny that Beriya was of Jewish descent and contend that he was pure Georgian.

Regardless of Beriya's ancestry, I made one discovery in Georgia which supports the picture of Beriya as a liberal. In a narrow twisting sidestreet of Tiflis I found a curious and interesting sight. It was a Jewish ethnological museum which was founded at Beriya's instigation. The curious thing was that while one of Tiflis' most ancient synagogues was closed in order to provide quarters for this museum, the exhibit itself was most comprehensive and bore neither an anti-religious nor an anti-Jewish character.

Instead, the museum was clearly designed to enhance among the Jews their knowledge of the cultural and traditional history of the Jewish people. Here there were paintings and models, depicting the ancient rites and customs of the Jewish church, scenes from the

Bible, reconstructions of early Jewish churches in Georgia, repre-
sentations of the oppression of Jews by the Turks and the Mongols,
pictures of beautiful Jewish women being sold as harem slaves or
traded for great Caucasus sheep dogs at the rate of three women
for one dog.

The director of this museum, a scholarly Jew of middle age, had
nothing but kind words for Beriya. He told me that by the time of
the Revolution the Jews in Georgia had fallen to almost unbelievable depths of poverty and ignorance.

"The Jews had come to Georgia in the fifth century before Christ,"
he told me. "They were invited here by the kings of Georgia and
they occupied an outstanding place in Georgian cultural and economic life in the early centuries of the Christian era."

But in the centuries of war with the Turks, the Mongols and the
Persians the Georgian kingdom suffered severely. The position of the
Jews sank lower and lower, and when Russia finally gobbled up the
little kingdom the Jews even lost the right to own land or property
and were banned from almost all business and handicraft. By the
time of the Revolution there were few Jewish communities anywhere
in the world more depressed and oppressed than that of Georgia.
Jews no longer knew how to read and write. They were beginning
to forget the rituals of their religion because education was forbidden them. The yellow ticket of the prostitute was the only way
a Jewish girl could get to the city.

In the twenties, the director told me, Beriya helped start a program for rehabilitating the Jews. Special schools, trade and handicraft centers were opened. Special Jewish farms were set up. A
Jewish charitable society was organized under Beriya's sponsorship
to help the people help themselves. This sounded very strange to my
ears because the Soviet, theoretically, frowns on any kind of charity.

And, as part of this program, the Jewish museum was founded.

The director took me about the building. Here were photographs
of the life and times of Sholem Aleichem, including a picture of his
funeral in New York. Here was a special layout on Albert Einstein,
telling about his achievements in the field of physical theory and his
struggle against oppression of the Jews. Here was a large section
devoted to Nazi persecution of the Jews, to the anti-Semitic out-

rages in Germany and the horrors of the Nazi cremation chambers. And beside it was a layout of Jewish generals in the Soviet Army and Jewish heroes in the Red Army during the Second World War.

So far as I could see there was nothing wrong with the museum. It was just what it purported to be, strange as this seemed against the background of open and notorious anti-Semitism in Moscow. Still, there was the curious bit about the synagogue being closed to provide a building for this institution. Perhaps, in fact, an effort was being made to discourage churchgoing. I asked the director whether there were any synagogues in Tiflis.

Yes, indeed, he replied. There are two. A big one for Georgian Jews and a smaller one for Russian Jews.

I asked him where the synagogues were located and went around to check up on whether he was telling the truth. He was. On a Friday evening both synagogues were busy and active, and seemingly, operating without interference.

So, perhaps, Beriya had some feeling of tolerance and consideration for the Jews of Georgia—natural enough, if he himself were half Jewish.

However, whatever Beriya may or may not have done for the Georgian Jews there was no doubt about what he had done for Stalin and, in particular, for the ever-changing, ever-growing Stalin legend.

Beriya it was who built the glass and steel and marble canopy over the little two-room slum house in Gori where Stalin spent the first four years of his life. Beriya even persuaded Stalin's strong-minded old mother, Ekaterina, to help him in reconstituting the furnishings of the shabby little home she had shared with her husband, Vissarion, a cobbler who drank too much. However, if the word of a history professor at Tiflis University was to be believed, Ekaterina came to Gori only once. She took a look at Beriya's grandiose creation, uttered a rude but expressive Georgian word and returned to her simple but comfortable home in Tiflis.

I met the history professor in the Georgian state museum one morning and when he learned that I was an American who was interested in Stalin's Georgian origins he offered to act as my guide. He took me to the famous shrine at Gori and I could understand

Ekaterina's reaction. The place was pretentious in the worst possible combination of Georgian and Russian bad taste. From what I knew of Stalin's artistic sense I was sure he loved it.

What interested me a good deal more was the fact that in the streets around the Stalin shrine there were many, many slum dwellings, identical with that in which the great dictator was born. And all of them still inhabited by families which looked to the casual eye very much like the early photographs of the Djugashvili family, poor, downtrodden and exploited.

It was clear as could be that what distinguished the Djugashvilis from all the other poverty-stricken mountain people was the iron will and single-minded purpose of Ekaterina, who was determined that Josef would be educated and that he would rise above the gutter level of his father's drunkenness.

Her ambition was certainly achieved, although not exactly as she had anticipated. She expected little Josef to rise through the Church, one of the few narrow staircases up which a poor boy in Czarist Georgia might with pain and fortitude mount toward a better life.

Just down the street from the Gori house I saw the white stone nineteenth-century Georgian Orthodox church where the Djugash-vilis went to services and where young Soso (the Georgian diminutive for Josef) sang melodious three-part Georgian hymns in the choir. Beriya had spent no money restoring the church. Pigs were grazing in the grass-grown courtyard and owls were nesting in the decaying tower.

In the museum which Beriya built beside the Gori house I saw a picture of Stalin as a thirteen-year-old Gori schoolboy, bright-eyed but somewhat smaller than his schoolmates, and I talked to an old man named Tzitatrishvili who said he was the only other survivor of that class and who remembered, or thought he remembered, that Josef Djugashvili was the brightest boy in the group. And one of the smallest.

I also saw the scholarship report of the Tiflis ecclesiastical seminary for the entering class of the school year 1894–95. That was Stalin's first year at the seminary and he had already come a long way along the path which his mother had set for him. Young

Djugashvili had taken five out of the six possible subjects—writing, Russian language, history, mathematics and Georgian language. The only subject he missed was Latin. He had a perfect scholarship record—all 5's which is the Russian equivalent of A's.

And I got confirmatory evidence of Djugashvili's good scholarship and early promise from a most unexpected source. I paid a call in his pleasant quarters behind the seventh-century Zion cathedral on the eighty-five-year-old Patriarch of the Georgian Church, a wonderfully pleasant old man whose white hair and beard, twinkling blue eyes and chubby red nose reminded me of my childhood dreams of St. Nicholas.

Between pleasant drafts of cool, dry Tsinondali wine, bites of candied melon rind and Georgian cakes the old Patriarch, whose name was Kalistrat Tsintsadtze, added his little contribution to the story of the young Stalin. In the 1890's, said the Patriarch, he was an examiner in the ecclesiastical seminary.

"It was my duty to examine students on their progress," said the Patriarch. "On two occasions Stalin appeared before me for examinations—once in the Russian language and once in Russian history. Stalin was small for his age but a very bright boy. All of his instructors at that time knew this although of course we none of us were able to foresee how far he would go."

The Patriarch said Stalin had done well in the two examinations he gave him. I learned, too, that Stalin had repeatedly gotten into trouble during his years in the seminary, principally for reading books from the so-called Cheap Library, sometimes romances but sometimes books with more social content, such as Victor Hugo. Eventually, to his mother's great regret, Stalin was expelled from the seminary during his fifth year of attendance. The cause was not as you might suppose, revolutionary activity. It was cutting an examination.

About a year after my pleasant conversation with the old Patriarch he died. While he had been interested in telling me about young Djugashvili he was considerably more interested in showing me his new Zim car. At that time this machine, something like a Buick, had just come out in Russia. The Patriarch's was the first in Tiflis, excellent testimony of the strength and influence of his position, but whether this bore any relationship to his contact with the young seminarian I could not say.

My history professor led me to another view of the young Djugash-vili and one, I confess, which I hardly imagined existed. This was of Stalin, the poet.

In the yellowing newspaper files of the Georgian State Library I found six poems by Stalin, five published in 1895 and one in 1896. The first appeared within a few months of his enrollment in the Tiflis seminary at a time when he was only sixteen.

I am no judge of Georgian poetry but the Georgians who trans-lated Stalin's youthful verses for me into Russian swore that they were excellent. That this is not entirely an ex post facto opinion is shown by the circumstance that the magazine *Iberia*, which pub-lished five of the poems, in each case gave the verses place of honor on page 1. This magazine was published in the 1890's by Georgia's outstanding literary critic, a liberal writer named Ilya Chavchavadze.

There is no doubt that Chavchavadze thought Djugashvili was a poet of promise. Moreover, twice in the years just before and after 1900 Stalin's verses were reprinted in Georgian anthologies of poetry. Long before Djugashvili won his spurs in the Bolshevik underground of the Transcaucasus and a full generation before he became an important figure in the Party he was well known, if not famous, in his homeland as a poet.

And his poetic reputation was based, primarily, on typical Geor-gian lyricism. True, there is a faint social content to two of his poems. But while this was eagerly pointed out to me by the Georgians in the Library it was plain that you had to stretch it pretty far to read anything revolutionary into the young Georgian's verses.

Take, for example, his first verse, published in *Iberia* January 14, 1895. It carried no title and was signed with the most obvious of noms de plume— "I. G–shisveli" (instead of "Iosef Djugashvili").

Here is the poem:

> The rosebud is opening
>   And all around are bluebells.
> The iris, too, has awakened
>   And all nod in the breeze.

The lark flies high in the sky,
Chirping and singing.
The nightingale with great feeling
And quiet voice, sings:

"Flourish, my dear country—
Wed and be happy, my land of Iberia—

"And, you men of Georgia,
May your studies wed
You to your homeland."

The only "ideology" in that poem is a faint hint of Georgian nationalism, with which if indications may be believed the young Djugashvili was deeply tinged. There was a slightly more social content to another Stalin poem called "To the Moon," in which he called on the moon to "awaken all the people, and the poor people who live under the moon in snow and ice, as well." In fact, the moon was a favorite image with the young poet, and a second of his verses was also called "To the Moon."

One of his poems was dedicated to the famous Georgian poet, Eristavi, whom he described as wandering over the earth, fighting for justice with verse and song and gaining as a reward "not the praise of the government but only poisonous glances." This may well have reflected Djugashvili's own hurt at his lack of recognition in the seminary. For, even if his verses had no great social content any such activity was strictly forbidden by the strict seminary rules.

It was unfortunately not possible at this time to visit the seminary where Stalin studied because after many years in which it had served as a hotel it was now being completely rebuilt, preparatory to being opened as another Stalin museum. This, too, was one of Beriya's projects.

One and one only of the Djugashvili poems had a curiously prophetic quality about it, a quality that may have foreshadowed a philosophy still germinating in the young Georgian's mind. It was called "Old Man Ninika" and it tells of Old Ninika, who has worked and labored his whole life through. Now he is old and tired and sick. In his youth he had been strong but his strength was drained away in ill-paid labor and in his age he has nothing. He is lying ready to die. No one helps him and as he watches the strong, full-bodied young workers hurrying at their labors his heart fills with envy. Then, comes the quick twist. The one which the Stalin ideology and the Stalin regime would use over and over again to justify any hardship, any sacrifice of the people. As he watches the hurrying, strong young people Old Ninika becomes happy because he realizes that while he was denied happiness in his life the younger generation will achieve happiness as a result of his sacrifices.

A curious and not very Marxian thought for an adolescent young Tiflis seminarian to have!

In fact, outside of such works as Beriya's *History of Bolshevik Organizations in the Trans-Caucasus* and the museums dedicated to the Stalin myth it was hard to find much firsthand evidence of Djugashvili's revolutionary activities. True enough, he had played a part in the "movement" in the Caucasus but when you pinned it down it didn't sound much more revolutionary than the career of a young CIO organizer in the steel towns of Pennsylvania in the early thirties. Even his role in the famous Tiflis holdup of the State Bank to get funds for the Bolshevik underground may be apocryphal.

With much difficulty I finally uncovered an old man who remembered Stalin as a "revolutionary." The old man was a carpenter in a Tiflis silk factory and he had worked in the same factory all his life. The only material difference was that before the Revolution the building was a tobacco factory run by a man named Bazhartzantze and now it was a silk factory run by a woman named Gaftadze. Previously the profits went to stockholders. Now they go to the state.

The carpenter's name was Georg Hatizov and he said he could remember Stalin in the days of 1898 to 1901 when he was a trade-union organizer in Tiflis.

"I got forty kopeks for a twelve-hour day," Hatizov said. "I remember Stalin very well in those days. He was a young thin man. Not tall at all. But full of energy. He used to come out here and talk to us. 'Why do you work twelve hours?' he would ask us. 'Eight hours a day is long enough.'"

I smiled wryly to myself, thinking of the working hours of some of the industrial establishments in Stalin's Russia. Maybe what the country needed was a new crop of young Stalins.

The old man went on talking, looking at his gnarled old hands as he spoke.

"He used to tell us that forty kopeks a day wasn't a living wage and that we should get more. Well, we knew that, too. But he encouraged us to fight for better pay and better hours. He was a good speaker and when he was talking you forgot everything else," the man said. "He used to say: 'Never be afraid. Don't be afraid to ask for your rights. If they don't give you your rights don't be afraid to take them.'"

The old man stopped there and was silent for a long time, as though that was all he had to say. Finally, I asked him how old he was. Sixty-seven. "I could retire," he said. "But when you have worked all your life you don't like to stop."

Later on, I wrote up that interview into a dispatch for *The New York Times*. The censor let it go through without very many cuts. But he took out Stalin's appeal to the workers not to be afraid and to stand up for their rights. Needless to say that kind of advice was no longer the fashion.

My history professor took me on one more trip which he thought would help me to understand Georgia and reveal a bit more about Stalin's background. First we went to the beautiful little village of Ateni or Athens on the limestone banks of the Kara River to see how the pale yellow wine of Ateni is made. This is the most famous of the wines grown around Gori in the general vicinity of Stalin's birthplace. It was a pleasant and relaxing experience. The wine growers of Ateni live wisely and well. They put their light dry wine into huge earthen pots and bury them completely in the sand floor of the wine vaults. The director of the Ateni vineyard said that Georgians had been making wine like this for thousands of years. "From time to time we open the pots and draw off a few liters so sample it," said the black-shirted wine maker. "Then we seal up the pot and within a few days the pot is full again. Nature restores what we drink." Why this was true he did not know, but I found that all Georgians believed in this implicitly.

Here, too, I witnessed the old Georgian custom of handing a guest a ram's horn full of wine. It must be drunk to the bottom before being put down because otherwise the wine would spill.

It was easy to see that life in the Georgian vineyards was not too difficult. Certainly not in the Ateni vineyards, which each year sent to the Kremlin the best wine of the crop.

Next, we visited the curious ruin called Uplis Tsikhe, or "God's Fortress," an ancient stone city literally carved in the wall of a cliff, about an hour's drive from Gori across the deep-gorged mountains. Here we had slipped right out of the modern world and into almost prehistoric times. The shepherds and their flocks might have been back in the time of another Joseph. And it was hard to believe that any philosophy of Marx or dialectics of communism had found a foothold in this rock-strewn landscape, almost devoid of any appliance more modern than the wheel and the forked stick for plowing.

Nothing had changed in this world since young Josef Djugashvili and the other youngsters from Gori roamed over the mountain trails and scrawled their names, as centuries of youngsters had before them, in the stone caverns of God's Fortress. Here, as in few other places in Georgia, was the combination of legend and romance—once, Uplis Tsikhe had been an imperial city, capital of a pre-Georgian empire—and utter poverty, backwardness and ignorance which formed the seed bed of young Djugashvili's inherited environment. Add his mother's resolute and unbounded ambition; add his own determination and a growing sense of hurt, unfairness and injustice and the makings of the future man of steel lay at hand and exposed. He had been a small boy and he grew up a small man—not the first nor probably the last small man from a backward kingdom to shake the world.

Yet, still there seemed something missing from the picture. Some ingredient, some spark, some catalyst which would make the smallest boy in the class, the youthful student, the budding poet, the promising seminarian, the energetic labor agitator come alive; which would set him apart from all others; which would transform this provincial tyro into a colossus who bestrode the fate and path of millions.

Where would I find this missing component? I did not know. I hardly knew what I was looking for and, even after I found it, it was not until much later, much, much later, that I became fully aware of what I had found.

Like many such discoveries it was rather accidental. Even before I had gone down to Tiflis I had heard of a remarkable Georgian actor, named Akady Horava, who many persons thought was one of the best in Russia if not the world.

Horava's most famous presentation was said to be Othello. The idea of Georgians playing Shakespeare at all seemed to me, on the surface, to be a bit of Soviet pretension. The Russians were forever going around and proclaiming that they understood or appreciated Shakespeare better than anyone else. They even had started to claim that he was "Russian in all but name."

Thus, it was in a mood of considerable skepticism that I found myself one night at the Rustaveli Theater, watching Horava's Othello. It proved, however, to be one of the most remarkable experiences of my life. Horava is a great, powerful man with a voice like a bell, the eye of a hawk and the figure of a gladiator. He was speaking in Georgian, a language of which I knew not a single word. But he could have been speaking in Urdu or Eskimo. It didn't make any difference. Five minutes after he stalked onto the stage he *was* Othello. Not just for me and not so importantly for me. He was Othello for every Georgian in the theater that night and every seat in the big house was taken although Horava has played the role hundreds of times in the last fifteen years.

I felt myself caught up in the performance in a way that seldom if ever had happened before. I could *feel* Othello's suspicion and Othello's jealousy and the inevitable unfoldment of Othello's tragedy. It was happening here and now in this theater except that the theater had vanished and it was real.

This happened so quickly and so naturally that I hardly had time to analyze it and it was only later as I began to take the experience apart and to think about it that I understood what happened when Horava came onto the stage. And when I did I realized that it was not only the projection of a great actor which I had experienced. It was the emotional reaction of a great audience.

I have never seen Horava perform Othello in Moscow. But I do not believe it could ever be the same thing. Because when he plays it in Tiflis it is not Shakespeare. It is not an historical period play from the seventeenth century. It is not a classic English play translated into Georgian.

It is life. Georgian life. It is the blood and the tragedy and the spirit of Georgia, just as contemporary as today's blood-red sunset behind the Georgian mountains, just as real as a dagger in a woman's breast or a muffled horseman galloping over the mountain pass. There is nothing alien in it.

Each Georgian who sat in the theater that night was experiencing just the emotions which Othello experienced. The tiny pinprick of suspicion. The quick spread and rise of the infection, so fast that the victim often as he has felt it before still is surprised and caught off guard. The futile fight to throw off the madness. The defeat and the ever-growing abandonment to the torture and the passion of jealousy, to the fire in the veins and the quick breath in the lungs as the poison grows more strong and more strong.

This was, as I came to look back on it, not merely an exciting night in the theater. It was that, of course, par excellence. It was an exciting night in life. Because as I looked at the audience I could see in their haunted eyes, in their distended nostrils, in their clenched fists, in the mounting blood in their temples the passions of Othello mount, higher and higher.

I even felt a momentary panic as I looked about me at the fixed and rigid gazes which saw not Desdemona, not Othello, but God knows what deceit of friends and foes, what treachery of wives and sweethearts in the place of the actors on the stage.

That night I left the theater limp and exhausted. For the first time I really knew what suspicion, what jealousy could do to men and women who outwardly appeared so gay, so lighthearted and romantic.

It was a long time, however, before I was able to apply the full moral of this lesson about Georgian character. But when the moment finally came it cast a strange and fitful brilliance over a complex of events which already emanated a somewhat phosphorescent glow.

I mean, of course, the terrifying and sinister happenings which came to be called the Doctors' Plot. It seemed, by then, to me that

my trip to Georgia had given me all the keys I needed to understand
the complex character of the man the world knew as Josef Stalin,
who might, but for a chance of fate, have gone down in history as
a romantic poet, or, perhaps, in an earlier day a star-crossed knight
of God's Fortress.

VII

A Pig, a Chinaman and a Stove

I NEVER thought when I saw the village of Saltikovka in a thin drizzle of rain in the spring of 1950 that I was taking the first steps toward half ownership of a Russian pig.

Nor did I suppose that I would meet a Chinaman, selling hot-cross buns in the village market, or find myself showing a Russian *pechnik,* or stove builder, how to construct a fireplace with the aid of an advertisement from the *Saturday Evening Post.*

Which only goes to show how little we can guess of what the future may hold and how many interesting things can happen in a Russian village even to an American in the coldest days of the cold war.

Had it not been for Saltikovka I should never have managed to stick it out in Russia through the grim years during which for all practical purposes I, like the rest of the correspondents and foreigners, was practically confined to the environs of Moscow. While it was possible during this period to visit Leningrad, Stalingrad, Odessa and Tiflis, I had been to all four places. There was little more to be seen in any of the cities and, except for a very brief trip to Leningrad, I was not away from Moscow from June, 1951, until September, 1953. It was a long grim haul but Saltikovka made it not only endurable but often even pleasant.

My introduction to the village which lies twenty-two kilometers east of Moscow on the paved Chaussee Entusiastov, or Highway of Enthusiasts, leading in the general direction of Vladimir, Gorky and, eventually, Siberia, was not auspicious.

Before learning that I was going home on leave in 1950 I had written a curious and uniquely Soviet organization, called Burobin, or the "Administration for Services to the Diplomatic Corps," and advised them that I was interested in renting a cottage for the summer. This organization is a kind of combination catering outfit, employment bureau and rental agency, which is operated as a subsidiary of the Soviet Foreign Office. If you are a foreigner and want to rent a flat, hire a chauffeur, throw a big reception or buy a Russian television set the chances are you will end up dealing with Burobin.

Only Russians who are hired through this outfit are allowed to work for foreigners and only apartments and summer houses provided by Burobin may (with a very few exceptions) be rented by foreigners. As can be imagined, the liaison between Burobin and the MVD is very close indeed.

Burobin, as was its custom, did nothing about my request for some time, but finally told me that, regrettably, it could not supply me with a summer cottage, or *datcha,* as they are called in Russia. However, they said that they could rent me a half-datcha if I did not mind sharing with someone else.

It seemed highly unlikely that there was anyone in the diplomatic colony with whom I would care to share a cottage. I had some vivid memories of cottage sharing in Minnesota when I was a youngster and I thought the hazards of such close association would be substantially greater in the abnormal atmosphere of Moscow.

However, I agreed to look at the Burobin cottage, chiefly out of curiosity as to what it might be like. But when I met the harassed little Burobin renting agent to go out to see the datcha I found to my pleasant surprise that the person to whom the other half of the cottage had been proposed was my colleague and very good friend Tom Whitney, one of the two Associated Press correspondents in Moscow. Tom was married to a talented and attractive young Russian girl whose career as one of Russia's leading composers of popular songs had been brought to a sudden end by a combination of two circumstances—a Communist Party edict against jazz and her marriage to an American.

The Whitneys were one of six American-Russian couples who had

been quite literally trapped in Moscow by the development of the
cold war. In each case the husband was an American citizen and the
wife was a Soviet citizen. And in no instance would Moscow give
an exit visa to the Soviet wife. Not until after the death of Stalin
did it prove possible to win the release of these involuntary victims
of the cold war.

At this time, in 1950, the prospect that any of the couples might
win their freedom seemed dim indeed. So dim, in fact, that Tom and
Julie Whitney, as I came to learn, tried quite consciously to put such
thoughts out of their mind because the pain of realization that they
might well face spending the rest of their lives in a virtual prison
whose walls each year constricted and contracted a little more was
too difficult to live with.

However, there was very little thought of such things on this
rainy morning when we set off together for Saltikovka. Despite the
drizzle the spirits of all three of us, I think, were buoyed somewhat
because we thought that it might, after all, prove possible to rent
a datcha on a share-and-share basis.

I must confess, nevertheless, that my first sight of Saltikovka was
depressing. The rain was cold and the spring was late. The village
lay off the highway to the right, down an old stone road that ran at
first through a small pine forest and then between two rows of
houses, some as patched as Joseph's coat, many built of plain hewn
logs and almost all of them devoid of any paint except, perhaps on
their tin roofs. We slithered over a road so deeply rutted that the
differential housing of the car scraped bottom and finally came to
a stop in front of a row of brown-stained story-and-a-half cottages.
Each had a front porch, a balcony on the second floor, steep
peaked eaves, vaguely reminiscent of a Swiss chalet, and about an
acre of patchy land over which grazed a good many goats and cows.
It looked a little like a seedy summer development on a backwoods
Wisconsin lake about forty years ago. All the houses were of identical construction and all, quite obviously, were inhabited year-
around by Russians, with exception of the house in front of which
we had stopped and that next door to it.

The houses were set out in a tall pine forest, planted fully sixty
years before, if one was to judge by the height and regular spacing

of the trees. Here and there was a gap where a tree had been taken out, and in the time I was to know Saltikovka I saw a good many more trees cut down to provide lumber for various local building projects.

To me the forest was singularly unattractive. There were no shrubs, no underbrush, and the houses, each in its plot, seemed naked in the featureless landscape, marked only by sagging fences and packing-case shacks for livestock or, in some cases, for people. The house the Burobin man showed us was just as dreary as its neighbors, both outside and inside. Downstairs there were two small dark rooms which would be the Whitneys'. Upstairs there was one large and more attractive room with nooks and deeply recessed windows which would be mine. I would have a back entrance up a narrow twisting flight of stairs. The Whitneys would have the front door off the porch. We would share a kitchen which possessed the only handsome feature of the house, a big whitewashed brick stove of the Russian type set at the corner of the room so that one radiating surface would heat the living room, another the bedroom and the fourth a very dark back hall. There was a large closet for food supplies and wood, and an outdoor toilet attached to the house. About a hundred feet away, hidden behind a little fence, was a rope-and-bucket well which served all the cottages on the lane. There was electricity of a feeble sort.

Looking off across the landscape I could see nothing but gray houses, fading and blending into gray background in which the green of spring was just beginning to show. On the vacant porch of the house next door three dirty goats huddled for protection from the rain, and beyond this was a low barrackslike building where two women in gray sweaters and gray skirts were digging up the reddish soil for a potato patch.

"Do you really think this place might do?" I asked Tom and Julie.

Tom hesitated a moment but Julie spoke quickly.

"Oh, yes," she replied, and it was evident from the glow in her eyes that she saw something quite different than I did. Perhaps she saw a summer sun and hammocks and roses and sweet-smelling tobacco plants and even the burnished gleam of a samovar on the porch table. I don't know what it was but she managed to communicate an enthusiasm to Tom and also to me which had not been there before.

The upshot was, after long discussion and much negotiation with Burobin, that we both decided to take the datcha. It was a much more important decision than I had any notion at the time and one which was to open up to me long vistas into Russian life and surprisingly close—although in some ways still sterile—associations with ordinary Russian people. And it was to make of Tom and Julie Whitney the best friends I had ever had or hoped of having. But of this at the time I had little premonition because almost immediately after negotiating to get the datcha I went back to America on leave, and so it was not until a full year later, in the spring of 1951, when Burobin again offered us the datcha, that I really began to know Saltikovka.

Saltikovka was the true anomaly of my Russian years. This was the experience which proved so completely that at any given time the reverse or opposite of whatever generality you may state about Russia is also true. This is a basic point. An important point. And one which I was very slow in coming to understand.

Because here I was isolated in Moscow in the most frigid period of the "deep freeze" when ordinary business contacts, let alone any kind of personal associations between Americans and Russians, had long since shriveled away. Yet, simultaneously and contemporaneously with this I was living in a completely Russian village community, surrounded by nothing but Russians, sharing almost every element of their life and getting to know them in the close and intimate way that is only possible on the long summer afternoons that seem to stretch away into infinity and the longer summer evenings of Russia, when even at eleven o'clock there is still enough light, out of the shade of the pine trees, to read another scene from *The Cherry Orchard* or finish the description of the opera in *Anna Karenina*.

I didn't make a single Russian friend in Saltikovka and yet when I came to leave Russia I found that almost my only warm memories were connected with that village and the people who lived there. And as I write about it now a tender feeling comes into my heart when I think of Dedya Vanya, the fine-looking old man in his hand-some embroidered Russian blouse who sometimes cut the grass with a great long-handled sickle and fed it to his goats; or the serious little Red Army colonel who was building his own house, brick by brick, across the grassy Datchnaya—Cottage—Lane; or the Chinaman with his hot-cross buns in the Saltikovka market place.

The first summer at the datcha presented practically no complications from the standpoint of news coverage. There was an electric train from Saltikovka which took me to Moscow in twenty-five minutes. I made arrangements for the delivery of the papers and periodicals from which almost all my stories, in this period, were derived, and by keeping in touch with my colleagues in Moscow by telephone was able to do the great bulk of my work in the country. The lid on news was battened down so tightly and the freeze was so complete that it was no trick at all to cover Russia from a country datcha. It was not until almost the end of the following summer, 1952, that a radical change came about. News, often big news, started to break with increasing and unexpected frequency. We began to get into the period of mounting tempo and tension which culminated eight months later with the death of Stalin. When that time came it was good-by to the datcha; good-by to experiments in growing Minnesota sweet corn in the acid soil of the Moscow pine forests; good-by to mushroom hunting and swimming in the mud-bottomed Saltikovka pond; good-by to playing *gorodki* with neighborhood small boys or visiting ambassadors.

Actually, the only ambassador who displayed a real talent for gorodki was Admiral Kirk. From the first moment he picked up the gorodki sticks and whirled them around his head it was evident that he had the touch. His son Roger, on the other hand, was so wild that he proved a menace to any spectators within a hundred feet.

Gorodki is one of the few Russian native games. It is played with sticks, about the size of but somewhat lighter than baseball bats, and small blocks of wood. The object is to hurl the sticks from a distance of about forty feet and knock the blocks of wood out of a square, scratched in hard earth, where they have been set up in a series of figures or patterns. It is a game for two players or two sides

and the object is simply to see who can first run through a series
of ten patterns, knocking the blocks of wood successively out of the
circle.

The Ambassador was excellent at this game and mighty proud,
as he well might have been, of his skill. The only persons who came
close to him were Tom Whitney, who had been a baseball pitcher
in college, and one of the barefoot Russian lads who was supposed to be minding cows in a vacant lot but was irresistibly drawn
to the spot by the sight of Americans playing this traditional Russian
game.

The small boys of the neighborhood actually introduced us to the
game, and, attracted by the chance of having a closer look at these
strange foreigners and the possibility of chocolate bars, helped us
cut the turf in the back yard of the datcha and lay out the gorodki
court. They also helped build a volleyball court—aided by a promise
that whenever they wanted to they might play on it. Volleyball and
basketball are two sports which are almost as popular in Russia as
they are in America.

However, this Tom Sawyer approach to mobilizing the local small-
boy labor potential came to an inevitable end not long afterward.
We heard that some of the neighbors were complaining that they
couldn't get their boys to do any home chores, such as chopping wood
or hoeing the potatoes because the boys preferred to work for the
foreigners. In view of the general state of relations between Russians
and Americans it seemed only too apparent where this kind of
grumbling might lead. So we were reluctantly compelled to discourage the children from embarking on further projects. Up to this point
we had encountered no hostility on the part of local residents and,
in fact, no outright hostility ever did manifest itself. However, there
was a certain coolness, and in the second year some of the boys who
had been most enthusiastic about gorodki and volleyball no longer
even bothered to say hello.

One of the most pleasant features about life in Saltikovka was that
it was completely unspoiled. There were no other foreigners living
there, although in the following year a diplomatic couple obtained
a cottage on the other side of the town. A very high percentage of the
Russians who live in Saltikovka commuted to Moscow to work.

Others were retired Army officers, schoolteachers or civil servants, and some worked in nearby textile factories.

A large peasant market on Sundays was a beehive of activity, filled with people selling fruits, flowers or vegetables from their personal garden plots or the communal surplus of collective farms. There was a big dairy pavilion for milk, sour cream, cottage cheese and eggs, behind which was an open space where people brought live chickens, ducks, geese, turkeys, lambs, piglets, dogs and cats, rabbits, goats and, occasionally, a cow or calf to sell.

That is how Tom and I came to go into the pig business. It was the custom of many of the *datchniki,* or datcha people, as most of the residents of Saltikovka called themselves, to buy a piglet in the spring for 150 to 300 rubles, feed it through the summer, and slaughter it in late fall. They fed the pigs scraps and slop plus some meal, bought from the Government stores, and figured that the fattened price of the hog in November was not more than 500 rubles, which is $125 as the ruble-dollar rate is computed by the Russian Government but which is a good deal closer to $50 if the ruble is valued in terms of comparable purchasing power.

A neighbor woman who did what the Russians call the "black" work at the datcha, that is, the cleaning, the scrubbing and much of the hauling and carrying, bought a piglet and asked if we didn't want one, too. We did. And that is how Masha, the Russian piglet, came into my life. As befits a Russian piglet Masha led a rather obscure existence in a gloomy pen and seldom saw daylight. Nonetheless, pig style, she grew and grew and by November had attained quite respectable proportions. And, by November, Masha presented to Tom and me, each of us for the first time in his life half owner of a pig, a rather major problem. For neither he nor I could properly carve a duck, let alone slaughter a pig.

What to do?

Fortunately, there was at that time in the American Embassy an agricultural attaché with unique qualifications. He actually knew something about farming, having been born and raised on an Iowa farm, and an Iowa corn-and-hog farm at that. He came to our rescue and said that, if we would get Masha into town he would refresh his slaughtering memory with a little study of a U.S. Department of Agriculture pamphlet and see if he could not reduce her to the appropriate loin cuts, bacon, ham and tenderloin.

So, one crisp November day shortly before Thanksgiving, Masha was stuck and bled and cleaned of bristles in the farmyard where she was reared. Then Tom and I stowed the carcass into a big burlap gunnysack, put it in the baggage compartment of my car and drove into town. The American Embassy, where our agricultural attaché lived, was still located at that time on the Mokhovaya, across Manezhny Square from the Kremlin.

We parked the car at the curb in front of the embassy and, as the ever-present two Moscow policemen eyed us curiously from the doorway, opened up the luggage compartment of the car and lifted out the bloody burlap sack. Tom took Masha's head and I took the rear quarters. Then, our backs bent by our burden, and leaving a gentle but unmistakable trail of blood behind us in the white Russian snow, we walked slowly past the Russian policemen and into the U.S. Embassay, where in competent fashion Berle Hamer quickly reduced Masha's bleeding corpse to the appropriate chops and roasts.

I have often thought that it would be worth a good deal to see the report those Russian policemen turned in to their superiors that night about the Americans, the heavy gunnysack and the blood trail over the sidewalk.

Masha was only one of countless projects which revolved around the datcha. I don't suppose it would be possible to put two Americans into a cottage so neglected and undeveloped without making their fingers itch to do something about it. Both Tom and I, brought up in the tradition of Midwestern "summer places at the lake," had very similar ideas about what should be done to improve the datcha. Julie had ideas, too, but they sprang from a different environment and the contrast made life more interesting and various.

Tom and I were great for building and constructing; for projects that involved physical labor and work with the hands. This was directly contrary to the tradition of the Russian intelligentsia or upper-middle-class intellectual life. To Tom and me life in the country meant breaking the sod and setting out a big garden. It meant a lot of carpentry (Tom's particular specialty); planting shrubs and flowers (my specialty). We enjoyed working and sweating and getting dog-tired. But this was not the Russian way of life for persons in our "social class." I saw many a curious Russian stare at me as I sweated, bare-backed, weeding the corn patch. (They thought it was crazy, anyway, to grow corn. Only Ukrainians grew corn and they, mostly as feed for cattle.) And while the colonel across the street might lay the bricks of his house with his own hands while his wife and daughters mixed mortar and carried water, this was not because they enjoyed working with their hands. They did it because they had to and because they didn't have enough money to pay someone to build their house for them. This was "black work," and while, because of the nature of the conditions in which he lived, the Russian intellectual had to do a certain amount of work with his hands, he did not do so by choice. He usually did it poorly and if he could avoid it he avoided it.

This, of course, is not a purely Russian attitude, it is fairly general in Europe. The psychology of doing physical work as a diversion is rather an Anglo-Saxon trait. I will never forget the utter astonishment which the late Lord Inverchapel, then Sir Archibald Clark Kerr, caused during the wartime years in Moscow when he laid out a vegetable garden on the British Embassy grounds, just outside his office. He would take off his shirt and dig in his garden, between callers, and sometimes walked back into his office, his hands grimy, sweat pouring off his chest and trailing a shirt, to shake hands with some protocol-punctilious Russian from the Foreign Office. "The Russians think I'm mad," Clark Kerr used to chuckle, "and I think it is very reassuring to them because that is how English diplomats have been seeming to them since Ivan's time."

Russian ideas of appropriate datcha diversions centered around such things as lying in a hammock and reading novels; long talks around a bubbling samovar; quiet walks through the village in the evening twilight; excursions into the pine and birch forests, looking for mushrooms; occasional visits to the village pond for bathing and sun-bathing but not really swimming (very few Russians swim well. They prefer to wade in shallow water or sit and watch others splashing along the shore).

These were the kinds of activities which appealed more to Julie than the sweat-producing projects of Tom and myself. And, most of all since she was a composer deprived of the right of composing, she enjoyed listening to music and was capable of sitting for hours beside the phonograph playing one collection of American popular songs after another. Nor was she the only Russian in the neighborhood who liked American music. Sound carries a long way in the evening quiet of a Russian village. And many times I heard American songs, sometimes songs of very recent vintage but sometimes old and scratchy from having been played again and again, sounding over the countryside. Just up the street there was a datchnik who had half a dozen American records which he would play over and over on a phonograph that could be heard for a quarter of a mile away. Apparently this did not embarrass him in any way. And occasionally there would be a party in a big white stucco house a block or so away which, we were told, belonged to a general. The general had a son and daughter of college age and the party would be for them and their friends. On such nights, our part of Saltikovka would be kept awake listening to "Some of These Days," "Stormy Weather," "Wind at the Windowpane" or some other American favorite.

I have been told and my observations at Saltikovka tended to substantiate it that American popular music which is generally called "jazz" in Russia, regardless of how we would designate it, has never lost its popularity among Russian young people. American records are purchased in substantial numbers by Russians in Berlin, largely, of course, Russian officers. They are sent back to Moscow and played over and over in young people's apartments and at young people's parties. Many times, walking the back streets of the Arbat or other old quarters of Moscow, I have heard American music coming from dingy rooms or flats, and I know that old, secondhand American records which wouldn't bring a nickel at a Goodwill store in the U.S.A. can be sold in Moscow for twenty-five rubles apiece.

One of the projects which Tom and I conceived was that of building a fireplace.

I had fallen in love at first sight with our Russian stove. Such a stove is built with a comparatively small fire pot but a very large surface of bricks over which hot air and smoke passes through a series of baffles. The stove is fired very strongly and continuously for several hours until the brick surfaces are thoroughly hot. Then the drafts are closed and the surface temperature of the brick structure rises substantially and continues to radiate heat for many, many hours. It is on much the same principle as the Dutch oven and I have been told that it is one of the most economical and efficient heating devices ever invented.

Beside a Russian stove a fireplace is a thing of whimsey. But it also is a delight, and I hankered for a fireplace. So did Tom. After all, we had been brought up on fireplaces and not radiating stoves. We were thinking about keeping the cottage for the winter to use it for skiing expeditions and snow parties. For that a fireplace was essential.

However, the controlling factor in this venture was the discovery that just a few houses away there lived a *pechnik*, or stove builder, named Ivan Ivanovich. Ivan Ivanovich, which is just about the most Russian name on the calendar, is the equivalent, in English, of John Johnson.

We decided to see whether Ivan Ivanovich couldn't build a fireplace in the Whitney's living room, which was heated by one face of the brick stove. Tom, who spoke Russian almost as well as a native, invited Ivan Ivanovitch up to the datcha and, after pouring him the customary drink of vodka, explained what we wanted to do. Ivan Ivanovich was not the world's most brilliant Russian but he was eager to please. Tom rattled off a vivid description of the project. We wanted to cut a hole in the face of the stove. Ivan Ivanovich nodded. We wanted to make an opening into the chimney. Ivan Ivanovich nodded. We wanted to put a fireplace here. Tom gesticulated. Ivan Ivanovich nodded. Was this possible? Ivan Ivanovich nodded—but remained silent. We stared at him. He stared back. Finally, he spoke. Would the *gospodin* please explain again just what it was that he wanted?

Certainly, said Tom. He went over it all again, using terms so simple and language so precise that even I with my bad Russian understood every word. Ivan Ivanovich nodded from time to time during this explanation. At the end he nodded again and smiled.

"*Panimayu,*" he said. "I understand. You want the opening of the stove in this room instead of in the kitchen."

No, said Tom. That is not it. We want a fireplace in this room. We don't want to disturb the opening in the kitchen.

"*Nu,* so," said Ivan Ivanovich, nodding again.

Julie had been listening to this conversation with growing impatience. Now she could contain herself no longer. She burst into a voluble, nonstop stream of Russian. Her eyes snapped. Her hands moved like lightning as she painted in the air a picture of the fireplace. Ivan Ivanovich watched closely. From time to time he nodded.

"*Nu,*" he said again. "So. Now I understand. In the kitchen nothing will be changed. But here you will have another fire pot. It will be a double stove. Yes?"

No! exploded Julie. No! exploded Tom. And they both started talking together. But I had a bright idea. It was plain to be seen that Ivan Ivanovich was never going to understand this business for a very simple reason. He did not know what a fireplace was. He had never seen one and he just didn't know what we were talking about. I ran upstairs to my room and started thumbing very quickly through a stack of old *Saturday Evening Posts*. Finally I found what I wanted and dashed downstairs and showed it to Ivan Ivanovich.

"There," I said in triumph. "See. A fireplace!"

Ivan Ivanovich studied the picture carefully. A fireplace. Yes. Well, why hadn't we told him what we wanted him to build. A fireplace. Surely. Of course. Now, there was something to build. He took a long look at the picture and then extracted a piece of black thread out of his greasy pocket and shuffled over to the stove wall and set about measuring it, mumbling figures to himself.

I have forgotten how many bricks he said it would take. About sixty, I think. I remember being surprised at the number he needed and also at the price, because it was comparatively cheap—eighty kopeks a brick, if memory serves me right. About twenty cents a brick at the official rate, and we were able to buy the bricks at a big hardware and building materials store at the Kolkhozni Ploshad, or Collective Farm Plaza, in Moscow.

Once he got some idea in his mind of what we wanted him to do Ivan Ivanovich fell to work with enthusiasm. I am sure he thought we were out of our minds but that didn't bother him in the least. Most Russian peasants and working people regard foreigners as a kind of unpredictable children, subject to the most extreme of whims, who must, so far as possible, be indulged and pampered.

Ivan Ivanovich was no exception to this rule, but this did not mean that he was not interested in his job. He was. He was, moreover, a rather exceptional Russian. He worked for himself. He was a stove builder and stove repairman. He worked for no factory, no trust and not even for a stovemen's artel or co-operative. He went around to people's houses and fixed their stoves when something went wrong, and he built new stoves for new houses and new stoves for old houses if the old stove fell apart from neglect and finally had to be replaced.

His materials were simple—bricks, and a few bits of old iron which he picked up from a blacksmith friend of his. For mortar he usually used a good blue clay which he knew where to get in the neighborhood and simple white piping to cover the stove with. He was an honest, industrious workman and he built good Russian stoves. He built them exactly the way his father built them and, in in fact, his father had been a pechnik as well. And his grandfather before him and probably a good many generations before that if the truth were known. He built sturdy stoves, suitable to the Russian climate. They cost little and were easily repaired.

But never in his life had anyone wanted him to build a fireplace, and when at last the job was done and we anxiously gathered around to see how it would work, no one was more nervous than Ivan Ivanovich. From the lighting of the first kindling it was obvious that the fireplace of Ivan Ivanovich, like that of so many of his masters before him, was not going to draw too well.

However, it worked. It burned, and Ivan Ivanovich's face relaxed in relief when he saw that. But a good deal of smoke curled out into the room.

When it became fully apparent that Ivan Ivanovich had, indeed, built us a fireplace, albeit a smoky one, a solemn glass of vodka was drunk to commemorate the occasion. Then he was paid the agreed sum, which was not just a sum of rubles. Like all traditional Russian artisans Ivan Ivanovich had fixed his price as so many rubles—let us say 150 because I do not remember exactly—plus a bottle of vodka. That is the way it always had been and so it still was. The workmen and the master argue and dispute over the price. This is as important as the bargaining over an Oriental rug in the bazaar. There must be offer and counter-offer and finally a price is agreed upon. Plus a bottle of vodka, to show that it is a real bargain and no hard feelings.

Ivan Ivanovich fussed over the fireplace for some time longer, trying to get it to draw better. He even rebuilt it once in order to install a grate to allow the fire to get more draft. There was some improvement but not much.

Finally, he came by one day with a sheet of iron in his hand. He had one last idea and this one, he was sure, we would like.

"You know," he said, "I have found this good sheet of iron. If you would like I will make it into a door and fit it onto the front of the stove. Then the fireplace will draw just as well as the firebox in the kitchen."

But, don't you see, we told him, if you put an iron door on the front it won't be a fireplace any more. It will just be a Russian stove.

Ivan Ivanovich looked at us with eyes that were serious and sad. He nodded his head again and said, "*Panimayu,* I understand," and finally went away. Certainly he did not then nor ever would understand, but the story of his adventures with the foreigners and the strange kind of stove they had insisted that he build for them would carry him through many a long winter's evening and many a glass of vodka.

It was quite possible with preoccupations like fireplace building and all the other pleasant and ordinary things that went to make up life in the country to get a very long way from the tensions and strains of Moscow and the grimly rigid pattern into which the life of most foreigners had been forced by the steady encroachment of Soviet restrictions. I never exactly understood why so few diplomats tried out summer life in the Russian countryside. All but one of the American newspapermen in Moscow at this time had places in the country. The American Embassy had a big estate outside Moscow that originally had been rented in 1941 as a hideaway in case bombing got too bad or the battle surged too close to Moscow. But it was badly run down and used comparatively infrequently. Two or three diplomats had cottages but for the most part the foreigners huddled together in their ghetto existence in Moscow and seemed almost without initiative to make the effort necessary to improve their way of life.

The contrast between the nervous and almost psychotic atmosphere which the "deep freeze" was producing in the diplomatic colony and the comparative peace and quiet of the countryside was so sharp that I went to Moscow no oftener than possible.

Instead, I took to roaming the countryside around Saltikovka. I found a wonderful lake with a sandy bottom and pine-sprinkled shore, blue and crystal, and far superior to our poor Saltikovka pond, which was little more than a glorified mudhole, formed by damming up a little creek that meandered through the settlement. The blue-and-crystal lake was harder to get to, of course. You had to have a car. That meant that very few ordinary country folk or villagers ever went to it.

Perhaps that is one reason why there were only seven datchas on this lake. Each of them was big and comfortable and pleasant. There were cars parked in the yards of each of these houses, Pobedas, Zims and even a Zis or two. The people who lived in the houses were well dressed, and if the size and shape of the older men and women were any indication, well fed.

After I learned who occupied the seven datchas I was not surprised a little bit later when the lake was placed out of bounds in one of the revisions of the restrictions on movements of foreigners around Moscow.

The seven datchas were all privately owned. They belonged to seven generals.

I suppose the place in Saltikovka which I most enjoyed visiting was the market. It was crowded on Sunday with both peasant sellers and datchniki buyers. On weekdays the crowds were not so big. I got to know many of the sellers, the old man who had the finest rose bushes, the fussy little woman who sold dahlia roots, a Georgian whose garlic came from Dagistan, a half-dozen blowzy bold-eyed peasant women with their sacks of sunflower and pumpkin seeds, sitting and eating and spitting, winter and summer.

Once there was a great crisis at our market. The police closed
down the huge Perovsky Moscow market where, for many years,
people had been permitted to carry on what the Russians call "hand"
trading—that is, they could buy and sell their old shoes, old overcoats, surplus furniture or whatnot. The militia, for I don't know
what reason, arbitrarily decided not to permit such trade in Moscow.
So thousands of Muscovites—plain citizens, poverty-stricken individuals, and not a few thieves and pickpockets—descended on Saltikovka to carry on their buying and selling and stealing.

This inundated the peasant market and threatened the whole
pleasant character of the village. But after a few weeks hundreds of
police suddenly appeared in Saltikovka one Sunday, which was the
big trading day. They posted huge signs that hand trading was no
longer permitted and set up loudspeaker cars that blared warnings
that any *spekulanti* or traders would be arrested. It took about a
month of such Sunday drives before the situation was cleaned up.
After that no hand trading was permitted closer to Moscow than
Klin, about ninety miles away.

But for the most part the Saltikovka market was quiet and countri-
fied. It reminded me not a little of my days as a youngster in Minneapolis when I used to go to the farmers' market with my father. The
stalls in my home town, to be sure, were neater and the vegetables
fresher. But something in the atmosphere and something in the
smell was the same. Of course there were no parchment-faced old
women in Minneapolis with gaudy religious paintings and new-gilt
ikon candle holders (and a few old ikons tucked away in a knapsack
under their skirts). Nor any men in sheepskin caps selling shovel
handles they had carved themselves or thin young girls, gingerly
holding up a bit of lace or a pair of stockings, half in and half out
of their *sumka* in case a militiaman should come along.

But what reminded me most of my childhood was the Chinaman.
When I was a youngster there was a store owned by a Chinaman
not far from the market. It was a fearsome place and yet too fascinating to stay away from. There you could buy candied ginger and
kumquats and lichi nuts and a thousand spices that I never knew
the name of but can still taste on my tongue. The Chinaman who
ran that store was a serious and a silent man but he had a way of

smiling when you had bought your ginger or tasted one of his spices as though there was something which only you and he knew and nobody else, a secret just between you two.

There was a Chinaman in the Saltikovka market, too. He didn't look very much like the one in that store on Western Avenue in Minneapolis. For one thing he was a good deal younger and he wore a faded khaki cotton-padded jacket, winter and summer. And instead of spices he sold hot-cross buns. Not real hot-cross buns, of course, because his were made without a cross by a Soviet bakery trust. But there was something in them, possibly a pinch of cinnamon or allspice, which reminded me of that long-ago store. And stranger yet was the secret smile the Chinaman gave me after I had handed him two rubles for his buns. As though there was something between us which only he and I knew, a secret just between us two.

VIII

A Spare Room Upstairs

A TALL, lanky serious-faced man strode toward the datcha with a loose-jointed boyish pace and came up to where I was wielding a paintbrush. We were glassing in the front porch and I was busy in my paint-smeared clothes putting the white trim on the windows.

"Do you have a spare room to let upstairs?" the tall man asked, rather solemnly, speaking in Russian.

I laughed and put down my paintbrush.

"For you," I said, "I think we do."

The tall serious-faced man was George Kennan, once more in Moscow and this time as the American Ambassador. He had come to call at the datcha, not to visit me, whom he had hardly met before, but to see Tom and Julie Whitney, whom he had known from his days in Moscow at the end of the war.

This was, I believe, George Kennan's fourth tour of duty in Moscow. No one would have guessed on this late May afternoon in 1952, a fortnight or so after he had arrived back in Moscow, that it was to be his briefest tour and that his career as U.S. Ambassador was to come to a sudden and almost tragic end under circumstances which to this day have never been fully clarified.

A machine-gun burst of Russian exploded around me as Tom and Julie greeted Kennan, the three of them speaking so rapidly that it was all I could do to follow the general direction of the conversation. I put my paintbrushes away in a can of turpentine, washed off the worst of the smears and settled down to listen to the first of an extraordinary series of conversations which were to provide a kind of counterpoint to the monotonous and sterile themes which, by now, were all that could be heard from the Kremlin.

I had long hoped to meet Kennan and now I quickly realized that I was in the presence of a rare phenomenon among men, a scholar with a practical ability for projecting his thoughts, a mind with a scope for global concepts, a sensitive personality with almost a poet's appreciation for images and sights and sounds, an individual with a true sense of dedication and responsibility to his own country and to the country which he had made his life work.

It was apparent that he was a complex man, full of contrast and conflict, whose mind encompassed vast corridors, never fully explored by himself. A man capable of deep feeling, deep happiness and deep tragedy. A man with both a mind and a heart.

And, above all, a man who loved talk and ideas and feelings, who liked to express himself, who wanted to express himself but who needed to feel a rapport between himself and those he was with in order to release the hidden springs which often gave him in public places and on public occasions an austere if not grim appearance.

The talk started that afternoon on the blue-and-white, paint-smelling porch. It went on and on. Dusk fell and it grew cool. We went inside the house and lighted our famous fireplace. As usual it smoked and quickly the atmosphere in the little room grew thick. Kennan sprawled out on a ragged bearskin rug in front of the fire. We sat on chair cushions in a semicircle around him. The room was dark except for the flickering flames which cast Kennan's deeply molded face into high lights and shadows.

It was Russian talk, spoken in Russian for the most part, and always about Russia. It was the kind of talk any Russian intellectual of the generation that came to an end in 1917 would have understood. It was the kind of talk they were familiar with. It simply picked up where they left off speaking. The generations since 1917 would have understood the conversation perfectly well, too. Many of them would have enjoyed participating in it. But the ideological baggage which they had picked up in the Marxist years would have cramped them and made them uncomfortable. And the atmosphere had changed too much. When Kennan first saw Moscow as a young secretary when William Bullitt re-established our embassy in 1934 it had not been like this.

In those days conversations such as Kennan was having with us were the rule, not the exception. Almost every night he and the other young men of the embassy, Charles Bohlen, who was to succeed him as ambassador the following year, Loy Henderson and the rest, sat around with Russians and argued and drank and talked. Men like Bukharin and Karl Radek visited Spaso House and even the Mokhovaya Street building. They were brilliant conversationalists and they were ready to argue until any hour of the morning with these equally brilliant young Americans from the great capitalist land to the west which every Russian admired so much, either secretly or openly.

But Bukharin had been shot and Karl Radek was shipped off to the notorious prison camp in sub-Arctic Yakutsk, there to waste away his days until a fellow prisoner's knife by accident or order from Moscow ended his life during the World War II years.

And, now, Kennan had come back to deep-freeze Moscow, to a Moscow where there were no Russians whatever to talk to and hardly any foreigners who either could understand his Russian, or, more grievous, the spirit and content of his conversation.

Here in this little Saltikovka datcha with the Whitneys to talk with and myself very much the quiet mouse in the corner, Kennan could recapture a breath of the Moscow which had vanished and could, in the interplay of conversation with two sensitive persons, one of whom was, of course, herself a Russian intellectual and the other who had spent nearly ten years in Russia and knew many phases of Soviet life, particularly in the economic field, better than Kennan himself, analyze and work out ideas and impressions of late Stalin Russia within a framework of intelligent truth-seeking.

Perhaps, to be sure, there was a little more to it. I never felt that Kennan was completely comfortable in his ambassador's role. It held him too remote from a country and a people whom he had known for so many years with the intimacy of a student. This gave a deeply nostalgic touch to his attitude which was apparent in the first remark he made to me when he came up to the porch where I was painting.

In asking if we had a spare room to let upstairs he was echoing the question he had put to good Russian datchniki in the first years of his service in Moscow, in the early thirties, when it had been possible just to take an electric train to the country, strike off along a country road and, when you came to a pleasant-looking house, knock on the door and inquire of the landlady whether she had a spare room upstairs to let.

Anything so simple, so normal and so human was, of course, completely out of the question in the present stage of the cold war. Not only for the American Ambassador. But for an ordinary correspondent as well.

Actually, I did rearrange my upstairs room at the datcha so that any time Kennan wanted to get away from Moscow and come out to the country to read or write or study he could make use of it. And he did this, once or twice, bringing with him a collection of Pushkin's poems which he was rereading, two or three contemporary Soviet novels which he gleaned for new ideological nuggets and rapidly discarded as pure trash, and the latest numbers of the *tolsti* or fat literary journals, like *Zvezda*, *Novy Mir* and *Oktyabr*, which he made a practice of following with considerable care. We gave him a key to the datcha so that he could come and go as he pleased, but actually, what with the routine at the embassy, he never got to spend as much time in the country as he hoped and when he did come was much more likely to devote himself to working out his ideas in conversation. Occasionally, he would read aloud, sitting in a wicker chair under the pine trees, a passage from Pushkin or one of Chekhov's short stories, many of which he virtually knew by heart. And he liked to walk over the countryside, sometimes with one of us, but often alone. Once or twice he sketched. The trouble with walking, of course, was that wherever he strolled he was accompanied by his MVD bodyguard, two men usually walking ahead of him and two behind.

He was much interested in every aspect of life in the village and particularly in the development of private home building, private home ownership and the extent to which, he felt, ordinary Russian citizens were trying to build self-contained lives, centered largely around their own houses and gardens, physically remote from Moscow and divorced as far as possible from ideology, propaganda or any of the shibboleths of communism.

There was evidence of this trend all about us. Across Datchnaya Lane there had been when I first saw Saltikovka an open pasture where villagers tethered their cows and where, in the evenings, the youngsters played football. Now, this plot had been allotted by the village authorities to some military organization. In addition to the pleasant little retired colonel who was building the red brick house, a series of other houses was going up, all for retired colonels or generals. One colonel was building himself a small frame house. Another with the aid of half a dozen soldiers from his regiment was putting up a more substantial peeled-log house, and a general, also using a squad of soldiers, was building a big two-story house which was obviously going to rival the two-story white stucco house of the other general that already existed.

Further along Datchnaya Lane, closer to the market and railroad station, there were eight or ten houses building, each being put up by the owner. In some cases, of course, the owners had help which they hired but they did the bulk of the work themselves. I heard later on of a certain amount of building "speculation," of individuals who got a land plot from the village Soviet and built a house on it. You can't buy land in Russia, nor own it. But if it is allotted to you and you build a house it usually is not alienated except by eminent domain, just as in capitalist countries. But the house you build is yours—your own property, to sell or to be inherited by your heirs. These individuals sold their houses after they built them—at very handsome profits. The price of a good datcha in the vicinity of Moscow ranged between 50,000 and 200,000 or even 300,000 rubles. A clever carpenter with access to a supply of state-owned timber and hardware could build one for not more than 20,000, including "gifts" for his building materials.

But I don't think much speculative building was going on in Saltikovka. It was too apparent that people were putting up their own homes and building their lives around the traditional symbols of family and hearthside. The new houses were raw and unpretty but in a year or two they planted vegetable gardens, set out berry bushes and strawberry patches, put in apple and cherry trees and began to raise flowers.

Given the basic differences in Russian taste and architecture and the comparative backwardness of Russian household conveniences it was quite possible to see the close affinity between the kind of life these ordinary Russian people were building for themselves and the kind of life which any suburban American knows so well.

This development struck Kennan as significant not just for itself but because it emphasized in rather dramatic fashion one of the basic postulates of his thinking about Russia. He saw in the stereotypy into which Soviet ideology had sunk, the monotone and grayness of its ideas, a kind of spiritual hardening of the arteries, a drying up or aging of the revolutionary lifeblood which he felt was increasingly reflecting itself in rigidity of policy and rigidity of doctrine. In this he and I felt very much alike.

Here in this little community of Saltikovka he sensed (if I do not err in the presentation of his thought) an example of the way the ordinary Russian people were reacting against the sterility and rigidity which were so manifest in Party doctrine and Party methods. The people, in effect, were turning their backs on Moscow and trying to sink, inconspicuously, into a quiet suburban background, the essentials of which were manifestly bourgeois rather than socialist.

And, what was equally striking to him was the extent to which the state itself was acquiescing in this development without, perhaps, full awareness of the implications. For in direct contradiction to the Communist doctrine of collective life, it was the state which was providing the individual building plots. It was the state which was providing individual loans of up to 20,000 rubles to some home builders. And many big Government trusts and departments had set up special procurement departments where their workers could get building materials at state prices. Government seed and shrub stores sold plants and seeds in competition with the peasant market for the first time.

It was obviously a strong and powerful tendency in Russian life and one which struck Kennan with particular force because it was a tendency in a direction opposite to the collectivist and socialist ideals which had apparently been so deeply rooted in the thirties when he first came to know Russia. In those days no Russian would have thought to turn his back on Moscow and a Moscow communal flat and make his life in a suburban house and garden. Now, it was evident, thousands of Muscovites each year were escaping from the capital and savoring the delights of private life and private ownership.

Kennan was, I think, amused a bit by some of the other aspects of datcha life.

There was the eternal question, for example, of the road. While the highway to the Saltikovka turn-off was not bad (after two years of rebuilding and bridge construction by Army troops, largely MVD) and the cobbled road to the village was an all-weather route, there was still a quarter mile of dirt track in to the datcha which was in spectacularly bad condition and impassable for passenger cars after a heavy rain.

We had repeatedly complained about the road but nothing had ever happened except that once a single truckload of ashes was dumped in one of the bottomless pits, vanishing without a trace within a matter of hours.

Now that Kennan was frequently driving out in the embassy Lincoln, escorted by the MVD in their heavy Zim, we thought that certainly the impassable stretch of road would be fixed. If the Foreign Office didn't insist on it as a matter of prestige surely the MVD would as a matter of practical mechanics because of the frequency with which the heavy cars got stuck.

Apparently, some of our neighbors felt much the same way. We both had complained before to the Village Soviet about the road. Now, several people proposed that we complain again.

The complaint was made but nothing happened except that luckily we had a long dry spell and the various mud lakes which formed the road dried up. The road would have been fairly passable had not several citizens dug deep ditches across it at various points, ostensibly for drainage but actually with the idea of making the road completely impassable and, thus, in the oblique Russian fashion forcing the village council to take action.

But we underrated the peasant ingenuity of the council. Some time later a neighbor told us that the complaint had actually been considered by the council. Previous complaints, I gathered, had simply been pigeonholed. However, this time the council discussed the question but finally decided against fixing the road on the following grounds:

We already have one house with foreigners in it in our village. They already have caused us trouble enough with their complaints about the road. If we fix the road, who knows? Probably, more foreigners will come to live in our town. In any event the foreigners we have will stay. That means more complaints and more trouble and not just about the road. If we leave the road unfixed it will get worse. No doubt, in time, the foreigners will get disgusted and leave. Better, therefore, not to fix the road because then the foreigners may go away and leave us in peace and quiet again.

Here, indeed, was real Russian psychology at work. True peasant psychology which so often lay behind Soviet actions and Soviet decisions once you stripped them of their protective covering of pseudo-dialectical language and Marxian terminology.

Almost everything in Saltikovka, which in many ways was a microcosm of Russia, was likely to be done in a fashion which was almost completely alien to Marx but completely familiar to Tolstoy or Turgenev.

For instance, Saltikovka did have a Road Plan, a veritable five-year plan for improvement of transport facilities. This plan and this project was truly grandiose in concept. It envisaged putting a tar surface on the cobbled road that led from the Chaussee Entusiastov to the Saltikovka railroad station, a distance of perhaps a mile and a half. I suppose that a crew of four men with a steam roller could have done this job in a week. But, the last time I saw Saltikovka, about half a mile of road had been surfaced and this represented three years of steady summertime work for a two-man crew. I would hate to estimate the amount of good pine logs this pair has burned up in keeping their pot of tar hot every day, or the wear and tear on the trucks and passenger cars which have had to bump up and down over the horrible detours which have become an almost permanent feature of the highway.

I am positive that five years hence if I go back to Saltikovka I will find these two men, if they have not died of old age by then, still laying their average of five or six feet of tar per day. And if they have finally come within sight of the Saltikovka station then, I am certain, it will be time for them to start back at the other end of the road, re-laying the surface and repairing the many, many places where the tar already has worn off.

That is the way most municipal improvement programs are carried out in Saltikovka and, as Kennan often pointed out, while what was true for Saltikovka was not necessarily true all over the country it did give you a pretty clear idea of certain basic trends and tendencies. It was a good thing to remember that there were a very great many Saltikovkas in Russia.

One thing I often marveled at in Saltikovka was the patient endurance of the ordinary Russian and his ability to put up with the most shocking and unnecessary inconveniences without ever raising much fuss.

One of the most scandalous of these concerned the village pond. The pond was a center of village life in the summertime and on hot Sundays several thousand people came out from Moscow to swim or picnic or go boating. There was a nice little outdoor restaurant called the Vodipad or Waterfall beside the dam which created the lake, and the pond itself stretched back along the little creek for a distance of a half mile or so.

Muddy it always was and dirty to be sure, after several thousand people used it on Sunday. But still it was a pleasant place and one of the reasons so many people had summer houses in the vicinity. The stone road passed over a small wooden bridge just above the dam which created the pond, and youngsters and old men congregated there with their fishing poles although I never saw them catch anything bigger than three- or four-inch shiners.

I think it must have been in the spring of 1951 that I noticed, lying beside the approaches to this bridge, a pile of long, freshly sawn pine logs, obviously designed for construction purposes. In Russia you seldom see finished lumber at a building site. The carpenters themselves shape the logs into timbers with ax and adze.

Since the bridge was a little rickety it was not hard to figure out what the authorities had in mind. The prospect that the bridge would be closed for reconstruction worried Tom and me considerably because if the highway were shut off there was no other way so far as we knew of getting to the datcha by car, and it was most inconvenient to have to depend entirely on the electric train.

We made inquiries and were told by Burobin that the bridge was going to be replaced that summer and to expect the road to be out of use for about two months.

But summer passed and nothing happened. No workmen appeared and the long pine logs lay untouched. By the following summer we had grown so accustomed to the logs that we no longer noticed them. Neither, apparently, did anyone else because for a second summer they lay untouched.

But early in the spring of 1953 workmen appeared on the scene. They built a small, temporary bridge across the dam and they opened the locks, letting all the water out of the Saltikovka pond. Obviously, the new bridge was to be built and I thought the authorities were showing a special consideration for the local residents by getting the work out of the way in early spring so that the summer bathing and boating would not be interfered with.

This was, indeed, a naïve idea. The pond remained drained and the bridge untouched all through the summer. The whole season was spoiled for the local inhabitants and for the Moscow people who had depended on the little lake for relaxation on Sunday afternoons.

But, surely, I thought, when winter comes the new bridge will be built.

Was it?

Of course not. I drove out through Saltikovka not long before I left Moscow, toward the end of summer, 1954. The little creek meandered mournful through the mud-bottom of the erstwhile pond. The outdoor tables of the Vodipad Café stood deserted. The pile of logs, weathered and worn, stood untouched. The bridge had not been built. How much longer this will go on I would not care to predict. Perhaps they are waiting for those two men who are laying tar on the stone road to finish their job. Maybe they are the labor force, specified under the Five-Year Plan, which is going to build that bridge.

Sometimes, of course, there is a happier ending to these Saltikovka stories. Sometimes, the people manage to assert their rights.

There was the row over the well, for example.

Up and down Datchnaya Lane for a block or more in each direction (and from more distant houses, too, in droughty summers when other wells went dry) the householders depended for their water on the rope and bucket well that was located about a hundred feet from our datcha. The well was protected by a little wooden housing and it was set back in a small jog taken out of land belonging to an old and well-managed datcha. The man to whom this datcha belonged was retired. He lived there year-round with his wife and two half-grown children. In summer they rented half their house at a good profit. He had his yard thickly planted with fruit trees and raspberry bushes which had spread almost into the lane.

Actually, there weren't enough wells to accommodate the growing population, what with new cottages going up all the time, and so we were not surprised one day to see some men start to drill a new well about a hundred yards to the rear of the datcha.

The new well was rapidly dug and put into service and about the same time the retired datcha owner launched a great improvement plan. He began to build a high board fence—fully seven or eight feet tall—completely around his property. The ostensible purpose of the fence was to protect his raspberry bushes and fruit trees from poachers but, in general, all Russians like to have fences around their property. When they set out to build a house they usually erect a good stout fence, first, and start on the house later. One of my prized exhibits along the Chaussee Entusiastov was a fine fence which had been erected around a pile of spare fence posts. I don't know whether I am right or not but I have always thought that the Russian love for fences was a Freudian clue to their general sense of insecurity which, among other things, may basically stem from living in a country which has few natural frontiers against invasion.

However, to return to the datcha owner and his fence. He rapidly constructed the paling around his property and when he came to the jog where the well was located he ran the fence around that, too, but fitted it with a tall well-made gate. I thought this was a bit of unexpected public-spiritedness until one morning I went down to get a pail of water and found the gate closed and chained from within and a handwritten sign in Russian which said: "Well out of order."

Possibly nothing in the time I was associated with Saltikovka caused the residents of the village, or at least of Datchnaya Lane, more indignation than this because it quickly transpired that the well wasn't out of order at all but had, quite literally, been stolen by the datcha owner who clearly proposed to keep it by main force, if necessary.

The story of this grasping property owner was quickly on every lip and all day long little groups of datchniki gathered in front of the chained gate to the well to discuss ways and means. The man, it seemed, was a retired employee of the Moscow Datcha Trust which owned almost all the datchas in the immediate vicinity. The trust owned the datcha this man lived in as well as the one which we rented from Burobin, Burobin merely leasing the datcha from the trust on a year-to-year basis. Originally, these houses had been built back in the early thirties by a co-operative building society, made up of employees of one of the big Government departments. The co-operative society, generally, was organized just about like an American co-operative building society and, just as has happened sometimes with our co-operative building groups, this one ran into financial difficulties and eventually the houses were taken over by the Datcha Trust which is a kind of section of the Mocow City Housing Department.

The retired worker had been the Datcha Trust manager for this block of houses and was given the house he still occupied as a per-quisite of that job. When he retired he simply refused to get out of the house and, under Soviet law, the trust was unable to evict him. It was whispered, probably correctly, that he had bribed the appro-priate Datcha Trust officials and that the house was now registered in his name.

The well which he had "captured" had been drilled by the Datcha Trust, or perhaps the original co-op, for the use of all the houses. But the man claimed that, actually, it was on his property and that he merely had been allowing the other cottagers to use it, out of the kindness of his heart. Now that a new fine well had been drilled close by he proposed to close off the public to "his" well.

Indignant as the cottagers were they were none too sanguine of getting their well back by means of protests to the local authorities because they recognized that their opponent had influence or he never would have tried this coup in the first place. Therefore, their talk ran more to retaliatory measures, such as putting dead rats, cats, or even larger animals in the well, which if not restoring the water to them would at least make it unfit for the datcha man to use. There was talk of sterner methods if this did not bring him to hand.

The situation, however, did not merely concern the other cottagers. It concerned us. We were indignant, too, because this was the well we also used. Tom and I made a particularly blistering protest to Burobin and threatened a personal appearance before the Village Soviet (I wish we had made it) unless the well were immediately reopened. For once, we got action. By the end of the week the chain came off the gate, the sign came down and the well was again open for use.

Such incidents as this, of course, are the real stuff and fabric of Russian life. Naturally, the propaganda, the ideology, the Party line, the dialectics and Government policy are important. But the paper work and theory, taken alone as so many "experts" do take them, give a distorted, slanted picture of Russia. Regardless of what they say about themselves Russians are Russians first and Communists second.

This was what George Kennan knew very well, and I like to think that Saltikovka and the talks we had, first around the fireplace and then, as summer advanced and Mrs. Kennan and the children arrived, sitting all together out under the tall pine trees, looking up at the blue, blue Russian sky helped him, in some measure, to get the picture into perspective and to test out many working hypotheses.

For Kennan had not come to Moscow just by chance. He had not accepted the appointment from President Truman simply because he wanted the prestige and honor of an ambassadorship. Nor did he agree to come just because it provided an opportunity for another look at Russia.

I would not want to suggest that Kennan came back to Russia because he felt he had an appointment with destiny but I do know that he felt that his fate, like that of his famous uncle, the Siberian traveler, was in some fashion inextricably bound up with Russia. Moreover, as the author of the doctrine of "containment" on which so much of our postwar policy toward Russia was, and still is, founded, Kennan felt he had very special responsibilities toward the United States and toward Russia.*

For the sake of clarity I think it should be recorded here that the so-called Kennan doctrine on Russia was not regarded by its author as, in any sense, a static policy nor as a policy which was to be carried out for ends which were comprised within itself. Rather, if I understand Kennan correctly, he envisaged it as setting up a series of strong points which would resist the expansive force of postwar Communist imperialism. Once these breakwaters had taken the brunt of the Soviet tide and its dynamism was somewhat spent then the vista of a new era and a new policy would open up in which, through pragmatic recognition of each other's paramount interests and needs, it should be possible to organize world affairs on a more peaceful and permanent basis.

I have doubtless stated the Kennan thesis rather crudely but I believe this was the essence of his position.

Holding views along these lines, Kennan had returned to Moscow, I think, because he felt that he had a real mission there; a duty which he as a man who had assumed public responsibilities must perform; a task to carry out which was, as a matter of fact, quite precise and exact.

* In his famous article published in *Foreign Affairs* for July, 1947, called "The Sources of Soviet Conduct," Kennan had recommended that we follow with regard to Russia "a policy of firm containment, designed to confront the Russians with unalterable counter-force at every point where they show signs of encroaching upon the interests of a peaceful and stable world." He predicted that such a policy would "promote tendencies which must eventually find their outlet in either the break-up or the gradual mellowing of Soviet power."

This mission (and again I take the liberty of stating in simple—perhaps oversimple—terms my own understanding of his viewpoint) was to be on hand in Moscow for the breakup and abandonment of the Stalin postwar "hard" line and the opening of a new era which would be marked by Soviet willingness to talk and to negotiate.

Not only was Kennan completely convinced that this radical change was coming. He was positive that it would come within the year—possibly sooner, but in no event later than a year from his arrival in May, 1952.

This was not a subjective impression based on intuition. It was the result of careful, thoughtful analysis of the Russian situation, paying heed to the historical factors involved; a great deal of attention to the aging process at work within the revolutionary heritage of the Bolsheviks; a sure sense for the realities of Russian character and intelligent evaluation of the shrewdness of the Communist leaders.

While I agreed with much of Kennan's reasoning and, in general, deferred to his judgment I privately felt that he was overoptimistic—that while changes might come in Russia they were further away than he supposed. For instance, he did not think the Stalin line would survive the old man's death. I thought it probably would. In this, as events were so strikingly to show, I was completely wrong and Kennan was completely right.

Kennan reasoned a good deal like this. The Communist leaders are not stupid. They are smart, able men or they would not be where they are. They cannot indefinitely blind their eyes to the reality of the world situation. Sooner or later—and undoubtedly sooner rather than later—they must realize the sterility of Soviet policy and the blind alley into which Stalin's postwar "hard" line has led them.

In fact, the evidence of Soviet failure, of their alienation from the rest of the world, of Russia's increasing isolation and the West's growing unity is so impressive that many Soviet leaders must already be cognizant of it.

Above all things, Communists are, in the end, realists. They do not invest any moral weight in a given political position. When they have reason to change their policy they can change it overnight because the essential test is pragmatic rather than consistent or principled.

Stalin himself should realize these facts. If he does not, however, change his line, conflict within the leadership is certain to arise because other men in the leadership cannot help seeing the imperative necessity for change. The Soviet leadership is not so monolithic as it wishes the world to believe.

Thus, the Stalin line carries within itself the seed of its own repudiation and is already burgeoning with that germinating seed. When the moment of actual repudiation and change comes we must be prepared to seize it; to grasp the unique opportunity which will present itself. At the nucleus of the talks then to be held must be mutual recognition that war between Russia and the United States is unthinkable because this war would mean mutual destruction and the end not just of the capitalist world or the Communist world but of the one world in which we all live. Thus, much as we would like to live in a world devoid of Communist Russia; much as the Kremlin would like to live in a world devoid of capitalist America we must for the sake of our own survival, like estranged members of a family forced to continue to live under one roof, work out some system of getting along.

Kennan thought that it might be possible to hasten this Soviet appreciation of the realities of the situation, as he viewed it, by a few positive actions. For example, he felt it very desirable, if possible, to cut down on the volume and heat of the propaganda recriminations between the United States and Russia.

This, he felt, was a prerequisite to the creation of an atmosphere in which statesmen of the two countries might begin to think and talk about the solution of problems. So long as the atmosphere was constantly heated by charges and countercharges he felt that talk was virtually impossible.

He was fully aware of the difficulties of achieving anything like this, because, for one thing, much of the name calling on the American side was done by private individuals and private publications over which the government had no control. However, he felt that if the Russians could be persuaded to take the first step in this direction—a much easier thing for them since all propaganda was fully within the control of the Government—he by the exercise of his personal influence could produce a comparable cooling down on the American side.

As a preliminary, he arranged even before he left America that the official U.S. propaganda, the broadcasts over Voice of America, etc., would be toned down as an earnest of the sincerity of his proposals.

However, from the start Kennan had no success in achieving a propaganda standstill. He found the Russians completely skeptical of everything he had to say including his informal suggestions about propaganda. Moreover, I think he was personally rather shocked at the vituperation in the Soviet press directed against the United States. This was an old story to those of us who had been in Moscow, but he had not seen it before. He tried several quiet, confidential approaches to the Soviet Foreign Office on the propaganda question without success. Indeed, if anything the propaganda got worse—so bad, in fact, that Kennan broke the rule he had laid down for himself and publicly protested against the anti-American content of some posters being used to advertise Air Force Day.

Nor was Kennan any more successful in his efforts to get started on another preliminary looking toward the "forthcoming" reversal of the Soviet line. This was what he regarded as Step No. 2— private exploratory talks between himself and some person or persons on the Soviet side which would be entirely informal, completely off-the-record, and in no manner commit either side to anything.

The purpose of the talks would merely be, in a most quiet and secret way, to begin to go over some of the ground which would have to be covered once the big Soviet shift occurred; to chart out some of the areas in which agreement might be expected with not too great difficulty; to locate the real and most serious points of conflict; to enable each side to gauge the amount of change and the amount of flexibility that would be needed in overcoming these difficulties.

The essence of such talks was secrecy and informality. But, though he made his ideas plainly enough known to Soviet officials who were in a position to act, nothing came of this initiative, either.

While he never admitted any discouragement I think that Kennan, being only human, was somewhat downcast by his failure to achieve any progress on either of these two steps. On the other hand he was fully confident of the accuracy of his analysis of the Russian situation and felt that the firsthand look which he had had at the bread-and-butter realities of Soviet life as well as at Soviet officials in action merely confirmed and fleshed out the picture which he had sketched in his mind long before he had ever accepted the appointment to the ambassadorship.

This, then, was more or less the situation in September, 1952, when he decided to go out to Western Europe for a week or two to consult with some of our people in London and Germany. He didn't plan to stay very long because the announcement had already been made of the calling of the Nineteenth Congress of the Communist Party which was due to meet shortly after the first of October and he was eager to be on hand to watch these proceedings at first hand.

There had not been a Party Congress since before the war and he was looking to this meeting to provide further and possibly decisive clues to the development of Soviet policy which, regardless of how it looked on the surface, he was confident was rapidly moving in the direction of the denouement which he had predicted before he left America and on which his position as Ambassador was virtually predicated.

I believe that all of the correspondents in Moscow went out to Vnukovo Airport on the morning of September 19 to see Kennan off. We had spent a good deal of time with him the afternoon before, discussing the general situation and his trip to the West. We wished him well and expected to see him back in ten days or so.

But fate—if it was, as I think, fate—played a curious trick.

When his plane touched down in Berlin that afternoon Kennan gave out a brief statement to the Berlin reporters. There was nothing extraordinary about what he said except that he used one phrase, comparing conditions in Moscow with conditions he experienced in Nazi Berlin, which hardly would sit well with the Kremlin. It was not a very diplomatic thing to say and I still do not know exactly why he said it except that when a man feels something as deeply as

George Kennan did sometimes those feelings come to the surface regardless of whether he is a diplomat or an ambassador.

In any event it quickly became apparent that this was just the excuse the Kremlin was waiting for. Doubtless, from the start, Stalin had not been comfortable about having a man who could look out his window on Mokhovaya Street and see right through the Kremlin walls into the heart of so many of his secrets. I had really been surprised that the Foreign Office accepted Kennan at all. However, his remarks in Berlin provided an excuse, and now the Kremlin wasted no time. Even before he could return to Moscow Kennan was named *persona non grata,* which meant that he would not be permitted to come back.

Thus, by a singular ill chance, Kennan's mission to Moscow was brought to an end and he was barred from the Soviet capital almost at the very moment when the curtain was to rise on a progression of events which was in most dramatic of fashions to bring about—on the surface at least—precisely the kind of changes of the Soviet line which he, studying the situation from afar in the quiet of his Princeton closet, had predicted would inevitably occur.

It was all going to happen. Just as George Kennan said it would. Right down to the brief standstill on propaganda. The only thing he hadn't forecast was that it would take the death of Stalin to bring this change about.

And when, in the following March, Stalin died and the Soviet leaders who took his place began to act and talk exactly as George Kennan had said they would he was back at Princeton again, virtually repudiated by the government he so long had served; the U.S. Embassy in Moscow was once more in the hands of a chargé d'affaires, capable enough but powerless to lift a finger, and Charles Bohlen, the man who was to succeed Kennan and who probably is Kennan's only equal in judgment of Russian affairs was preoccupied in the United States Senate, defending himself, essentially, on the curious charge that he had had, in the past, some small experience (and success) in dealing with the Soviet Union.

So, one of the most remarkable long-range international political forecasts of our time was confirmed by the day-to-day progress of events in Russia.

But not only was Washington at the time unable (if not unwilling) to take advantage of the situation. It was hardly willing to admit that any change had occurred. And the fantastically accurate predictions of the American who knew Russia best were carefully tucked away in one of the streamlined modern pigeonholes of which the State Department in its new Foggy Bottom building has so many.

IX

The Doctors' Plot

IT WAS February, 1953, and as I sat in my gloomy Empire room in the Hotel Metropole little curlicues of fear made their way up and down my back. It was real fear and it came from an only too real cause. Terror had been let loose in Moscow once again. Not the quiet, customary everyday sort of fear which everyone in Russia had to get used to living with but Terror with a capital T.

I had been spared the experience of living in Moscow during the purge days of the thirties but I had often heard of those times from friends. And, even more vividly, I was familiar with them through the dramatic pictures given by Koestler and other sensitive persons. And I had myself experienced the *petite terreur* of 1949–50.

Now, as I sat in this ornate room which had always seemed so unfriendly, so totally lacking in cheer, I was afraid—afraid for myself and afraid for some of my friends in the tiny Russo-American colony, which had survived actually only in the correspondents' corps, itself so small as to be really only a vestigial remain.

Fear seemed to sift invisibly into the room like dust from a storm on the desert. I had drawn the great plush draperies to shut out the grimy sight of the Metropole Hotel courtyard and sat trying to read by artificial light. But the fear which I had felt in the city had come into the room and was sitting with me. It was a physical thing. I shuddered and tried to think what was likely to happen and where it would all come out.

This feeling of fear and terror had been growing day by day in Moscow for a month. I knew how unreliable subjective appearances are in Russia but it seemed to me that, by now, I could recognize fear in the streets, in the straight-walking crowds on Gorky Street and the pushing, shoving shoppers on the Stoleshnikov. And I was sure that I could recognize it inside the Metropole Hotel. The maids, I thought, went about their work with a wary eye. More often than not when I was about to say good morning to the supervisor she "happened" to be looking the other way. Mrs. Grey, the quarter-Russian, quarter-English, quarter-Viennese, quarter-French "administrator" no longer tried to inveigle me into conversations about her perennial English lessons when I came into the hotel late at night.

One thing was perfectly clear. The Russians knew only too well how dangerous it was to be a foreigner in Russia at a time like this and how doubly dangerous it was to be a Russian who had contact with a foreigner. So it had been in the time of Ivan the Terrible. So it had been down through the centuries of terror which marked Russian history like a streak of red. So it had been at the time of the purges in the thirties and so it was now.

I sat under the sparkling light of the crystal-hung chandelier in this baroque chamber which had been my home for more than three years and tried to shake the cobwebs of fear out of my brain sufficiently to be able to estimate in practical terms my chances of surviving this rising whirlwind. But it was quite impossible to assess the situation just as it was impossible to determine how far the terror would spread. It was obvious that it was going a long way and it was equally obvious that the capitalistic correspondent of the leading American newspaper might well be cast for a role of some importance at a later stage of the developing plot.

After giving very serious consideration to the question of recommending my recall to my editors I finally decided to wait a while longer, at least until the opening of the second act of the developing tragedy which I felt would not be long delayed.

The immediate source of my alarm was, of course, the so-called Doctors' Plot and the events connected with it. While the ramifications of this plot were by no means clear at that time (nor have they become completely clear since then) it was quite apparent

that Russia stood on the brink of a reign of terror beside which that
of the thirties would seem trivial.

It was equally apparent that the motivating factor in this was a
new and horrible dementia in Stalin's mind, a return of the plot
psychosis which had caused him to ravage Russia during the years
of the thirties.

What was brewing within the secret walls of the Kremlin, clearly,
was a new massacre of the Streltzi—a blood purge of the men standing closest to Stalin, similar to that of Peter the Great or to the
demoniac slaughter in which Ivan the Terrible struck off the heads
of the boyars of Novgorod and of thousands of men who had been
his firmest supporters.

I have seen at Zagorsk, an ancient monastery some forty miles
outside of Moscow, a great fat book of parchment pages, about the
size of an old-fashioned family Bible. On these pages were written
down at the orders of Ivan the Terrible the names of all those men
whom he ordered executed. The old book bulges with pages and
yet it is only a partial list. No such book exists to list the victims of
Stalin's purges yet it is safe to say that the bloodshed of the thirties
would have seemed but a few drops compared with the slaughter
which was being prepared in the weeks before the old dictator
met his death.

And it is traditional in Russia that whenever an ill wind of this
sort blows up the casualties are thickest among those Russians who
actually have or falsely are charged with having connections with
foreigners and among foreigners who have associated with Russians.
Since, as a Western correspondent, I was already considered nothing
more than a kind of licensed spy by the authorities, my apprehen-
sions were not mere fancies of the imagination.

However, to feel something of the real atmosphere of the winter
of 1953 in Moscow and to understand a little more about the witch's
brew which had been stirred up, it is necessary to turn back a few
pages in the extraordinarily complex and terrifying sequence of
events which brought the thirty-year period of Russian history,
which even in his lifetime was known as the "Stalin epoch," to an
end.

The emotional soil in which this strange story was rooted was provided by the tortured, pride-conscious, suspicious Georgian land where I had seen Othello come to life because he lived within the breast of every jealousy-haunted man. In Georgia to suspect was to believe and the only hand you could really trust was that of your enemy because you knew it held a dagger. Stalin was a Georgian and to the Georgian mind the phantasmagoria of a Doctors' Plot was only expectation of treachery confirmed.

The curtain went up on the opening scenes of this final drama of Stalin's years in a manner which little foreshadowed the conclusion. It began in the autumn of 1952 when the Nineteenth Congress of the Communist Party was summoned to assemble in Moscow on the fifth of October.

For thirteen years there had been no Congress of the Party, not since one held in 1939, on the eve of the war. Party rules calling for the holding of Congresses had simply been ignored, just as Stalin ignored any rule or regulation of government which happened to interfere with his personal wishes.

There had often been speculation that a Congress was about to be held. In fact when I had arrived back in Russia in the winter of 1949 there was a series of Republic Party Congresses going on and most of my colleagues felt sure that a general Congress would be held that year.

But no Congress was held in 1949. Nor in 1950. Nor 1951. And no subject had seemed deader than the question of a new Party Congress in the summer of 1952 until suddenly one morning at about 4 A.M. as I was peacefully sleeping at the datcha in Saltikovka my telephone rang. It was one of my colleagues.

"You better get dressed and come right into town," he said. "The papers have just come out and there is an announcement that a new Party Congress is to be held."

The date was August 20. Along with the call for the Party Congress there was made public, nearly two years after it had gotten under way, the outline of the new Five-Year Plan.

I hurried into town, catching an electric suburban train in the thin five o'clock morning twilight, and sped to the Central Telegraph Office through Moscow streets, empty of people except for the inevitable *dvorniki*, or building porters, almost all women, in their white aprons, busily sweeping the streets with long-handled brush brooms or watering them down with hoses.

It was a familiar sight and one which became more and more familiar in the months that followed as event piled upon event in Moscow in dizzy succession until the clock and calendar lost all meaning and the predawn hours of the capital became more familiar to me than normal working times. It was the last time I saw the datcha that summer and almost the last time I was to know any feeling of relaxation in Moscow.

"This means that Stalin has finally made up his mind about his successor," one of my colleagues told me after reading the call for the Congress. I thoroughly agreed. Stalin was approaching his seventy-third birthday and it was time that he gave the Party a clue to what was to happen when he should die.

It was true, as I had noticed, that Stalin like many elderly men had offered certain indications that the thought of death was almost too repugnant for mention in his presence. There seemed no doubt to me that the enormous and unusual concentration of Soviet medical work in the field of longevity and the frequent press articles about persons in the Soviet Union who had lived to the age of 120 and even 140 was not accidental.

I had often smiled wryly on reading accounts of the long life of Georgians, in particular. Still, it seemed fairly obvious that Stalin would hardly, at long last, have summoned the Party to meet if he did not propose to give it a clear line as to whom he wished to inherit his mantle. So I thought and so I wrote. Furthermore I thought it was quite certain that the choice would lie with Malenkov and I tried in the indirect and clumsy fashion which was forced upon me by the censorship to put across this idea in my dispatches.

But to my stupefaction nothing of the kind happened. Stalin did not anoint the brow of a favorite son. No crown prince was designated. No successor. The only brow to be touched with laurel was that of Stalin himself.

It had seemed at the start that the great roles at the Party Congress were to be played by Malenkov and Khrushchev. But this notion was quickly dispelled. There were no really great roles at

Each year the Russian Orthodox Church regains some of its pre-Revolutionary strength. This is an Easter scene at a village not far from Moscow. The women carry traditional *kulitch* and *pashka*, the Easter cakes, in white linen bags to the priest for blessing. (*All photographs courtesy of The New York Times, by Harrison E. Salisbury.*)

Outside the beautifully decorated refectory of the ancient Trinity Monastery at Zagorsk, an elderly believer of the Orthodox Church waits for alms on Easter eve.

Along the Volga—today as always—onion-turreted churches dominate the scene. This ancient church is at Yaroslavl on the upper river.

The Saltikovka datcha. The picture shows the author with Dedya (Uncle) Vanya, a retired Russian railwayman who cut the grass with a long-handled scythe, cut firewood with a two-bladed ax, and did other chores.

This "road" led to the summer datcha from Saltikovka highway.

This magnificent flight of steps leads up from the Volga River steamboat landings to the main promenade which has been constructed upon the rubble fields which marked no man's land between the German and Russian lines at Stalingrad. The building to the right is a Children's Theater.

Aboard the S.S. *Lermontov*. A bearded Rostov professor snaps a picture of Captain Yertakhov with the new Kiev camera. The picture is taken against a background of the Stepan Razin heights, the hills where the leader of a famous Russian peasant revolt of the 17th century hid with his rebel band.

Life changes with incredible slowness on the middle Volga. Here a bearded beggar holds out his cup for kopeks, a barefoot woman drowses in the sun and peasants gather to sell eggs. The only new sign—a boy with a bicycle.

It is early morning in Bukhara and this boy has just come in from the desert with a load of twigs and dried grass. In theory he has completed four years of rural schooling and is now a full-fledged worker. Actually he probably is hardly literate enough to write his name.

The author was arrested for taking this in the local bazaar of a tiny mountain village along the isolated "highway" which leads from Alma-Ata to Frunze, close to China and the Hindu Kush. This old scissor grinder is a direct descendant of the fabulous "golden horde" of Mongol invaders

This handsome Uzbek tambour player strikes the drum with incredible rapidity. He has an audience of all nations. The little boy in the foreground is a Kazakh. The little dark-faced girl is a gypsy. The two men to the rear of the player are Uzbeks and the man with cap and cane is Russian.

The bright side of things in Bukhara, Central Asia—a group of schoolchildren standing in front of a library which has been set up in an old mosque as a memorial to the Arab scholar Ibn Sin. The older girls pictured here are students in a midwives' school. All of these children are of Central Asiatic nationalities.

The Jewess in this photograph is riding down the ancient Street of Jews in Bukhara, a few steps from the Jewish synagogue, one of the oldest in Central Asia. She is a member of a small colony of Bukhara Jews who have survived war, revolution and anti-Semitic excesses. Note her daughter, cradled on a big pillow in her lap, and the rug and bedding which are wrapped about the donkey to form a saddle.

This is the grimmest gate in all Russia and, perhaps, the world. It is the steel portal leading into the Lubiyanka, the remodeled insurance building on Lubiyanka hill which serves the MVD both as headquarters and as its central prison for important political captives. Many condemned men, including probably Beriya, have entered through this gate. This is probably the only picture ever taken of the Lubiyanka gate. It was snapped without focusing from a rapidly moving car.

A Czarist prison at Chita a hundred years ago. It is almost identical in style and construction with the present prisons used by the Communist regime in Siberia.

This is Lenin Square, in the heart of Khabarovsk, Far Eastern headquarters of the MVD. The building is a hospital. To the left behind the just visible low wooden fence is being constructed an addition to the hospital with a forced labor group, largely women. If you look closely at the fence you will see at each corner the telltale wooden watchtowers in which the tommygunners stand on guard.

In Tadjikstan, the Russians have forcibly resettled many Germans who had lived since the time of Catherine the Great along the Volga and in the Ukraine. These industrious, able people have constructed many fine buildings in this backward Asiatic area, but they are forced to live in squalor. Fine houses go to Russians

This is Yakutsk, a city in Russia's Siberian sub-Arctic. It is a wooden city—wooden sidewalks, wooden houses and wooden paving blocks for the street. There isn't, however, a tree in all Yakutsk, and hardly a spot of grass or green.

Here is a close-up of a building being constructed in Yakutsk by prison labor. Behind this high wooden palisade, men and women workers, guarded by the eternal tommygunners of the MVD, are building a printing and publishing plant.

Here is the Red Square as it appears since the death of Stalin. To the left is the big new GUM department store, biggest in Moscow and one of the biggest in Europe. The man has bought his child a tricycle there. The woman is a peasant with a pack on her back. In the background is St. Basil's wondrous cathedral. The car in the foreground is a Moskvich station wagon similar to the German Opel.

This Chinaman sells hot-cross buns (without crosses) in the peasant market at Saltikovka for a State Bakery Trust. His fresh buns are packed in the wicker basket at the right. The little sign in back says "Hand Trading in the Collective Farm Market, Strictly Forbidden."

More evidence of the new Government's drive to provide consumer goods. The little girl is in raptures over the display of dolls and toys in this sidewalk showcase.

These women are polishing the windows of the Mostorg department store in Moscow. The new consumer goods may be turned out by factory methods but the most primitive methods of hand labor still prevail in even such simple tasks as washing the show windows.

This is an unusual picture of part of the Kremlin walls, taken from across the Moskva River. The half-built skyscraper in the center is the Zaradya building which Stalin started and which, if continued by the new Government, would have dwarfed St. Basil's Cathedral and the Kremlin and sharply altered Red Square.

An exposition of Soviet automobiles, trucks and farm machinery. On the lower floor is the sports model Zis, something like a Packard, used either as an escort car by the MVD or for open-top sightseeing around Moscow. Beyond the Zis are the newer Zims, Pobedas and Moskviches. The Zis was Stalin's favorite car. Its production has been halted by the new Government.

Here are the faces of the Russian people. The flat cloth cap gives away the fact that one is a worker. The stiff-brimmed cap is worn by a countryman. They are looking at an experimental stand of wheat at the Moscow Agriculture Exposition.

These are Muscovites, sitting on a bench in a park in the heart of the city on a cool spring day. The bearded old man is reading his copy of *Pravda*. The man sitting at the other end of the bench has a *Pravda* too. But he is sitting on it, probably to protect his coat from the freshly painted bench.

Here is the Russian land in all its infinity, a vast sea of land that has no ending. In this space is born Russia's temperament, her fears (of invasion across the open plain), her grandiose dreams (of empire without end), her timelessness (for time is only the tick of a watch), and her resignation (how can man conquer the infinite?).

the Congress. The star role and the only important one was played by Stalin and with exceptional cynicism, even for him, it was played not at the Congress but before it opened and in such a way as to reduce the Congress itself to a mere claque.

This Stalin achieved by issuing a few days before the delegates met in Moscow a new "master work," a kind of Stalin gloss on Karl Marx's *Das Kapital*. It completely stole the thunder of the Congress, as it was obviously intended to do. After this all the Congress had to do was to make speeches praising Stalin's genius and quoting extensively from his new Economic Theses. He succeeded in reducing the speeches of Malenkov and Khrushchev to the customary level of Party hackwork.

It was an unusual display of contempt, even for Stalin, I thought, although the Generalissimo had never been backward in showing his disdain for his lieutenants and for the constituted agencies of Soviet Government. But why, I puzzled, should he go to the trouble of summoning the great Congress only to treat it like a bunch of kindergarten children—or was that the whole point?

As the Congress proceeded it seemed, indeed, that perhaps this was the point which Stalin wished to make. He, himself, was careless and erratic in attending sessions and confined his own remarks to a brief and rambling speech about the role of the foreign Communist parties.

It seemed, also, as though another extra-Congress event could hardly have been better timed. This was the ouster of Kennan, which was bound to impress the country delegates to the Party meeting.

Stalin could say to the delegates from Kamchatka or the mid-Volga: See how big and powerful Russia is. We can kick out the American Ambassador and Washington has to bow its head and take it.

It was a heady demonstration and one calculated to stir up the nationalistic tendencies of the delegates to a considerable extent.

In addition to teaching his "children" a lesson or two it became plain before the Congress had long been over that Stalin had another purpose in mind. What he was actually trying to do, I was convinced, was to conceal and confuse the lines of succession rather than clarify them. And confusion he certainly sowed with a broad and generous hand.

Before the Congress, there had existed a twelve-member Politburo of Party leaders. It at least had the virtue of being a compact and recognizable body of leaders. Now in place of this well-known group there was substituted an amorphous Presidium with twenty-five full members and eleven alternates, so big a body that it obviously could play no role in government. But an excellent screen behind which to confuse the leadership picture.

Stalin played the same trick with the Party Secretariat, which had always been a tight little group and which was, in fact, the device which he himself had utilized for his climb to power. In recent years, in so far as Stalin ever let any strings out of his fingers, the Secretariat had been run on a day-to-day basis by Malenkov.

Now, it was suddenly expanded to a total of ten members, headed by Stalin and including Malenkov and Khrushchev. But there were so many new and unknown secretaries, fresh from the provinces, that it was difficult to visualize in practice how such a body could function. I even had trouble in identifying some of the new personnel—so obscure had been their previous Party posts.

In fact, the net effect of the Party Congress and the personnel changes was to give me the impression that someone was deliberately shuffling the cards in such a way that only he would know who was to come out on top. Or maybe no one would. Because the person who was shuffling the deck, of course, was Stalin. Some diplomats took a different view. One man from a Mediterranean country who knew Russia quite well told me that he was sure Malenkov was behind all the shadow work and camouflage. I didn't argue with him. Perhaps he was right but I had long since reached the conclusion that in any changes of Party or Government it was Stalin and only Stalin who was the prime mover. He might, at times, act through Malenkov or Molotov or Voroshilov but he was the boss and any plans or any decisions were his. The responsibility and usually the initiative were his.

While I was still trying to puzzle out the events of the Congress two very curious things happened which were far beyond my powers to analyze at the time but, as it transpired, they were deep portents of what the future held in store.

The first occurrence was the hanging of the portraits of the Government leaders in the days of the annual November 7 holiday. All foreigners, myself included, and many Russians watched these displays with hawklike interest, as a barometer of changes up and down in political fortunes. It was the absence of Nikolai Voznesensky's portrait from such a display in March, 1949, which gave the first hint that he had lost his job as top state planner.

Now, with the pictures going up for the first time after the Party Congress, I was intensely interested to see what would happen. I kept my eye on the Moskva Hotel, the Maly Theater and the Central Telegraph Office for the crews of workmen to start putting up the pictures. Finally, I saw the work beginning and went over to the Moskva Hotel to watch. It was interesting all right. First the great portrait of Stalin was hauled up and anchored outside the seventh and eighth story windows. Then a smaller portrait of Molotov was hoisted up and fastened just below that of Stalin. In a single row at the level of the third-story windows were the rest of the men who, with the elimination of the Politburo, came to be called Stalin's "comrades at arms" or *sorotniki*. And here was a big and startling change. Beriya, who had long occupied No. 4 spot, below Stalin, Molotov and Malenkov, suddenly was dropped to position No. 6. Voroshilov and Bulganin, the two military members of the top hierarchy, moved up ahead of the Secret Police Chief. It looked as though Beriya was slipping. And the military rising. I watched Beriya closely at the big Bolshoi Theater Party meeting on the night of November 6 and again the next day on the podium of the Mausoleum in the Red Square. I couldn't see any change in his manner. He behaved just the way I had become accustomed to seeing him in recent years, talking and joking most of the time and most of the time directing his conversation to Malenkov. To my eye he seemed the most jovial member of the top leadership.

But there must be an explanation for his slip to position No. 6 even if Stalin was just continuing his policy of mystification and confusion, and I could not help recalling some previously unexplained happenings. Six months before, in April, there had been a great upheaval in Georgia which was, virtually, Beriya's private province. The henchmen whom Beriya installed before coming to Moscow in 1938 had been ousted and a new crew substituted. Beriya himself went to Tbilisi and, so far as the reports in the papers went, apparently supervised the purge. The new Georgian party leaders paid him fulsome tributes. But I had thought at the time that there was something fishy about the situation since the men whom Beriya ostensibly ousted were his close friends and associates whereas the new crew did not seem to have these personal ties. Moreover, any scandal attaching to men whom Beriya appointed inevitably left his own hands not quite clean. However, up to this moment there had been no sign of any loss of political favor for Beriya. Now, however, I tentatively concluded that the political tides must be running against the police chief.

By this time I was beginning to miss the wise guidance and counsel of Kennan acutely. There were few enough persons, at best, in Moscow with whom it was possible to carry on any intelligent discussion or analysis of Russian events. Outside of three or four of my newspaper colleagues who had spent many years in Russia the foreign colony was almost bereft of individuals with any real background in Russian affairs. There was no one of Kennan's insight or interest in the "ghetto" of the diplomatic colony and yet it was increasingly plain that events in Russia were assuming a pattern so complex that only the most exhaustive scrutiny and study would make clear what was going on.

Before it was possible to do much more than note that Beriya seemed to have suffered at least a temporary fall from favor and that possibly the military were being given a boost up another and more curious thing happened. One evening I opened up the Kiev newspaper *Pravda of the Ukraine,* to read on the back page a notice of a kind which I had never seen before in the Russian press. It was simply headed "Chronicle" and it announced the verdict of a special military court which had sentenced three men to death and a group of others to long prison sentences. The three death sentences had been carried out by shooting. The crime with which these individuals were charged was "counter-revolutionary wreck-

ing." Quite a story to headline "Chronicle." But this was only the
first "Chronicle." More were to come.

Familiar though I was with the Russian habit of using sledge-
hammers to kill flies the Kiev case broke all precedent because the
accused men were not traitors in any ordinary sense nor even in
some far-fetched Russian sense. They were, so far as the "Chronicle" went, a group of executives in the Kiev retail and wholesale
trade network who had, apparently, been engaged in black market-
ing, theft, embezzlement and other forms of commercial skuldug-
gery. It was difficult to see how their alleged activities, however
reprehensible, constituted any threat to the security of the state.

And I noticed some other very strange circumstances such as the
fact that the Russian criminal code makes no provision for military
trial of persons accused of this type of crime. Nor does it make any
provision for death sentences for persons found guilty of such
crimes.

And, I noticed, too, with a kind of a this-is-where-I-came-in feeling that most of the persons accused seemed, by their names, to be
of Jewish extraction.

For the moment this was to be a single unlovely blossom, flowering suddenly and with no apparent connection with any other event
of which I was aware. But within six weeks it was to be revealed
as only a small harbinger of other unlovely blossoms of the same
species, suddenly springing up almost everywhere you cast your eye.

But at the time I could only note that the victims were largely
Jewish (in the same old Ukraine where, as I had seen in wartime
days, anti-Semitism ignites with the ease of meadow grass in a dry
autumn); that they were fairly prominent members of trading organizations directed by Politburo member Anastas Mikoyan; that
they were fairly prominent members of a Party organization still
largely dominated by Nikita Khrushchev; and that their prosecution
seemed to have been taken out of the hands of the justice organizations controlled by Beriya and vested in an unusual, temporary military body.

It was a bone with plenty of meat to chew on. What did it mean?

All that I could see was that strong and unpleasant forces,
stronger and more unpleasant than any I had seen before, were

being let loose in Russia. So far, like the cards of the Party Congress, the pattern was too mixed for intelligent interpretation. Perhaps, I thought, it was not accidental that before this strange phantasmagoria began to unfold, Kennan, the one foreigner in Russia most capable of understanding what was afoot, had been barred from his ringside observation post in Moscow.

In late December the cards were given another confusing shuffle. On Christmas Eve *Pravda* came out with a sudden and bewildering demand for a new round of *mea culpas* from persons prominent in the Party, particularly persons who had played a leading role in ideology and economics. It demanded apologies and explanations from everyone who had been so uncautious nearly five years before as to praise a study of Russia's World War II economy which had been written by Voznesensky a couple of years before his still unexplained downfall as the Party's chief planner.

The views for which apologies were now demanded in summary fashion had all been on public record for the past five years. It was obvious, therefore, that no current question was at issue but, rather, that in the Florentine fashion of Kremlin politics someone, for some hidden motives, had fashioned a poisoned dagger out of a completely meaningless question and proposed to use it against a number of persons in high positions in the Party, particularly against persons connected with organizational and ideological questions, such as those who might be expected to be associated with Malenkov and with economical and industrial questions with which Kaganovich dealt.

I have an old-fashioned habit of spending some time on New Year's Eve or New Year's Day looking back on the year just past and ahead to that which is in prospect, and trying to see, if I can, where the world in general, and myself in particular are headed. I must confess that on the New Year's Day of 1953 I felt more than a little confused as to where Russia might be headed. This was rather unusual for me since (regardless of whether I am right or not) I usually prided myself in having some fairly clear idea of the general direction in which Moscow was steering.

That was not true on January 1, 1953. I felt adrift. There were too many clues and they seemed to point in all directions of the compass. If Stalin was erecting a camouflage barrier behind which to carry forward some unknown intentions he certainly seemed to be succeeding. But clarification, of a kind, was close at hand.

Only thirteen days later like a terrifying burst of St. Elmo's light, green and sickly, everywhere and nowhere, the terror came back to Moscow with the publication in *Pravda* of a ten-paragraph announcement which was again simply headed "Chronicle."

Behind that bland and colorless word was concealed the most deadly and sinister event, in all probability, that had occurred in Russia since Stalin had murdered his way to power. In form it was as simple as a rattlesnake's fangs. Only a thousand thousand times more potent. It was an announcement that a group of nine doctors, six of them Jews, had been arrested on charges of plotting against the lives of a group of members of the Soviet Government, principally against high military officers. The group of doctors was said to have had connections, through Zionist organizations, with British and American intelligence and to have been able to carry out its operations through the slackness of the Soviet security organs.

I will be frank to say that the hair rose on the back of my neck when I read this statement and the editorial which accompanied it in *Pravda*. There was not the slightest doubt in my mind that this was no mere flash in the pan. It was the basic scenario of a desperate and deadly drama which was about to unfold. The patchwork of puzzling events of the past four months suddenly jogged together. For whatever the reason might be—sheer mania, intra-palace plotting, an old man's deadly desire to tighten the stranglehold he already had upon his associates—it was certain that we were headed back to the days of the purge and that this time the blood bath would likely be more terrible than Ivan's, some 350 years before.

It was now only too plain that what had gone before—the confusing Party Congress and the rest—was only by way of setting the stage for this new and more horrible drama. It was designed to create an atmosphere in which terror could strike without end.

It took no analytic ability to see two obvious and immediate targets of this campaign. One was Beriya, chief of security services. The other was the Jews.

Nor did it take any master mind to see that no matter who had

written the particular lines of this scenario or had stage-managed
the arrests of the doctors and their "confessions" that the sponsor,
the guiding genius, the man who had placed his imprimatur upon
this new chapter from the Grand Guignol was none other than
Stalin.

As one practical and irreverent American said: "The old man has
reached for that bottle again. Watch out!"

Watch out! Sound advice but hard to take if you were staying in
Russia. It was plain as could be that this wildfire would not halt
with Beriya and the Jews. They were stage effects for a new and
greater Georgian *Othello*. Every day the sickness was spreading.
Each fresh batch of provincial newspapers that was brought into my
office reported new scandals, new exposures, new arrests. At first
the victims, almost invariably, were Jews, usually in trade organizations but also in professional posts. Doctors, lawyers, writers and
actors were involved. Any Jew was a fair target.

The heaviest run of cases was in the Ukraine—that old seedbed
of anti-Semitism. It was also Khrushchev's territory. First came the
exposures and arrests of the Jews. Then the drumfire was laid down
against the Party organizations which had permitted the "corruption." The target quickly broadened out. Khrushchev was involved
because his Party chiefs were being attacked. Beriya was involved
because of the security angle. Mikoyan was involved deeper and
deeper because of the alleged scandals in the trade organizations.
And Malenkov was dragged in because in one city after another
his Party lieutenants were implicated.

But implicated most deeply and most dangerously of all was that
dry and pedantic little man who had survived so much before,
Viacheslav Molotov. For years Molotov had suffered being the public butt of Stalin jokes and Stalin sneers almost every time the Great
Man decided to grant a state audience to some distinguished foreigner. He had taken all this and gone on serving his master loyally.

Now, Molotov was getting his reward. Almost every day I saw
in the central press itself, or heard over that mysterious grapevine
which still operated somehow or other in Moscow, of the arrests
and confessions of persons closely connected with the Foreign
Office; persons who worked in the Foreign Office; persons who were
connected with foreign correspondents.

It was of such items that my fear was composed as I sat in my Metropole Hotel room and wondered whether the odds were growing too short to justify my staying on in Moscow. By this time I could see that even the military were not immune. Scandals had begun to appear in connection with Jews in the Army and Navy although, in general, I felt that the military were to be spared in the initial phases of the onrushing purge. I deduced this from the fact that it was largely military men who had been named as the supposed "victims" of the Jewish doctors. And it was a military court which had executed the first Jews in Kiev.

Trying to make a pattern to fit the events I thought that the military were to be cast in the role both of "victims" and, perhaps, as "saviors" of the country. Yet, if history was to repeat itself, as seemed possible, a horrible thought came to mind. The purges of the thirties racked every level of Soviet society. Then, finally, the madness came to an end with a purge of most of the general officers of the Army. It is not likely, I told myself, that any Russian general with a memory as long as the hair on his bullet-shaven head can have forgotten the thirties. It is not likely that the generals can be any more easy in their minds than the rest of the people.

And steadily as February wore on the terror deepened in Moscow. Was it my imagination? I think not. Certainly, I was not the only person who was wondering where it would stop this time and whether there was no limit to the blood sacrifices demanded by Stalin. Every day the rumors circulated. There had been arrests in Tass, the news agency. The head of the agency, Palgunov, a man known for years to be very close to Molotov, had vanished . . . arrested. . . . Madame Molotov (a Jewess) had disappeared . . . banished to Siberia. . . . Arrests in Moscow University . . . Arrests in the Academy of Science . . . More Jews dismissed . . . Protectors of Jews arrested . . . Arrests in the Central Committee . . . The Jewish jazz band leader, Utuesov, arrested . . . Mekhlis, the Jewish security administrator who had been ill for several years, died. Kaganovich (a Jew) headed the funeral procession. . . . Window dressing, Moscow said.

Who in the Politburo could feel safe by late February? No one, I thought. Not Molotov. Not Malenkov. Surely not Beriya. Possibly Voroshilov because he pulled no weight, anyway. Bulganin? Hardly,

Kaganovich? Mikoyan? Khrushchev? There wasn't a safe name on the list.

And what of Stalin, himself? In the pink of condition. In the best of spirits. Good health. Lively mind. That was the word of three foreigners who saw him in February—Bravo, the Argentine Ambassador, Menon, the Indian, and Dr. Kitchlu, an Indian active in the "peace" movement. Only Menon had one strange thing to report. He saw Stalin on February 17. He found the Generalissimo in striking good temper but throughout the interview the old man kept doodling on a pad of paper with a red pencil. This was an old habit of Stalin's, but Menon has sharp eyes. He saw that Stalin kept drawing wolves, one wolf after another. And presently Stalin began to talk, too, about wolves. Russian peasants, he said, know how to deal with wolves. They exterminate them. And wolves, said the Generalissimo, know this and they behave accordingly. A curious remark and one which Menon didn't know how to interpret. He thought Stalin might have been referring to the capitalist wolves of America or, possibly, making a veiled criticism of the Indian doctrine of nonresistance.

I didn't know how to interpret it either when Menon told me about it. I remember that back in 1944 when Eric Johnston called on Stalin he had doodled, also. But it had been pretty girls that time. I didn't like the sound of wolves any more than I liked the deepening tension in the Moscow atmosphere. In retrospect this incident may have been quite significant. It may, perhaps, have been a tiny visible evidence of a mind that, behind a façade of seeming brightness and normality, was only too preoccupied with the subject of "eliminating wolves."

It seemed certain that great and sinister events were in the making. Exactly what I did not know, but I could not believe that my instinct was deceiving me. All straws pointed in the same direction. One day I ran into a man I had known a long time, a Westerner who had taken the Communist side. It was a casual encounter in the Metropole Hotel. But somehow too casual. Without putting it into so many words he let me know that it would be better not to speak to him any more in public places—not that I often did. There were rumors—even among the small circle of Russians with whom I had contact, mostly servants and minor officials—of more doctors arrested. Frumkin, whose wartime fame for regenerative grafting of male sex organs had spread as far as Hollywood and whom I'd interviewed in 1944, had suffered a heart attack. Or was it a diplomatic "heart attack" and was he actually being questioned in the Lubiyanka? No one knew. No one would even ask. It was said that investigations had been ordered in a whole series of deaths, particularly deaths of all general officers since the end of the war. It was whispered that young officers almost never survived admission to certain hospitals. It was whispered that even the "black help," the peasant slop women in the hospitals, had known that something was wrong but were powerless in the face of the Jewish doctors. Terrible things had gone on in the hospitals. If people only knew . . . Whispers . . . Jews . . . Doctors . . .

Over the whole scene I seemed to sense the ghostlike, sinister presence of the man who was so seldom mentioned and so seldom seen—Stalin's *chef de cabinet*, the silent, inscrutable General Poskrebyshev—the man who vanished without a trace with the death of his chief.

Something was going to happen. And soon. I arranged with two of my colleagues for an all-night watch at the telegraph office to guard against sudden developments. With great difficulty we managed to make arrangements to get *Pravda* and *Izvestiya* at their editorial offices, soon after publication. I thought at the time, and still think, that the only reason we were able to make such arrangements was the fact that night after night we prowled about the back doors of the great *Pravda* plant, looking for individuals leaving the publishing house early who might be persuaded to part with their copy of the newspaper. And I also wondered then and still do how we escaped being arrested in the gloomy alleys behind the *Pravda* building or why the numerous sentries with their ever-present tommyguns never took a shot at us. It was a risk but the news which we all felt was in the making seemed to justify taking risks. After all we reckoned it was no small risk in itself simply to remain in Moscow in such times.

By this time my colleagues of the news agencies had all managed to set up telephone circuits to their offices in London in order to dictate hot breaks directly to this communications center. This was almost obligatory because of the fantastic slowness of transmission from Moscow over the ordinary cable circuits. Even if you paid five times the usual press rate and sent your message "urgent" it was often many hours en route. I sought to persuade my New York office of the necessity for setting up similar facilities to London or Paris but the reaction of my editors provides a commentary upon the efficiency of the Moscow censorship and its success in preventing me from conveying to New York any real feeling of the developing situation. My editors could see no reason for any special arrangements and, indeed, among the most curious souvenirs of my newspaper career is a cablegram which bears the time of receipt in Moscow of twenty-two minutes after midnight, March 4, 1953. The message reads: "Salisbury, dubious about setting up London Paris dictation posts simply for late breaks Moscow."

The cable was delivered to me shortly before I went down to the Central Telegraph Office at 2 A.M. on March 4. It so happened that on this night I was the man on the dog watch. That morning the papers seemed to be extremely late and I had plenty of time to worry about the situation and wonder what was going to happen next and how I could manage to get my news to New York in time for the paper. Daylight was just breaking when a call came through from Tass to stand by for a special bulletin. The Russian editor wouldn't say what it was but he was very excited. A little before 8 A.M. we got it. It was the announcement that Stalin had suffered a stroke, and it was perfectly plain that the last days of the old dictator were at hand.

As I sat at my typewriter that morning, pounding out bulletin after bulletin, a great feeling of relief flooded over me. It seemed that the black, black storm clouds which had deepened and strengthened over Moscow for months inevitably were going to break up. I could not tell then whether this announcement was coming as the last chapter in a sequence of events which had opened the previous August or as the first chapter in a brand-new Russian era. Nor did I care too much. It did not seem that the terror, this particular terror at least, would survive Stalin.

What a strange quirk of fate, I thought, that Stalin should lie dying just a few weeks after the Kremlin's own doctors had been accused of plotting precisely such a death. A very strange and curious quirk of fate.

But was it just a quirk? I did not know. Was it possible that these powerful and able Soviet leaders, together with their colleagues in the Army, had stood idly by and taken no step to halt the creeping terror that was certain to destroy almost all of them before it finished?

It was possible, certainly, since no one was able to halt the terror of the thirties until it had eliminated most of the prominent leaders of the Bolshevik party. But there was a difference this time. The plot was not aimed at men with whom Stalin had ideological or leadership quarrels. It was aimed at his own trusted and respected lieutenants.

Of course, a cerebral hemorrhage could not be regarded as uncommon for a man of Stalin's type and age and strenuous life. He had, it was said, suffered at least one mild stroke some time before.

Whatever the case may have been I have since been told by a person who has at least secondhand knowledge of some of these events that the full story of the Nineteenth Party Congress and the events that culminated in Stalin's death will never be written. For good and sufficient reasons.

I suspect that the real cause of Stalin's "illness and death" will never be known with certainty. It is by no means impossible that he was murdered by a group of his close associates, the men who now run Russia. And many people in Moscow believe that, as they put it, the old dictator was "assisted" in his exit from mortal life.

While murder cannot be proved there is no question that motive to murder existed. For, as I thought to myself that morning in the Central Telegraph Office, if Stalin was dying a natural death it was the luckiest thing that had ever happened to the men who stood closest to him. To all of them. And, I suspected, to all of Russia as well.

X

The Seventy-five Hours

A FEW minutes before 6 A.M. on the morning of
March 6, 1953, I left the Central Telegraph Office and drove down
Gorky Street, across the wide asphalt field of Manezhny Place,
where the American Embassy was then located, and up through the
narrow passage between the State Historical Museum and the Lenin
Museum, where the chapel of the Iberian Virgin stood until it was
razed in 1929 by the Bolsheviks, and into the Red Square.

Just under two hours before this my sleepy and dull-witted
chauffeur, sitting in the car outside of the telegraph office, had
listened to a dictation speed broadcast of the Tass News Agency,
directed to provincial Russian newspapers, in which the death of
Generalissimo Stalin at 9:50 P.M. the previous evening had been
announced.

The chauffeur, whose name was Dmitri Grigorievich, had walked
into the stuffy little international call office of the telegraph building
where I sat with the four other Moscow correspondents of Western
countries waiting for precisely this news and whispered into my ear
what he had heard.

I got up from my typewriter and handed in to the telegraph clerk
a bulletin which I had already prepared, and within two or three
minutes the small room was a bedlam as agency men filed their
flashes and shouted to the telephone operator to connect them with
their London offices.

The shouting and excitement went for nothing, however, because the Moscow censors refused to pass our bulletins and, in fact, sent a telephone technician down to rip out the backboard connections in the international switchboard so there could be no communication, accidental or otherwise, between Moscow and the outside world.

Since it was obvious that no copy was going to be moving from Moscow for some time I decided to see what effect Stalin's death was having on the city. It proved to be a startling experience and one whose significance I was long to ponder. Repeatedly, during the night, I had driven through the center of the town and had seen little that was unusual. About 1 A.M. a number of limousines pulled into the Kremlin garages which are set under the Great Stone Bridge of the Moscow River, below the Borovitzky Gate of the Kremlin. It looked as though they had been taking Government men home from an evening meeting. About 3 A.M. several big Zis limousines had parked outside the Moscow City Soviet building just up Gorky Street from the telegraph office and lights had gone on inside the building—the first intimation that something unusual was afoot.

As late as five o'clock there was no sign of any change in the center of the city. No extraordinary movement in the streets and only the usual all-night traffic policemen at the corners of the main squares surrounding the Kremlin. It was a chilly March night but not especially cold by Moscow standards. The snow had all been cleaned from the streets except for a very light film left by a few vagrant flurries during the night.

But now as the great golden hands of the clock on Spassky Tower moved to six o'clock a subtle change was occurring. Smooth and quiet convoys of trucks were slipping into the city, down the broad incline of Gorky Street, down the steeper pavement of the Lubiyanka Hill, over the Great Stone Bridge and the Moskvoretzky Bridge from the other side of the Moscow River. From all directions the convoys were flowing toward the central squares of the city.

Sitting cross-armed on wooden benches in the green-painted trucks were detachments of blue-and-red-capped MVD troops— twenty-two to a truck, the special troops of the Ministry of Internal Affairs. They were arriving from their camps, located just outside the Moscow City limits. For an hour or so the precise disposition

of the troops was not apparent as the truck lines crossed and re-
crossed the city, and the fleeting thought entered my mind that,
perhaps, a coup d'état might be in the making. But then, as little
clusters of trucks began to accumulate at the principal intersections
and in the principal squares and prospects, the design became more
clear to me.

What was in progress was one of the most remarkable military
exercises I have ever seen. And, as it transpired, one of the most
fateful. With clockwork precision the Internal Affairs troops were
taking over every one of the main streets leading to the center of
the city and disposing their trucks in such a fashion as to block all
access from side streets and *pereuloki*. The trucks were parked hub
to hub along the street and two or three deep at intersections. Later,
some intersections were more completely blocked by hoisting trucks,
front end to rear platform, in jigsaw style.

By nine o'clock when, the ban on communications abroad having
been lifted, I completed filing my dispatch on the announcement
of Stalin's death and again emerged on Gorky Street I found an
extraordinary transformation. The Internal Affairs troops were everywhere in the center of the city, running their lines across streets
and completing their disposals. In upper Gorky Street columns of
tanks had made their appearance and I could hear their low-
throated murmur in other thoroughfares leading to the central
squares. All the troops and all the trucks and all the tanks belonged
to the special detachments of the MVD. Not a single detachment
of regular Army forces was to be seen. I confess this aspect of the
maneuver did not, at first, deeply impress me, perhaps because I
had so often in the past watched the MVD troops come into the
city and set up special lines which cut off traffic during and preceding the big demonstrations on May Day and November 7. I had,
often enough, seen the big camps of MVD troops along the highways, just outside Moscow. I knew the troops were there and I
knew they were maintained for just such an emergency as had arisen
on this particular day since among the multitudinous tasks of the
MVD the function of preserving internal order and security rated
very high. Moreover, I was too busy trying to absorb what was
going on to analyze very deeply the significance of events. Thus,

for the moment, at any rate, the presence of Internal Affairs troops in such numbers struck me more as to be expected than as sinister or alarming. Ostensibly, at least, it was obvious that the task of the troops was to control traffic during the period in which Stalin's body would lie in state.

Although the dwindling number of busses and automobiles showed that traffic into the center had already been blocked off it was still possible to enter the Red Square and I walked over to see what was happening. Just beyond the center of the square I saw a cigar-shaped crowd that extended almost up to the Spassky Gate. There were a thousand or two thousand people collected there, waiting, I deduced, for Stalin's body to be brought out of the Spassky Gate, since his death had, at least according to official announcement, occurred within the Kremlin. This was the first ordinary, voluntary street crowd of any size which I had ever seen in Russia and the first time I had ever seen people gather in the Red Square of their own volition. Among the spectators in the Red Square I met several young people from the American Embassy and they were just as bug-eyed as myself.

In Stalin's Russia people gathered in the Red Square only for formal parades or demonstrations. In fact casual assembly of citizens in any circumstances automatically brought the militia into action to disperse the gathering even if the people merely were staring at two cars which bumped each other at an intersection. Yet, here, within a few hours of Stalin's death, a group of ordinary people had collected in the Red Square, in the holy of holies, and was standing in defiance of all militia regulations right in the center of the pavement without any sign of interference.

It was a startling sight and a premonitory one.

However, it was not long-lasting, for even as I stood amid the crowd trying to sense its mood (for the most part the people were silent with a semi-suppressed look of expectancy although here and there an old peasant woman sobbed a little—the easy-flowing, almost conventional Slavic expression) a thin line of troops was thrown across the streets leading into the Red Square. At first the MVD units merely barred the way to any more people entering the square. Then, gradually but very efficiently, the lines began to inch forward in a concentric movement into the square itself, pressing the crowds away from the Spassky Gate and back toward the entrances at the State Historical Museum end.

It was apparent now that the MVD intended to clear not only the Red Square but the enormous adjacent squares—Manezhny Place and Theater Square—and seal off the whole inner center of Moscow. Later, I discovered that the MVD had, in fact, isolated almost the whole city of Moscow. The Russian capital is built in a system of concentric rings which, roughly, follow the lines of the ancient city walls. The Kremlin with the big adjoining squares is the core. About a mile out is the first circular boulevard. Half a mile further out is a second similar ring, the Sadovaya Circle. Avenues radiate through these circles, like the spokes of a wheel, giving access to the heart of the city.

The special troops of the Ministry of Internal Affairs had taken possession of this system of circles and spokes as well as the arterial streets beyond them and, by the use of thousands and thousands of trucks, parked hub to hub along every street, had cut off all vehicular and pedestrian traffic. They threw barriers of trucks and tanks across the streets and placed double or triple lines of troops, shoulder to shoulder, in front of them. Tank squadrons were parked three deep at key points in case of need.

By ten or eleven o'clock of the morning of March 6, 1953, no one could enter or leave the heart of Moscow except by leave of the MVD.

I did not quite realize this, however, on that morning as I allowed myself to be moved back with the crowd by the steady pressure of the troops, out of the Red Square and along past the Lenin Museum, which in another time had been the Moscow Duma, toward the Hotel Metropole. I had more immediate problems on my mind. It was apparent that for the duration of the MVD's pleasure I was going to be confined within the eye of this hurricane and I was not at all certain whether it would be possible to make my way from the hotel through the central squares to the telegraph office, a distance of half a dozen blocks, in order to file my dispatches. (By chance, my car was inside the lines also, and by an inexplicable quirk of fate, it proved possible to operate it for the entire period

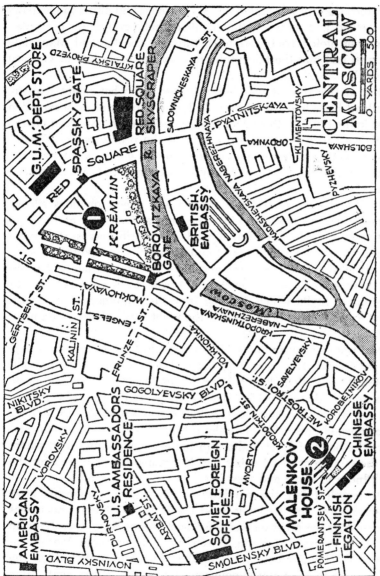

Map of Central Moscow (from *The New York Times*, September 23, 1954).

in which the city was sealed off. MVD troops and officers repeatedly threatened and impeded the chauffeur but never quite prevented him from going back and forth through Theater and Manezhny Squares and into the telegraph office by the back door of Gertzen Street.)

But at this time it was impossible to tell what might happen. Walking back into the Metropole Hotel I took up an observation post in the big bay, third-floor front, window of the Mexican chargé d'affaires and watched the troops herd the people out of Theater Square until nothing could be seen in the great sweep past the Kremlin toward the Alexandrovsky Gardens but MVD special troops.

In the absence of traffic a strange and almost ominous silence seemed to hang over the city. The only activity was at the Hall of Columns, the former Club of Nobles, just visible across the square at the corner of Pushkin Street and Hunters' Row. Workmen were hastily affixing festoons of red and black bunting, garlands of fresh-cut spruce and, in the center, a great story-and-a-half canvas painting of Stalin which, judging from the brightness of its colors, painters must have been up half the night freshening and retouching.

As I watched, an ordinary blue-painted Russian motor ambulance swung around the corner from the Red Square and past the Grand Hotel. It proceeded along the far side of Theater Square and came to a stop beside the Pushkin Street entrance to the Hall of Columns. Two or three Zis limousines followed the ambulance. The back door opened and a file of husky soldiers lifted out the coffin and bore the body of Josef Stalin into the chandelier-hung hall, where on the same spot that Lenin's bier had rested it was placed for the multitudes to come and view.

At length I left the window on the square. Limousine after limousine was now drawing up at the Hall of Columns and it was evident that the great men of the Soviet regime were assembling to pay their respects to Stalin. I went back to my room, located on one of the interior courtyards of the Metropole, switched on the radio so as to hear any announcements by the government, drew down a book from my bookshelf and sprawled out to catch a few minutes' rest. I had had only a couple of hours of sleep since the night of the 3rd. It was now midday of the 6th and not before the 9th was there to be anything more than a fifteen- or twenty-minute cat nap for any of the handful of foreign correspondents who had managed to survive the long winter of the Stalin era in order to be present at its finish.

The book whose pages I now began to turn was a collection of dispatches by Walter Duranty, including his account of Moscow at the time of Lenin's death.

Some foreigners have said that the reason so many hundreds of thousands of Russians came to view Stalin's bier was to make certain that he was dead. Besides being a cheap joke which must seem in singularly bad taste even to a Russian who hated Stalin it just isn't true. In the course of his long reign Stalin had come to satisfy what I suppose a psychologist might describe as the fundamental Russian need for a father image. By his own choice and to a considerable extent through his own seeking, Stalin had placed himself in that niche in the domestic iconography of the ordinary Russian peasant and worker which so long before had been filled by the Czar.

Thus, when Stalin died it seemed to many Russians a little as though God had died. And ceremonially, if in no other way, they, and particularly the women, made an expression of grief. Tears come easily to the eyes of the Slav woman. And, I suppose a cynic might say, they dry easily, as well.

Reading Duranty's account of Lenin's death I immediately felt the contrast between the two events. When Lenin died the grief of the people was deep and sincere. Not only did the ordinary man on Moscow's streets feel a sense of personal loss but many members of the Party hierarchy were actually prostrated.

Now with Stalin dead the feeling of the people, if I sensed it accurately, was rather different. There was a display of the signs of grief but the chief impression was a numb sense of shock; the kind of shock which I imagined a work horse might feel which for twenty years had been hitched to the shafts of a heavy cart when suddenly the leather bindings dropped off. But the animal stands still in his tracks, unable quite to perceive what has happened, long since having lost even the ability to sense what freedom of movement actually is.

Such, or so it seemed to me, was the aura of the Russian crowds at this moment of Stalin's death, and the curious numbness and deadness of sensation was to persist all through the four days in which the country as a whole and Moscow, in particular, was in the grip of the formal mourning and funeral ceremonies. Looking back on that time I find that what has left the most indelible impression on my mind is not the garish spectacle of Stalin, waxlike on a bank of flowers under thousand-candlepower movie lights; it is not the faintly carnival atmosphere of the five-mile queues of people, slowly shuffling toward the Hall of Columns through double and quadruple lines of militia; it is not the strong feeling of powerful undercurrents, half grasped, half concealed in the funeral speeches of Malenkov, Molotov and Beriya.

It is the sense of numb shock which I felt in the Moscow crowds, particularly in the first twenty-four hours that Stalin's body formally lay in state. Little, indeed, of this feeling was it possible to convey to the outside world. The censorship allowed passages describing grief and sorrow among the people to be transmitted abroad. This, after all, was a mood appropriate to the occasion in the minds of the masters of Glavlit, as the organization charged with censorship responsibility is called. But of shock and numbness no hint was permitted. For that might have suggested weakness.

In the time that has passed since Stalin's death many people, and particularly Americans, have asked me about the mood of the Moscow crowds at that time. How could the Russians display grief at the passing of this terrible man; why didn't the people joyously celebrate the end of this era of burdens and of terror? I don't know the full answer to those questions but I think they lie somewhere deep in Russian character. I do not believe there was dancing in the streets when Ivan the Terrible died; nor when so many others in the long history of Russian oppressors passed from the scene. Perhaps the people know too well that when one tyrant departs another is almost certain to take his place.

But whatever the reason may be, I sensed no mood of jubilation nor deliverance in these wooden Moscow masses. I myself felt "delivered" and I knew some others who must feel the same way and I suspected there were men in the Kremlin who felt this most strikingly. But not the masses. And the instinct of the masses in Russia very often is right.

As events developed it was quite obvious to me, having read Duranty's account of Lenin's death and funeral, that I was not the only person who had recently refreshed his recollection of the ceremonies attendant upon this earlier time of Bolshevik mourning.

For the arrangements for Stalin bore the closest resemblance to those which had been made for Lenin. The fact that this resemblance was actually highly superficial was a testimony to how times and feelings had changed. For there was quite obviously a relative freedom and spontaneity about the Lenin funeral days which the stage managers of the Stalin spectacle were not able to recapture.

For instance, Duranty walked with the Communist leaders as they bore on their own shoulders Lenin's coffin from the railroad station to the Hall of Columns. He stood chatting outside the building with the leading Bolsheviks as Lenin's body was put in place and then went in with the others to pay his last respects.

But MVD troops barred ordinary citizens from the hall while the Government leaders visited Stalin's bier and when I tried to go through the lines an MVD colonel sharply turned me back.

So, it was not until the next day that, together with the diplomatic corps, I joined the fantastic procession that was hurried and jostled, sixteen abreast, past the open coffin where Stalin lay, his face as waxen as a calla lily. I stumbled in the blinding glare of the klieg lights as I was forced at a half-trot past the bier and, now, when I try to bring back the picture to my mind I see only the masses of flowers, the guard of honor half hidden in the greenery and the face of Stalin, blanched as an almond, and his old hands which seemed still clutching, in pain or terror, at the edge of his coverlet. And to my ears come the doomed strains of Chopin's funeral march, played by a military band of two hundred men, most of whom seem to be trumpeters. I hear again the constant admonition of the sweating MVD troopers to keep moving and to hurry along, and to my nose come the overwhelming odors of the cooking in the basement of the Hall of Columns where huge kettles of borscht simmered to feed the masses of troops. A far cry from the simple grief of the people when Lenin died!

An even stronger contrast came to light the next day, a Sunday, and it was a contrast which sharply illumined the real significance of what was happening in Moscow in these curious hours between the announcement of Stalin's death and the funeral ceremonies in the Red Square, Monday, March 9.

A rumor spread through Moscow on Saturday that thousands of persons were arriving from all over the country to view Stalin's body as it lay in state. According to this report every train entering the city was crowded with citizens and some persons were said to have ridden all the way from Leningrad (in subfreezing weather) on the roof of trains.

What particularly interested me about this report was the fact that this was actually what had occurred at the time of Lenin's death. Lenin had died in January in a very severe cold snap and many persons were seriously frostbitten, riding long distances in the open in order to get to Moscow for the lying-in-state.

The only way of checking this rumor, of course, was to make my way to the railroad stations and see with my own eyes what was going on. And there was no way of getting to the railroad stations, all of which lie at or beyond the second circle, except by walking. This meant that I would have to penetrate countless military barricades—just how many I had no way of knowing since I had not been beyond the first circle since the MVD forces had taken over the city.

Later, I was very glad indeed that I decided to check up on this rumor because the effort gave me, for the first time, a somewhat more coherent picture of what had happened to Moscow.

I started out on my venture not long after dawn. The first thing I learned was that no one had any very reliable information as to what was going on in the segmented, sealed-off city. In response to inquiries I got two or three conflicting reports about the subway system. It was not operating to the center of the city, of course, but no one seemed to know exactly which lines were still working.

I strolled leisurely through one sleepy sentry line after another.

At some places there were curbside campfires and troops whiled away the long hours playing the accordion and stomping out tunes with their soft leather boots. At some places I had to scramble under truck barricades. At other places I clambered over them and at one point I squeezed, very gingerly, between two medium tanks whose dozing crews paid no heed to me whatsoever.

There was a curious, half-holiday atmosphere in the back streets but what was most impressive was the iron grip which the MVD forces held on the city. Their tentacles went back, back, back all the way through the city to the outskirts. And, once you were beyond the city limits, they controlled almost every nearby highway through their camps and establishments.

By the time I reached the Kursk railroad station I was considerably enlightened as to the state of affairs in Moscow. Further enlightenment awaited me at the station. There the true state of affairs proved radically different from the rumor. Handwritten notices were posted up at the ticket offices where they were being read and irritably discussed by little knots of citizens. The notices said that trains out of Moscow were running on schedule. But no trains into Moscow were running at all with the exception of a few long-distance trains.

In other words, Moscow was truly sealed off—not only from the inside. But from without as well.

I pondered the significance of that fact as I made my way back to the hotel. Probably because of the earliness of the hour I had no great trouble in arguing my way back through the MVD lines, although when I came out into Dzerzhinskaya Square from Kirov Street I had to make a long detour before I was able to find an officer who would let me through into the central squares.

Even after this excursion into Moscow's back areas the full impact of what had happened did not strike me until about midday on Sunday when, by dint of simply walking past the sentry posts with a resolute air, I strolled right into the Red Square. A strange feeling came over me. The square was deserted. Troops stood guard at all the entrances to keep everyone out. Only in the very center, around the famous Mausoleum, was there any activity. Here power cables had been strung out from inside the Kremlin

and a few workmen with power chisels and hammers were busy
carving the name of Stalin into the stone beside that of Lenin and
making other, more practical arrangements within the tomb's stone
inner chamber for the reception of a second sarcophagus.

I made my way into the center of the square and stood for a
while, watching the workmen. A colonel of the MVD was super-
vising them. Neither he nor anyone else paid the slightest heed to
me. It was obvious that they presumed that anyone within these
innermost lines must have the right to be there.

Except for the intermittent sound of the hammers and chisels it
was deathly still in the Red Square, so still that I realized that the
quiet must be noticeable to the men inside the Kremlin walls. And
it was then that the thought which had been on the edge of my
consciousness since Friday morning struck home with full force.

What troops were these which held the city? MVD troops. Were
there any other troops in the city? No. Could any other troops enter
the city? Not unless they had the permission of the MVD or were
prepared to fight their way through, street by street, and barricade
by barricade. What about the Air Force? No good. Even if it bombed
the whole city to rubble it could not break the grip of the MVD
troops, who held every route into the city, the approaches to every
route and every strategic corner.

What of the Kremlin? The men who sat there today sat there by
leave of the MVD. They came by MVD permission. They could go
only by MVD permission. They were, in fact, the actual prisoners of
the MVD whether or not they recognized their status and, I thought,
men as well trained as those in the Kremlin in the tactics and methods of civil war could hardly fail to grasp the reality of their situation. It was a hard and striking fact and one which must touch the
military leaders with particular force.

Because the MVD was not just a group of initials. It was not just
a department of the government. It was an individual. A powerful,
ruthless man of extraordinary ability named Laventri Pavlovich
Beriya. And it was Beriya's troops and Beriya's tanks and Beriya's
trucks which had accomplished this small military miracle and taken
over the city of Moscow while the radios were still blaring out the
news about Stalin to the dumfounded citizens.

Using the basic movement plans which for many years had been employed on May Day and November 7th to control traffic in the center of the city and simply extending the control back into the city and its environs Beriya had with the smoothness of clockwork put Moscow into his grasp.

And once he had Moscow Beriya had, for all practical purposes, Russia as well. From mid-morning of March 6 until late afternoon of the 9th Beriya was the master of Russia. He was supreme. There was no one who could challenge him. Not Malenkov. Not Khrushchev. Not Molotov. Not even the Army.

At any moment within those fateful seventy-five hours or more Beriya might have proclaimed himself dictator, all-supreme ruler of Russia, heir of Stalin.

He did not do so and in his failure to act he sealed his own fate. The life that came to an end on Christmas Eve, 1953, probably in the blood-stained cellars of the Lubiyanka, was doomed from these days in March when Beriya failed to use his power.

Because Beriya's exhibition of strength was too smooth, too complete and too good. No military man could watch that demonstration and ever draw a quiet breath again—unless he trusted Beriya completely or unless Beriya was the top boss. It was too apparent that by giving a single order Beriya, between two and seven o'clock of any morning, could take the Kremlin, take Moscow, and, with the capital in his pocket, make himself, in all likelihood, the master of Russia.

The essence of this flashed through my mind as I stood there in the center of the Red Square, listening to the hammers and the chisels, on that Sunday before Stalin's funeral. If it was apparent to me it was, I thought, reasonable to suppose it was apparent to Beriya's colleagues and, of course, Beriya must have been only too conscious of his power at this moment.

It is very, very likely, indeed, that it was only in Stalin's final days that Beriya regained his full and unchallenged control over the forces of the MVD. It is extremely probable that it was only in the coalition of forces which occurred over Stalin's deathbed that Beriya resumed the police authority which was obviously slipping from his grasp in the weeks immediately preceding Stalin's fatality.

Perhaps this is why Beriya overplayed his hand at a moment when he could not hope to take open and full control of Russia. The exact motivations are difficult, if not impossible, to untangle in the dark jungle of Moscow intrigue.

ИНОКОРРЕСПОНДЕНТУ

Пропуск № 013

г-ну *Солсбери*

Гаррисон

для ПРОХОДА на КРАСНУЮ ПЛОЩАДЬ
НА ПОХОРОНЫ
Председателя Совета Министров СССР и
Секретаря Центрального Комитета КПСС
Генералиссимуса
Иосифа Виссарионовича
СТАЛИНА

A pass to Stalin's funeral, which reads: "Foreign correspondent Pass No. 013. Mr. Solsberi, Garrison [there is no letter "h" in Russian, so "h" is transliterated "g"] for admission to Red Square for the funeral of the Chairman of the Council of Ministers of the U.S.S.R. and the Secretary of the Central Committee of the C.P.S.U., Generalissimus JOSEF VISSARIONOVICH STALIN."

But on the next day, on Monday, when Stalin was formally laid to rest beside Lenin Beriya spoke in the Red Square along with Malenkov and Molotov. As I stood in the thin March sunshine listening to Beriya it seemed to me that there was an undercurrent in the speech which flowed from his confidence in his power and which he was unable to keep from expressing just as he had been unable to keep from showing to one and all his ability to seize the city of Moscow.

Beriya seemed just a little condescending toward Malenkov and Molotov—possibly not so much in his language as in his delivery.

And, what interested me even more, he seemed to be trying to convey without exactly saying so that he spoke for the Army as well as himself and the police power. With reference to this latter point, I noted in my dispatch that evening to *The New York Times:* "Mr. Beriya's tones were particularly confident. He spoke of the government's concern to maintain the security of the Soviet state and . . . said Russia had all kinds of contemporary weapons and could in case of necessity meet any aggressor who dared to attack, with forces tempered in battle."

It took only three and a half months to demonstrate that condescension toward his colleagues was not exactly called for on the part of Beriya and that, regardless of what he thought at the time, he was not in a position to speak for the Army. He had shown the Army only too clearly the power of his position. But powerful as his position was it had a fatal defect. While he was terribly dangerous to any other ruler or rulers he was not strong enough to rule by himself and this he tacitly admitted when he failed to take power in the Stalin funeral period. Beriya's danger in the unstable coalition of Party, Police and Army which assumed power on Stalin's death was that he had too much sheer military power, concentrated in such a fashion that he could quickly apply it to the center. He was too big for the triumvirate but not big enough to be dictator.

The only surprise about Beriya's end was that it came so soon and created such a small ripple—comparatively speaking—when it came. I was perfectly convinced that there was going to be a showdown over Beriya as were a number of other persons in Moscow. While the deletions of the censorship concealed from the outside world much of the substance of the events of March, 1953, it required no great genius in deduction for a person in Moscow to foresee that there would be a contest of power revolving around Beriya.

In my private correspondence of this period I confidently wrote that a settlement would certainly be forthcoming between Beriya and the Army. It was my feeling that Beriya did not expect to be able to step into Stalin's shoes. I felt that he was astute enough to realize that the Great Russians would never stand for two Georgian dictators in succession. But I did believe that Beriya (and this would have been in full accord with what is known of his character) probably hoped to be the kingmaker, wielding the real power behind the throne on which he might seat Malenkov or almost any other individual who proved malleable and acquiesced to Beriya's desires.

Such an ambition seemed not beyond Beriya's capabilities. After all, the Police Chief in Russia was, in many ways, the most powerful single individual, since Russia, of course, was a police state. The police penetrated all other branches of the state and all branches of the Party and the Army, as well. And in Beriya's pudgy fingers rested control of such enormous repositories of power as the MVD super-state in Siberia, the Far North and Central Asia. He had vested rights in all border areas and border states. He had a veto right over (if he did not run) the policies of satellite countries and, in particular, East Germany.

And, not the least important, Beriya ran Russia's nuclear plants. He it was who made and presumably controlled Russia's A-bomb. He it was who was directing the effort which within a few weeks of his arrest gave Russia the H-bomb.

Any man with such assets as these might be pardoned for harboring vaulting ambitions. But ambition, particularly overweening ambition, is not always a wise counselor. The men who took the power of Russia into their hands in March, 1953, were ruthless, experienced and, almost certainly, desperate. No one was in that group because of the color of his eyes or the pleasantness of his after-dinner conversation. These men were realists and they had not rid themselves of one threat to their lives and positions only to bow their necks to another.

Thus, when Beriya stayed his hand in March it was only a matter of time and opportunity before his "comrades-at-arms" would remove the possibility that at some future date he might display more boldness.

For the moment, however, the watchwords of March were unity and solidarity. Stability had been achieved, possibly over Stalin's dead body, possibly in the hours before his death. How long the new status quo might endure I was not prepared to guess, but as I walked back to the Metropole Hotel, dog-weary, in the early hours before dawn of March 10, having filed my final dispatch about Stalin's funeral, I chanced upon a little spectacle which an ambitious man might well have pondered. Turning into Hunters' Row from Gorky Street I saw half a dozen workmen clustered in front of the Hall of Columns where Stalin had lain. They had rigged up two ladders and were working in the ghostly blue of a great carbon-arc floodlight.

As I approached two men on ladders loosened the ropes with which the huge story-and-a-half portrait of Stalin was bound to the façade of the building and the heroic painting slipped crazily to the ground and canted over into the street at an oblique angle.

"Careful there," one of the workmen shouted.

"*Nitchevo* . . . Never mind," his comrade snapped back. "They'll not be needing this one again."

XI

A Toast to Justice

THE time was spring, 1944, and the place was the Ukraine—a vast sea of black mud which stretched from horizon to horizon and across which slithered and struggled column after endless column of tiny figures which at a distance looked like variously burdened ants but which when you came close turned out to be men and units of the Red Army.

The Red Army was on the move across the Ukraine that spring and nothing stopped it. Not the mud which was shoulder deep nor certainly the Germans who were retreating as fast as the mud would let them.

There was nothing very military looking about the advance of the Red Army but there was something extremely impressive about the way the columns surged slowly across the landscape. The men came on and on with the slow irresistible movement of lava down a mountainside.

Many of the soldiers walked, mud-spattered and dirty. Some, like the black-caped Cossack troopers, rode horses. Others rode mules. Most of them, however, sat stolidly on horse-drawn, wooden telegas, the springless, traditional, indestructible peasant carts which have borne the Russians across that black land sea of theirs from time immemorial.

The telegas were pulled for the most part by horses. But sometimes by mules and donkeys. Sometimes by snorting tractors. And even, occasionally, by camels.

176

Of course there were tanks and trucks moving over the black gumbo, too. But they moved haltingly and by fits and starts, constantly bogging down and having to be pulled out of sloughs and seemingly bottomless pits while the horse-drawn Army flowed steadily and constantly around them.

The Red Army was not advancing along roads or highways. It was surging forward across the open fields of the Ukraine. The roads and highways would have been quickly choked, in any event, and now they were impossible because there, frame deep in mud, occasionally scarred by aerial gunfire but most often untouched by flame or bullet, lay the wreckage of the German Army's Transport system, the thousands of trucks, thousands of tanks, thousands of motor-drawn artillery units on which the Wehrmacht depended.

It was an impressive sight and I have never forgotten the words of a Red Army colonel who looked down at his battered boots and said: "Those are the second pair in two months. They don't last long when you are marching every day and here in the Ukraine you have to keep moving. If you move and the enemy tries to stop or rest he is gone because he is never able to get going again. He simply sinks into the mud and is lost."

The Red Army may not have been able to match the Wehrmacht in equipment but it knew how to use its natural allies—General Winter, General Mud, General Distance.

When, in present times, I hear people speculating, as they sometimes do, about the possibility of war between the United States and Russia the picture of those miles of abandoned German transports inevitably comes into my mind, and I think of the American Army which, long since, has eliminated every horse from its rolls; which hasn't a wagon to its name; where even the mule is a rarity. I think of our dependence on the gasoline engine, the typewriter and the mimeograph machine and I wonder whether our generals, buttressed by their battalions of stenographers, filing cabinets, Dictaphones and commercial machinery, have given as much study as they really should to the tactics and methods of the Red Army.

I have always had, since those World War II days, great respect for the Soviet Army and its leaders. I saw a good bit of behind-the-lines operations of the Russian Army and command and I shared the belief of most foreign observers who were in Russia during the war that it was a fine battle force, skillfully managed and led.

True, it did not resemble a Western army. Orders were usually verbal, not written. Paper work was practically nonexistent. Units often foraged for their own supplies. Generals were lavish in expending the lives of their soldiers and comfort and convenience were nonexistent by our standards. Men were sacrificed instead of materials because materials were scarce and men plentiful.

No doubt the United States could not operate an army like that of the Russians. No USO. No PX. No pin-ups. No movies. No packaged rations except what they got from us. Yet the fact remained that the Soviet troops fought the Germans to a standstill; that they withstood the shock of losing millions of men and much of their best equipment in the opening weeks of war (largely, I am certain, due to blunders by Stalin himself); they gave up thousands of square miles of homeland, including the best industrial regions and the Ukraine breadbasket—and yet the cadres were vast enough and strong enough and the leadership had sufficient resilience so that the Russians were able to turn the tide of battle and, inch by inch, drive the Germans from their soil.

Only able men could have accomplished this feat of arms and it had been my feeling for some years that the military men of the West, including not a few American specialists, were inclined to undervalue Russian strategy and Russian generalship. It became fashionable after the misbehavior of Soviet troops in Austria, Hungary and Germany to dismiss the Red Army as a peasant rabble, led by brutish commanders. Sometimes I heard Western military men speak in much the same narrow terms as the worst of the postwar Russian propaganda. Our men would talk as though the Nazis had been defeated by our supply of Lend-Lease materials to Russia which, of course, was just as ridiculous as the claims I read in *Pravda* that the Red Army had smashed Hitler, despite rather than with the help of the Western Allies.

It seemed to me that the military minds which conceived and executed such bold and successful maneuvers as the operation in the vicinity of Moscow in November-December, 1941, which gave Hitler his first defeat since he had invented his blitzkrieg, or the brilliant encirclement at Stalingrad in the following year, December 1942–January, 1943, or the little-known (in the West) operations on the salient Kursk-Orel were forces which, eventually, the world would have to reckon with.

Moreover, I was convinced that the planning and strategy of such campaigns as these did not spring full-born from the brain of Stalin. I was (and am) willing to concede that Stalin may have been something of a genius at things military. Certainly he seems to have had his share of patience, endurance and Oriental cunning. But the type of genius who crowded his first-line troops along his frontiers, together with his tank striking forces, who massed his best airplanes at advanced bases and then allowed them all to be sitting ducks for a Nazi blitz stroke which, obviously, even at the fifty-ninth minute of the eleventh hour he did not believe was coming—that type of genius, who certainly was Stalin assisted by his old cronies, Marshals Voroshilov and Budenny, did not impress me as the one who had planned the successful counter-blows.

My feeling was shared, I might say, by a number of high-ranking Western military figures who visited Russia during the war. They were never completely sure of the role of such men as Shaposhnikov or Vasilevsky, who served as Chiefs of Staff. But they were positive that men like Chuikov, Rokossovsky, Zhukov and Konev were extremely gifted.

The Communist Party, of course, sought to claim for itself and for the principal figures of the Politburo the major share of credit that remained after obeisance had been made to the shrine of Stalin's military genius. This was to be seen in the fact that each of the Party leaders, in the course of the war, assumed a military rank and title, donned a military uniform and by being attached to the "Military Council" of this front or that front attempted to seize credit for the successes of the Red Army which occurred.

Thus, the late Andrei Zhdanov, party boss of Leningrad, assumed the rank of Lieutenant General, early in the war, and was given credit for the successful defense of the city. Malenkov was attached to the Stalingrad Military Council and given such credit for that operation as was left over after Stalin had absorbed the lion's share. Beriya was attached to the Military Council of the Caucasus and claimed credit for ousting the Nazis from Maikop, etc.

And so it went. But it seemed to me that the manner in which the Party sought to get the uniform on its back and steal the spotlight from the generals was, actually, a tip-off as to where the credit lay. In fact there was a general tendency for all civilians to identify themselves with the Army in so far as possible by the end of the war. It expressed itself in many ways. For instance, almost all doctors were mobilized into the Red Army during the war. After the war wherever possible the doctors tried to retain their military rank even after returning to purely civil duties. The Army and the military rank carried more prestige. One civilian Government department after another put itself into uniform. True, it is an old Russian tradition to wear uniforms. Before 1914 there were more uniforms on the streets of St. Petersburg than of any other European capital, simply because almost every Russian civil servant under the Czar had a uniform. But the uniform custom would not have been revived after World War II if the Army had not come out of the war with unprecedented prestige.

The Party leaders, the petty bureaucrats, Stalin himself—everyone wanted to get under this great umbrella of Army prestige.

That being true it was very natural to think in 1944 and 1945 that in the postwar era the Army, and particularly some of its leading generals, was going to play an important role in Russian life and Russian policy. I thought so and many American observers thought so. In fact it was just this kind of reasoning which led directly to the appointment of General W. Bedell Smith as our first postwar Ambassador to Moscow.

General Eisenhower had gotten acquainted with Marshal Zhukov, who was the most prominent and surely the most brilliant Soviet military figure to emerge from the war during the early days after the capitulation in Berlin. The two men seemed to get on very well and there was a general feeling that Zhukov was "the kind of man you can talk to." He invited Eisenhower to Moscow and acted as the general's host. It was a pleasant and companionable occasion.

Not unnaturally a theory arose among some American diplomats that Zhukov was going to carry much weight in postwar Moscow and that if we were to name as our Ambassador to Russia someone who could talk Zhukov's language a great many of the obstacles which were already looming large in the path of Soviet-American relations might be removed.

And so Smith was selected as Ambassador since he, too, knew Zhukov and seemed to get on well with him.

However, the hunch of our diplomats never had a chance for a practical test because Stalin whisked Zhukov off the scene so rapidly that no one ever got to see what good might come of talking to him. He simply wasn't there to talk to. He vanished from Moscow in 1946 and didn't reappear publicly in the capital until after the announcement of Stalin's death. In the interim the only thing which is known about Zhukov is that for a time he held a provincial Red Army command in Odessa.

Zhukov's re-emergence from the shadows in March, 1953, was a highly dramatic event and it symbolized the maturation of the Soviet military as a political entity. In a sense it was the delayed fruition of the tendency which had been apparent to the observers in wartime and immediate postwar Russia.

In other words, the military finally had come into their own.

And it seemed to me as I looked back on the events of the six months preceding Stalin's death that quite possibly the Soviet Army had been playing a considerably more important role in them than had been apparent at the time.

The truth is that when you study the few tangible pieces of evidence which tend to support the thesis that there was some premeditation involved in Stalin's death they seem to point toward the Army.

Some of this evidence concerns a rather obscure young general named Sergei Matveevich Shtemenko who was Chief of the Soviet General Staff until about twelve days before the announcement of Stalin's fatal illness and who has not been seen nor heard of since that time.

Perhaps Shtemenko is still alive, serving in some obscure Army capacity. Perhaps not. There has been one report that he now has a command in western Siberia but his fate actually is just one minor missing piece in a fascinating jigsaw puzzle.

Not much is known about this ambitious young general but enough has come to light to interest me considerably. He was not a prominent officer in World War II but served on the General Staff and at war's end was rewarded with the Order of Suvarov, First Class, and like dozens of other officers of equal rank, his picture was published by *Pravda*.

So far as I have been able to determine Shtemenko was not heard of again until November, 1948, when, in a general shake-up of the top Army posts he succeeded Marshal Vasilevsky as Chief of Staff. He held that post for a little more than four years. Then, a few days before the annual Red Army day celebration, February 23, 1953, he was removed without any public notice and replaced by Marshal Sokolovsky, a very close associate of Marshal Zhukov.

Although I do not remember any previous occasion when Moscow had failed to announce a change in the post of Chief of Staff Shtemenko's removal was secret and became public knowledge only accidentally. The Chief of Staff traditionally holds a reception on the evening of February 23 to which foreign military attachés are invited. The first and only indication that Shtemenko had been displaced came when these invitations were issued in Sokolovsky's name.

The next day a little item in *Red Star*, the Army paper, showed that Shtemenko had attended the Red Army day reception in Berlin, as a guest. From that day on his name, so far as I know, has not been publicly mentioned.

Possibly Shtemenko's sudden removal was quite unconnected with the events which so quickly followed—the announcement of Stalin's fatal illness and death. But perhaps not. Shtemenko was one of five military figures who were named as intended victims of the infamous Doctors' Plot. As I have pointed out there were signs that this plot had been constructed in such a way as to be used as a weapon against all of Stalin's closest aides with the possible temporary exception of the military, or at least a group of the military. In other words the favor of the military was being solicited while a purge was conducted of all other elements in the Soviet ruling circle.

What arouses suspicion so far as Shtemenko's role is concerned is the fact that the other four supposed "victims" of the plot were all veteran and very senior figures. And each of them has kept his job in the period which has followed Stalin's death. The other men were Marshals Vasilevsky, Govorov and Konev and Admiral Levchenko. Shtemenko didn't fit in that company and he has vanished.

I suppose that this recitation must sound complex and labyrinthine but if so it is only because the actual facts are so complex and intricate. The forces which activated the Doctors' Plot and which were set in motion by Stalin's death and, a bit later in the Beriya affair, were not simple. Events in the Kremlin under Stalin usually had the intricate design of a Bukhara carpet and, since they were often seen only from the under side or only in part, their reconstruction can be as tedious and tenuous as an exercise in archeology.

One thing, however, is certain with regard to the military. Due to a fortuitous or planned change in the Soviet High Command the post of Chief of Staff at the time of Stalin's death was occupied by Marshal Sokolovsky, who has been more closely associated with Marshal Zhukov than any other Soviet officer.

The second thing which is equally certain is that from the moment of the announcement of Stalin's death the military, and I mean the real generals rather than the political ones like Bulganin, or the old cronies of Stalin like Voroshilov and Budenny, has begun to play the important and prominent role in Soviet affairs which Westerners had expected ever since the end of World War II.

The very first picture to be published by *Pravda* after Stalin's death recorded this symbolic change. It showed twelve men standing beside Stalin's bier—six in civilian clothes and six in uniform. The civilians were Molotov, Khrushchev (way back in the corner), Kaganovich, Mikoyan, Beriya and Malenkov. The men in uniform were Bulganin, Zhukov, Sokolovsky, Voroshilov, Konev and Govorov.

The moment I saw that picture I felt certain that a fundamental change in the disposition of power had occurred in Moscow. Such symbolic pictures in Russia are carefully and thoughtfully prepared and executed in order, in simple fashion, to convey to the Soviet public some political truth. The lesson of this picture was obvious. The civilians occupied the most prominent positions in the photograph. Some of the faces of the generals, including that of Zhukov, were half concealed, but never during Stalin's life had the military bulked so large.

And if anyone in Moscow failed to see the significance of the picture, he could read the next day in the announcement of the reorganization of the government that Zhukov had emerged from banishment and, at a single stride, regained his old prominence. He was named, with Vasilevsky, as deputy minister of defense.

Zhukov and the younger and more handsome Marshal Rokossovsky were the two real military heroes to emerge in Russia from World War II. Zhukov's popularity with the masses in Russia was genuine and considerable. There is no doubt that it was this popularity and Zhukov's great influence with the top leaders of the Army which caused Stalin to banish him to the hinterland.

The fact that he immediately emerged into the public spotlight within twenty-four hours of Stalin's death indicates not only the depth of his hold on the Army leadership and the stability which his association with the new Government would suggest to the public. It also raised certain questions in my mind which are still unanswered.

For instance, Zhukov would seem to have been waiting very close in the wings for this call back into the spotlight—naturally enough if the February change in the Chief of Staff was a curtain raiser to the events of March.

While it was evident enough to those of us in Moscow that the new post-Stalin government had successfully met the initial crisis revolving around Stalin's death there were signs aplenty in the following weeks that complete political stability had not been achieved.

The chief evidence of this was a continuing series of changes and shake-ups in party and governmental setups throughout the country. The biggest sensation, of course, was the blunt announcement, issued under the signature of the Ministry of Internal Affairs, that the whole Doctors' Plot was a phony and a frame-up. This was a real blow to public confidence in the Stalin regime, or its later aspects, and was undoubtedly designed as such.

In addition, Beriya and the other members of the government who had been most dangerously involved in that "plot" were obviously getting their revenge. A new purge of the battered and bewildered Georgian Communist Party and Government was carried out and the men Beriya had supposedly put into office just a year previous were all kicked out as traitors and grafters. Another lot, headed by one of Beriya's oldest and most reliable cohorts, a granite-jawed Georgian named Dekanozov, who had been Beriya's man in the Foreign Office during World War II and one of his chief lieutenants in Berlin in the postwar period, was handed the job of rebuilding Beriya's Georgian organization.

As I have said earlier, I have sometimes seen it asserted that Beriya was the real "liberal" in the post-Stalin regime and that with his arrest the junta lost its more moderate character. The supporters of this theory cite the fact that the reversal of the Doctors' Plot was announced over the signature of the Ministry of Internal Affairs. They also point to certain statements of Beriya's pledging the government to abide by "Soviet legality"—in other words, not to use the customary extralegal police powers of the Stalin regime.

This doctrine never impressed me very much. Beriya continued to exercise arbitrary police powers so long as he held office and the only evidence of any lessening of police authority which I became aware of occurred after he was arrested. There were signs aplenty after July of police demoralization.

One piece of evidence which was sometimes cited to support the theory of Beriya, "the Liberal," was the fact that for many months after his arrest no announcement was made of what had been done with a police official named Ryumin, who had been blamed for concocting the evidence on which the Doctors' Plot was based. It was pointed out that Ryumin's successor, an accomplice of Beriya's, was executed along with the MVD chief, whereas Ryumin apparently had escaped punishment. In other words it was claimed that a man who played a leading role in the Doctors' Plot was getting off lightly while Beriya's clean-up man was shot.

However, even this minor point was lost in the summer of 1954 when Ryumin finally was executed.

All over the country, in this spring of 1953, there were changes, particularly in the police organizations, but there were so many appointments and dismissals that one could not be certain exactly what forces lay behind all these shifts.

However, curiously, or perhaps not so curiously, there were no important military shifts until just a few days before the famous

Berlin riots of June 17 and the arrest of Beriya which quickly followed on June 26.

Just as there was an important military change—the shift in the Chief of Staff—just before the events of March, so there was a major Army shift before the events of June.

The tough, hard-bitten commander of the 62nd Army at Stalingrad, Army General Chuikov, was suddenly "transferred to responsible work in the Ministry of Defense" from the post of Commander in Chief, Germany, which he had held for the past five years.

The shift occurred June 6, eleven days before the riots, twenty days before Beriya's arrest. Chuikov was replaced by an active young general named Grechko, a Ukrainian who had held the important Kiev command under the watchful eye of wise old General Konev. Both Grechko and Konev were leading members of the Ukrainian branch of the Communist Party and Grechko, while an Army man, was a protégé of Nikita Khrushchev, the man who is now first secretary of the Communist Party but who for many years was Party boss in the Ukraine.

This was a very important shift. So far as I know it marked the first but by no means the last occasion in which the political forces represented by the Army and by Khrushchev joined hands. It was those two elements, the Army and Khrushchev's Ukraine and Moscow Party organizations which stood side by side with Malenkov and gave the present ruling clique the power to deal with Beriya.

Grechko was a young general but his political reliability was vouched for by Khrushchev. He was put into Berlin at a moment when great events were in the making while Chuikov, who eventually went to Kiev and took over Grechko's post, was brought back, probably to report to the General Staff regarding conditions in Germany.

Germany and the satellites in general had to a considerable extent fallen under Beriya's control in the years since the war. The Interior Minister exercised a veto over policy and, most of the time, ran German affairs directly through his own agents, dictating to the Army command.

Possibly as a riposte to the Grechko move Beriya six days later raided deep into Khrushchev's territory and secured the ouster of

Leonid Melnikov, the man Khrushchev had installed to run the Ukrainian Party apparatus. It was a pyrrhic victory. Five days later the Berlin riots broke out.

I do not know and have not been able to find anyone who is able to describe satisfactorily just what relationship the Berlin riots had to the Beriya crisis. That a connection exists is generally conceded by everyone who has studied this affair. But the whole thing is so involved that it may never be completely clarified.

One most curious fact I noted at the time. *Pravda,* which usually publishes only carefully slanted and ideologically "correct" versions of the news, broke this rule in the Berlin crisis. For the first two days of the Berlin riots *Pravda* played it straight. It published undoctored news accounts of the happenings in Berlin and put the blame on the East German authorities and the Communist Party. It was only forty-eight hours later that the usual bias was injected and the whole thing was attributed to American "agents." I am sure *Pravda's* action was linked in some way to the burgeoning Beriya crisis. But exactly how I do not know.

The first indication I or any other foreigner had in Moscow that something might have happened to Beriya came just before 6 A.M. on Sunday morning, June 28, 1953. My newspaper colleagues and I were waiting as usual at the telegraph office for *Pravda* and *Izvestiya,* which were extremely late in appearing. This usually meant that some important news was being published. We grabbed the papers from the hands of the messenger and scanned them quickly. At the bottom of page 1 there was a small announcement. It said that the members of the Government, headed by Malenkov, had attended a performance of the new opera, *The Decembrists,* on the previous night, Saturday, at the Bolshoi Theater. The announcement listed the Government members who were in attendance. All were there except Beriya. One man who was not a member, Malyshev, was also listed.

It was very late to hope to get anything into the Sunday edition of *The New York Times* but I sent off an item anyway. However, the censor killed the sentence in which I pointed out that Beriya had not been present and I doubt if the *Times* printed the innocuous paragraph that remained. Probably, the editor wondered why I had started sending out social notes at urgent rates at six o'clock Sunday morning.

Sunday afternoon I tried again to send a speculative story but the censor was very alert. The story was killed in its entirety. Of course I did not know then whether Beriya was out of the Government but the question was hot. In the next few days every correspondent in Moscow and most of the diplomats occupied themselves almost exclusively in efforts to learn what, if anything, had happened to Beriya. No one was more active in this than the American Ambassador, Bohlen. He was particularly eager to nail down the rumor because he was planning to go out of Russia on leave immediately after July 4.

Despite all our efforts only two small pieces of dubious information came to light. The first was a report which one of the senior ambassadors in Moscow had received from a Russian source. This report was that Beriya had been arrested. However, the source was not regarded as reliable and I felt that if the news was true it would be circulating more widely in the city of Moscow and that we should be hearing it from other Russian sources, such as maids and chauffeurs.

The second item was equally dubious. It had long been whispered that Beriya lived in a big wall-enclosed, tree-shaded house at the corner of Kachalova Street and the Sadovaya Circle only about three blocks from the new American Embassy building. On the Saturday afternoon of the day the Government had gone to the Bolshoi Theater without Beriya some young Americans had looked out the windows of their flat and had noticed a detachment of Soviet tanks coming down the Sadovaya. The column came up to Kachalova Street and turned into the street Beriya lived in.

This did not impress me too much, either, since tank columns often moved around the Sadovaya Circle. Military movements of this kind were common on the Moscow streets—so common as hardly to arouse interest.

Actually, no one yet knows the precise mechanics by which the Beriya affair was brought to a climax. It is doubtful, however, that the tank column had anything to do with it since it later developed that Beriya was arrested on Friday, June 26, rather than Saturday, June 27, when the tanks were seen and the Government went to the theater. My own guess was that probably it was done very simply, possibly two Army officers may have stepped up to him as he arrived at the customary Kremlin conference room and taken him into custody with no ado whatsoever. One thing I can say with certainty and conviction—there was no deployment of military forces on the Moscow streets at the time of Beriya's arrest. Such fanciful reports are sliced from the same green cheese as those that Beriya actually fled Russia and took refuge with Franco.

The Beriya business was still very much in the unconfirmed-rumor class when Bohlen left for Western Europe. Later a rather ridiculous effort was made by someone in the State Department to claim that Bohlen went to Western Europe in order to be more readily accessible for consultation on the Beriya crisis.

This, of course, was sheer nonsense. It was not until the day after Bohlen left that we began to hear from Russian sources that Beriya was out and arrested and that something like a panic was on in the lesser ranks of the MVD—that MVD colonels were going about wringing their hands and burning their papers and acting as frightened and bewildered as their own victims usually did.

This convinced me that the news was correct, especially since a number of Soviet diplomats who were members of the Communist Party Central Committee were now arriving back in Moscow, obviously for a special meeting.

From this time forward I practically lived at the Central Telegraph Office. I wrote up in advance a series of bulletins on Beriya. I carried his biography, written down on handy cards, wherever I went. The suspense did not long continue. On the morning of July 10 the papers were again very late. The messenger did not arrive with them until a few minutes after 5 A.M. I saw the word Beriya on a copy of *Pravda* sticking out of the man's pocket and handed in my bulletins to the telegraph clerk. I knew what the news was without having to read it, except for the details.

Regardless of how Beriya was taken into custody the dominant role of the Army was never in doubt. Confirmation of that is provided by the fact that the same plenary meeting of the Central Committee which denounced Beriya elevated Zhukov from the status of candidate member to full member of the committee.

Announcement of the arrest was immediately followed by a series of meetings of military groups at which the Government's action was approved and Beriya was denounced as a traitor. The biggest of these was held in Moscow and was attended by all the top Army commanders. Bulganin spoke and Marshals Zhukov, Vasilevsky, Sokolovsky, Gorovov and many others stood beside him. It was made clear to everyone that the "Zhukov group" was 100 per cent behind the Government if it had not dictated the Government's action. The Moscow meeting was quickly followed by a similar one in Beriya's personal bailiwick of Georgia. Army General Antonov, who had been quietly running the Trans-Caucasus Military Command through one Georgian political upheaval after another, was the speaker at this meeting, which was notable for the absence of political and MVD generals who usually crowded the platform of every party meeting in Georgia. Later it transpired that most of these men, people like Dekanozov and old General Sergei Goglidze, had been arrested along with Beriya.

The place of Beriya's henchmen was taken by three men. First among them was Army General Antonov, Zhukov's friend who so long had guarded the Caucasus approaches to the Soviet Union. Second was the new Georgian Party secretary, a Georgian named Vasily Mzhavanadze with unique characteristics. He is a military man whose career has been in the Army since 1924. He has held one military post after another and in recent years has been the political chief of the Army in the Ukraine. In his person he combined ties to the Army and ties to Khrushchev's political organization. He practically symbolized the forces which ousted Beriya. And the third member of the triumvirate now installed in Georgia was also an Army man, a general named A. N. Inauri, a native Georgian born in Stalin's home town of Gori but a man whose career had been outside of his own country. He was put in the key position of Georgian Interior Minister.

Thus, Georgia, the heart of Beriya's power, was placed in control of three Army men, one closely connected with Zhukov, one closely connected with Khrushchev and, perhaps, although this we do not know, one closely connected with Malenkov.

In the months that followed the role of the Army in the Government appeared to harden into a permanent and accustomed thing. It did not seem to me that the Zhukov group sought to dictate Government policy so much as it was holding a watching brief.

But there is little doubt that the Army sought successfully to obtain modifications in foreign policy in an effort to reduce the swollen commitments of the Stalin era and, in general, to try to lessen immediate possibilities of shooting war. The Army strongly supported the Government's drive to boost consumer goods, perhaps because the Army with its millions of raw levies was in an excellent position accurately to gauge the real strain and moods of the people.

It was not until November, 1953, however, that the Army felt called upon to show its hand publicly, but it was a significant act— a nudge to the civilian leaders to get on with the business of meting out to Beriya the fate which the Army felt he deserved.

The nudge was administered by Zhukov himself in a fairly dramatic way at the big diplomatic reception which is traditionally held by the Foreign Minister on November 7. All of the Government chiefs, except Malenkov, Khrushchev and Voroshilov, were present when Zhukov was invited to the inner-room table by Molotov. The principal foreign ambassadors including Bohlen were present and toasts were flowing freely in the Russian tradition.

Bohlen, who is something of a veteran at this game, had offered a toast to justice. Then Zhukov was called upon to speak. He said he desired to support the toast which had just been drunk. He wished to drink again "to justice." This was a very unusual thing to do. In Russia it is the custom to offer your own toast and Mikoyan rather rudely reminded Zhukov of this fact. Moreover, in the present state of strained relations between Russia and America not many Russians would choose the words of the American Ambassador as a public platform on which to plant their feet. But Zhukov did and when he was heckled he stolidly and a bit angrily repeated that he proposed a toast to justice. The toast was drunk.

The significance of this demonstration was lost on no one present. Justice, in the context in which Zhukov spoke, could only mean a decision in the still pending Beriya case. He was publicly and in the presence of diplomats of all countries calling on the Government to speed up the adjudication of Beriya. Why he felt this necessary is not known. Perhaps someone in the Government was temporizing. But regardless of the reason he got results. Within six weeks Beriya and a group of his associates, including Deganozov and Goglidze, had been tried by a special court, headed by Marshal Konev, and sentenced to execution. On Christmas Eve it was announced that the men had been shot. The justice which Zhukov demanded had been done.

Five days later the papers published a two-paragraph item, reporting that a statue of Zhukov had been erected to him in his home town. This honor to which Zhukov had long been entitled by Soviet law had been denied him during Stalin's lifetime.

But a more unusual tribute was paid to Zhukov and to the role of the Army when the quadrennial elections to the Supreme Soviet were held in the winter of 1954. The customary appeal to the electors was signed by twenty names, the first five of them being Marshals of the Soviet Union, Budenny, Bulganin, Vasilevsky, Voroshilov and Zhukov. It was an accident of the Russian alphabet that the five Marshals were listed first. But it was no accident that for the first time in history one quarter of the names on the election list were military figures.

So far as I can judge the influence of the Army and of Zhukov continues to be conservative and moderate. I should guess that Zhukov and the generals like himself who actually led the Red Army to victory over Germany have very sound and realistic ideas about both the strengths and weaknesses of Soviet military power. And I do not believe they blind themselves to the truth about America's nuclear striking power. They know too much of war to be likely to stumble into the catastrophe which Soviet-American war with atomic weapons would inevitably be.

Zhukov gets along well with Westerners. This is not just the impression he made on General Eisenhower. It is the impression he consistently makes on foreigners. While not tall, he is a big, rather handsome man with a smile somewhat like that of Omar Bradley, except that his face is squarish where Bradley's is longish. He is a man of easy manners and one whose appearance inspires confidence. He does not have the hard round-headed Prussian conformation which is so common among Soviet officers of general rank.

Moreover, Zhukov quite obviously is a man with his own ideas—ideas which not necessarily always coincide with those of the other top figures in the Soviet government. The relationship, however, appears to be a smooth-working and generally successful marriage of convenience. The prestige and weight of the Army grows steadily. It was recently seen in the stripping of uniforms and epaulettes from the civilian bureaucrats who had worn them with increasing frequency in the postwar years.

Zhukov gave one insight into his ideas with his nudge to the Government on the Beriya question. He gave another broad and interesting insight on the ninth anniversary of the capitulation of Germany in May, 1954. He contributed an article to *Pravda* that was not just the usual piece of propaganda handed out by the Party to a general for publication under his signature. There were the usual number of hack articles published that day, including one by Zhukov's associate, Marshal Vasilevsky.

But Zhukov's article was different. It paid tribute, for example, in an honest and soldierly way to the role played in the war by the Western Allies and particularly the United States and England. He had a few gracious words for General Eisenhower and Field Marshal Montgomery. He did not in the usual hoggish fashion which Moscow has made customary in recent years claim that the Soviet won the war single-handed.

In these respects, Zhukov's article was sensible, polite and reasonable. But along with this he appended some sharp phrases, too, directed against American foreign policy, which he blamed for the deterioration of relations between the U.S.A. and Russia and for intensifying world tension. He warned that Russia was not a country to be meddled with lightly and had some harsh things to say about American bankers, which sounded very much like the old Stalin line that U.S. businessmen were more interested in profits than peace.

Despite these propaganda touches there was over the whole of Zhukov's statement a relative aura of decency and good sense which inevitably recalled the idea of our diplomats toward the end of the war that Zhukov was the sort of a man whom it might be useful to talk with.

At the time of writing, Zhukov is actually drawing a long oar in the Soviet Government and I can't help but think that it would do no harm and possibly some good if that war's end hunch were put to a little test.

XII

For Lust of Knowing

NEVER go back again. . . . The words echoed
through my mind as I paused a moment and sat down in the living
room of my apartment on the Sadovo Samotechnaya before leaving
on a long journey. It is a Russian custom before leaving on a long
trip to sit a moment in silent contemplation, and I was indulging a
slightly superstitious feeling which the thought of this expedition had
given me.

For I was retracing my footsteps on a path I had never thought to
take again. It was September, 1953, and I was once more taking the
golden road to Samarkand which first I had traveled in 1944.

Samarkand . . . The golden road . . . For me they had been the
fairest words, the most romantic of the English tongue. But, now, as
I sat there in the already darkened room, my typewriter waiting and
my bag packed, my heart was like lead and I was tired before the
first step.

This should be a thrilling moment, I told myself. You are doing
the thing which you dreamed of doing ever since you first went to
Samarkand. You are going back on the high road of adventure. Only
the fewest of the few ever get to Samarkand. Think of the dreams
encrusted like jewels in the syllables of that word. Where is the man
in whose heart the spark of adventure still lives whose eyes do not
flash at the whisper . . . Samarkand . . . Tamerlane . . . Kublai
Khan . . . Genghis Khan . . . pleasure palaces . . . slant-eyed
horsemen cruel as steel . . . bowmen supple as a Damascus blade

. . . a whole world bent to their will for a century or two and then the fat Khans, the rich Khans, the powerful Khans sitting on Asia's patient back for another half a thousand years or so.

Samarkand . . . Slowly I picked up my things and went out to the car. I tried to figure out where the thrill and the excitement had vanished. I was older, of course, and that was probably part of it. When we are young we think the Samarkands of the world are like golden nuts which we can crack in our strong white teeth. And inside, of course, will be "the secret"—the kernel of knowledge, the heart of the mystery of life. And for this we travel halfway around the world and back again.

But when we are older, I thought, we wonder whether it is all so simple. We get to Samarkand. Some of us do. And how much the wiser are we? How much the wiser would I be for going a second time? I honestly didn't know, but of one thing I was sure. If, the first time, I had gone to Samarkand in search of mystery and enigma, this time I was going in search of facts.

I had hardly been out of Moscow since the spring of 1951 but, now, as one of its first acts in a program of ameliorating the harsh restrictions on the lives of foreigners in Russia, the new Government had suddenly removed a large number of barriers on travel, including the ban on visiting Central Asia which had existed even in Czarist days.

With only a minimum of delay due to bureaucratic red tape I had been given permission to make a great swing through Central Asia, far more extensive than my trip of 1944 with Eric Johnston. I had permission to visit four of Russia's five Central Asiatic republics— Kazakhstan, Uzbekistan, Kirghizia and Tadjikstan. Turkmenia, or at least the area I wanted to see around the famous old center of Khiva which I had proposed to visit by steamboat down the Amu Darya (the Oxus of the ancients), was still closed to me although it was seen a bit later by some British diplomats.

Even so the journey which I had projected was to be more extensive than any foreigner had made into Central Asia in many years. I proposed to visit Alma-Ata, close to the Sinkiang frontier; Frunze, the capital of Kirghizia; Tashkent, the great Asiatic metropolis which was the capital of Uzbekistan; Stalinabad, the capital of Tadjikstan;

the Fergana Valley which was said to rival Kashmir for beauty and wealth; Samarkand itself, and ancient Bukhara. It was a fabulous trip in a kind of Richard Halliburton sense, but instead of excitement my mood was one of grim anticipation, a little bit like that of a soldier who is going out under fire after a long time in a concrete dugout.

The plane for Alma-Ata was airborne at 2:58 A.M. and we quickly headed east over the golden glow that was Moscow. The city looked big and diffused and warm with lights. Different from an American city because you could not see the red and green of traffic lights nor the many colors of the advertising signs. It was all softly glowing gold.

After flying half the night and half the day we came down with a conked-out motor at Karaganda. It seemed to me that nothing could be more appropriate than the fact that the golden road to Samarkand led through Karaganda. Karaganda is one of the largest and most successful of the new prison cities which the Soviet regime has created. It is a sprawling, kidney-shaped industrial town, patched with black and red and whitish-gray from the coal mines, the copper refineries and the limestone and gypsum works. It looks like a city of 300,000 or so people and, from the air, you are struck with the fact that it is laid out in perfect rectangular squares—as regular as cell blocks. You are also struck by the number of large compounds and fenced-in areas which may or may not be prison areas. Karaganda has two satellite towns, Temir-Tau, or iron mountain, and Saran, a coal center. Both are laid out on the same cell-block principle as Karaganda.

There was pleasant warm sunshine when our plane came down at Karaganda but I felt myself shivering a little. I had heard of Karaganda from my earliest days in Russia. It was mentioned in a hushed breath when it was mentioned at all by Russians. I sometimes had thought that, perhaps, we foreigners were inclined to overdramatize the role of the MVD in these industrial prison cities, but as we walked from our plane to the airport building I heard a Russian passenger in a joking way say to the air stewardess: "Better notify the militia we are here—quickly. We have no visas for Karaganda, and we do not want to be *rasstrelyat!*"

A joke but a grim one. *Rasstrelyat* means "to execute by shooting." We spent ten or twelve hours at Karaganda but there was no need to worry about the militia. We were not allowed off the airport grounds. So it came about that by an accident of airplane mechanics I got to visit one of the most notorious MVD industrial centers in the U.S.S.R. although I must admit I didn't see much of it.

The most interesting thing about Alma-Ata was that it provided a take-off point for a bus trip right back into the thirteenth century, into the time of Genghis Khan himself. I don't suppose any foreigner had ever made the trip before. It probably would not have occurred to him. Nor would it have occurred to me if I had not happened to pass the bus station and seen that there was a daily service to Frunze, 250 kilometers to the southwest over desert and mountain. I had permission to go to Frunze and I could see no reason why I shouldn't go by bus if I wished to.

So, ticket in hand, I clambered aboard a truck to which had been attached, as a body, a kind of wooden box, and set off on a chilly morning with fifteen other passengers. Our route led us straight along one of the paths which the horsemen of the great Khan followed when he ordered them west to avenge the events which are still known in Central Asia as the "catastrophe at Otrar." Time is marked on a different calendar in Asia and the catastrophe at Otrar seemed close at hand as I bumped and joggled along the mountain trail. It was at Otrar, as almost anyone familiar with Central Asia can tell you, that in the summer of the year 1218 the Grand Vizir, acting on orders of the Emperor Mukammad of the great satrapy of Khorezm, seized a caravan of five hundred camels laden with gold, silver, furs and silks belonging to a man whose name had not yet become famous, Genghis Khan. Nor was that the end. When the great Khan sent an ambassador to protest the incident the envoy was beheaded and his attendants shorn of their beards.

There was little traffic along this mountain trail but what there was would have been more readily recognized by the Khan than by me. There were slant-eyed black-mustached horsemen; horsewomen with their babies cradled on their backs, Indian-style; warriors with conical black and brown felt hats and belts and daggers of beautiful filigree silver; nomads who looked as though they had ridden right out of the year 1219 when Genghis Khan ordered his men to avenge the incident on the Jaxartes River.

They lived in felt tents or mud hogans and it was hard to believe the Communist Party or the Soviet Government had laid a very heavy hand upon them, and yet when I tried to take some pictures in a mountain market place five MVD men, four of them in plain clothes, sprang up out of nowhere and took me into custody. Of the many times I have been arrested in Russia for taking photographs I think this incident frightened me most, for I was so deep in the interior that I could imagine being held for weeks before Moscow ever was notified. But I was spared the horrors of the jail at the village of Torgatz. I had been talking on the bus with two youngsters who were going from Alma-Ata to Frunze to enter law school there. They saw me in the hands of the MVD and drew one of the plainclothes men aside for a little talk after which, grudgingly, the police released me.

"What happened?" I asked them when we got back on the bus.

"Oh," said one in an airy fashion, "I told them you were a distinguished foreign guest. And then I happened to mention that my father was the secretary of the regional Communist Party organization. So they decided to let you go."

For once I was glad of a little Party influence. The boys apologized for the local police and told about various times when they had had trouble with the MVD over their *dokumenti*. Once, en route, the bus was stopped and four young uniformed MVD men started to check documents but the passengers complained and they gave it up after looking at two or three. But every time an MVD trooper appeared I noticed a little chill come over the bus, and when two closed vans, guarded by armed MVD troopers, passed us, I saw people looking the other way.

I was glad when the bus finally bumped into Frunze and back into the twentieth century, even if it was the Russian version of the twentieth century. The young legal students plied me with one question after another about the United States until I began to get embarrassed because the picture I was drawing was so obviously superior to Russia. They asked me, finally, about our television. Did it really extend from coast to coast? Yes, I said, it did. And did almost every city in America have television? Yes, I said, they did. Well, said one of the youngsters, we have color television in Russia. I knew Russia didn't have color television and he knew I knew it but I said *"Da, da,"* because I thought it was time Russia came out ahead in some comparison.

While I was sitting in the restaurant of the Hotel Kirghistan talking with these youngsters I saw another youngster, twelve years old or so, enter the place and go from table to table, begging. He wore a sign around his neck saying: "Help me, Comrades, I am deaf and dumb." At every table he was given a handful of change except at one where an MVD officer, his girl and a friend had just ordered a bottle of champagne. They were so busy watching the waiter open the bottle and fill their glasses it was some time before they saw the young beggar and when they did the officer motioned him to go away.

It was in Frunze that I heard about Mr. Quinn, the American painless dentist. A taxi driver told me about Mr. Quinn when I asked him if he had ever met an American before. He said no, he hadn't except for Mr. Quinn.

Mr. Quinn had lived in Frunze twenty-five or thirty years ago. What had brought him there the taxi driver couldn't say but he was apparently a jolly fellow who laughed when you came to see him and joked about "extractions." One reason I believed the driver's story was that he used the English word "extraction" in describing Mr. Quinn's conversation.

Apparently Mr. Quinn drifted into Frunze about the time the famous Turbsib railroad was being constructed, a project which was bossed by an American, Bill Shatov, an ex-I.W.W. Whether there was any connection between Mr. Quinn and Shatov I don't know. Shatov of course has long since vanished from the scene and his very name has disappeared in the Russification of all Great Projects.

Mr. Quinn, also, has vanished. He worked a while in Frunze and then, the driver said, drifted on to Prezhvalsky. If Frunze is a far-off place, Prezhvalsky is literally on the edge of the world, the high shelf of the Tien Shan Mountains lying next to China. Whether Mr. Quinn went on from there or whether he still may be there, telling yarns about the United States and carrying out extractions, American style, no one could say.

Somehow, I am unable to get the story of Mr. Quinn out of my mind. It comes back again and again. What forces ever started him on the journey that was to lead to Frunze and Prezhvalsky? At night, occasionally, I find myself thinking about Mr. Quinn. A rather precise little man, I believe, with rimless glasses and thin lips. I fancy him in practice in some American city, possibly Des Moines, with offices in one of those two-story corner buildings with a drugstore on the ground floor, and a blond, not very good-looking assistant to help him with the instruments. One day I like to think Mr. Quinn hung up the little dental office sign which he put on the door when he went out to lunch. He fixed the metal hands of the sign to show that he would be back at 2 P.M.

And never returned . . . took off on a tramp freighter and wound up after many an adventure and many an extraction in Frunze . . . and Prezhvalsky.

When I think of Mr. Quinn I think that maybe I was too hasty in deciding that there was no more romance and no "secret" in Samarkand. And in moments like that I am a little sorry that I did not carry out the impulse I had to go to Osh. I had never heard of Osh before I went to Frunze but there I learned that it was the place travelers used to go to to outfit for journeys into the high Pamirs. I could have taken a plane to Osh, en route to the Fergana Valley to which I had permission to travel. But at the last moment I got cold feet. Because another thing I learned about Osh was that it was in the center of a mining area for radioactive ores. I thought I would probably get to Osh all right but perhaps I would never get out of it.

Instead, I took the plane for Tashkent, which is the Communist showplace of Central Asia and a lot more important in a pragmatic way than Mr. Quinn or even Osh.

Most Americans have never heard of Tashkent but it is a city of more than a million people, a great political and industrial metropolis which each year becomes better and better known to the people of Asia and plays a central role in all Soviet propaganda directed toward Asia. Its propaganda role becomes apparent even before you land because as the plane circles the field it flies around a high wireless mast which comes up almost to flight level. This is the beam of the powerful Radio Tashkent which twenty-four hours a day in every language and dialect of Asia carries the Communist propaganda line from Mandalay to Cairo and from Khyber to Malabar.

And the message which Radio Tashkent broadcasts is backed by the practical demonstration of Tashkent itself. For to Tashkent are brought each year hundreds and thousands of visitors and delegates and sightseers from the Asian lands, from India and Egypt, from Siam and Malay, to see the progress which Asiatic people have made under Soviet rule.

It is easy for a European to undervalue that message because, for instance, to my eyes Tashkent is a singularly unattractive city. There is a shabby old European city, dating from Czarist times. There is a garish section of Soviet buildings which, except for a beautiful Opera House, illustrates some of the worst features of Stalin-epoch architecture—what I call the "Gorky Street" style. And there is a large Oriental city—typical mud houses, whitewashed, around which irrigation ditches meander, and the streets are donkey-cart width.

Tashkent is not as picturesque as a Westerner expects an Eastern city to be nor so clean and up-to-date as he expects a Western, even a Russian city, to be. However, the irrigation waters are fairly pure. They are not used, simultaneously, as water supply and toilet as in Tehran. The native city does not smell. The market is sanitary (and therefore lacking in "color"). There are some beggars but relatively few by Oriental standards, and a notable absence of running sores, blind people and other by-products of Oriental disease.

Thus, to me Tashkent is a dull, unattractive city.

But to an Easterner it is an exciting, even a thrilling city because it shows him the kind of progress he would like to see in his cities— relative absence of flies, pure water supply, good schools, health facilities, etc. That is why Tashkent and its big modern agricultural machinery and textile factories, its cotton gins and fertilizer plants is Russia's No. 1 advertisement in Asia. I had seen Tashkent nine years before and I was not overly impressed with its progress during the interim. However, few visitors had any such standard of comparison. I could see, of course, that the great Stalin textile works had been expanded by one-third or more. And I could see that considerable progress had been achieved in clearing out some of the Oriental city and turning it into a park, lined with apartment blocks in the Russian style. But I could also see that the Oriental city had grown and expanded toward the outskirts of the city at a rate more rapid than it was being cleared away. The city did not live up to the boast its officials had made in 1944—"Come back in ten years' time and you won't recognize the place."

Not that I would suggest that the Communists have done nothing for this Asiatic world. They have. As always the cost in human suffering has been fantastic but they have their achievements. One night I walked about the Tashkent Opera House. The fountain was playing and colored searchlights made it look like fairyland. The night was pleasantly cool and young couples, Uzbek and Russian, strolled in the square.

Two pictures came to my mind. The first was of a kindly old Uzbek man and his wife whom I had encountered in the old city when I had been in Tashkent in 1944. They invited three or four of us into their courtyard for a bowl of tea. On the wall of their house was a picture of their son, a Red Army captain. The old man said with a simple dignity which I have never forgotten: "Before the Revolution I was nothing. Now I am a man." It was the first and only time I have met someone who has experienced the unique pride and joy of becoming a man.

The other picture was of the Kazak MVD man at the market place in Torgatz who arrested me. I could see his cruel piggish eyes, his face without eyebrows, his heavy cheek bones. And I remembered how he and four companions had sprung, as though out of the earth, in one tiny village and I thought of how many tiny villages and how many market places there were and how many men, in plain clothes and in uniform, there were constantly watching and watching, ready to spring.

Progress—but at what a price! Still, one should not forget that the Asian has a different scale of values than we have.

By any scale of values it is a lot easier to get to Samarkand by DC-3 transport plane than by caravan across the desert. The flying time is less than two hours from Tashkent in a plane provided with a hostess who has a supply of *Pravdas* and *Izvestiyas* for you to read if you get tired of looking out the window.

I found there had been some changes in Samarkand since I was

last there. The little movie house across the street from the famous
Registan had a new picture, of course, but still an American one. In
1944 it had been showing Samuel Goldwyn's epic *North Star*. Now
the feature was *Tarzan in the West*. I had an idea that Tarzan was
doing better business.

Romeo and Juliet was playing in the Uzbek language at the drama
theater and the Park of Rest and Culture advertised that classes in
ballroom dancing were starting shortly. You could buy the same kind
of cheap coral earrings and necklaces which the Moscow jewelry
stores were featuring, the same Pobeda wrist watches, Kremlin per-
fume and Moskvich radios. You could call a Pobeda taxi by dialing
No. 686 on the telephone or you could call a droshky by shouting
"*Kocher!*" in the street. There was daily airplane service from Samarkand to twelve large cities and for one hundred rubles you could hire
a little two-seater plane to fly you out to a more remote collective
farm.

I dutifully visited the Registan, Tamerlane's tomb, Ulug Bek's as-
tronomical observatory, and the Street of Kings where the beautiful
mausoleums in blue mosaic are located. There wasn't a thrill for me
in the whole lot. Nor a single new fact worth reporting . . . Never
go back . . . How right my instinct had been. I hurried on to
Bukhara, where the clash of cymbals still echoes over the flat-topped
roofs of the ancient city to tell the artisans that the working day has
started and mingles in a curious cacophony with the shrill blast of
steam whistles from the engines in the distant railroad yards.

In Bukhara I found a little of the romance that was so lacking in
Tashkent and Samarkand. Here was a city wholly Oriental with no
Russian quarter and little evidence of Russian influence except for
the schools. There was no new building going on and it appeared
that the ancient center of Moslem learning was deliberately being
allowed to deteriorate while the railroad center of Kagan, some
thirteen miles away, was built up.

Bukhara was the first city in which I encountered the custom of
the local chief of the MVD installing himself in the hotel as manager
in order to simplify his task of keeping foreigners under surveillance.
The police officer said his name was Kruban and that he was an

Uzbek. He had a bland and oily smile which seemed to me to conceal measureless evil.

Two diplomats from Moscow were in Bukhara at the same time as I was and one evening we stopped to have our shoes shined. A great crowd of natives collected to watch the operation. A thin young Russian came up and addressed me in broken English. "Excuse me," he said, "but I am the teacher of English in the Bukhara school. I heard you speaking English and I wanted to talk to you."

I asked him a few questions and learned that, so far as he knew, there were no English-speaking people in Bukhara. "Sometimes, I listen to the B.B.C.," he said, "or to the American radio. It is the only practice in the language which I have."

In the midst of our conversation Kruban appeared out of nowhere. "Who are you?" he asked the young man. "What is your name?"

A grimace of fright came over the man's face. "My name is Petrov," said the young man. "Teacher of English at the middle school."

"Ah," said Kruban. "Petrov. Teacher of English at the middle school."

He rolled the simple words on his tongue as though they were sweetmeats and stood looking with a bold stare at the nervous teacher.

Hurriedly Petrov spoke to me. "Excuse me," he said, "I must go now."

He melted into the crowd but a moment later I saw him only a few yards up the street. He had been stopped by a dark-faced man in plain clothes who motioned him over to the wall and engaged him in earnest conversation. I had my shoes shined and finally went on back to the hotel. Petrov was still being interrogated.

One of the diplomats and I took many pictures in the market place, which annoyed Kruban. He repeatedly cautioned us that we should only take pictures of "historic" buildings. He didn't actually forbid us to take other pictures. He merely said that other pictures were "Ni khorasha—not good."

I think what bothered him most was the fact that we attracted so much attention on the part of the natives. Business practically halted in the bazaar when we entered. I think Kruban regarded us as a dangerous influence on the local population and was afraid the people might get ideas of liberty into their heads. If foreigners were now permitted to come to Bukhara perhaps other things were permitted as well.

In any event he decided to stage a small demonstration. One day when the diplomat and I were in a store in the heart of the bazaar (looking at what was on sale, as it chanced, rather than taking pictures) a swarthy-faced militiaman came up to us, gave a slouchy salute and said: "It is forbidden to take pictures here. Come with me."

I laughed in his face. "We aren't taking pictures," I told him. "But we have permission to do so if we wish."

With the militiaman nagging at our heels we emerged from the store to find another policeman waiting for us.

"Come to the militia station," this man said in a loud voice. "The captain wants to talk to you."

Already a cluster of people had started to gather around us and it was immediately apparent to me what had happened. Our MVD friend had decided to stage a demonstration for the benefit of the bazaar, to show the people that the police still had the upper hand and they better be careful about emulating the free and easy manners of the foreigners.

However, I resolutely refused to go to the militia station and told the officers that we were going back to the hotel. If the captain wanted to see us he could come there.

This was not in the scenario the militiamen had been briefed for. At first they were bewildered and then angry. But when we stubbornly turned in the direction of the hotel they had to make a decision—either to grab us and detain us by force or to let us go. I was not at all certain which the decision might be since I didn't know how far the instructions of our host, Kruban, might have gone.

However, after a moment's hesitation, the militiamen permitted us to walk back to the hotel although they accompanied us, one on either side, arguing and gesticulating at a great rate for the benefit of the crowd of two or three hundred people which had now gathered.

When we got to the hotel I found Kruban waiting there. He had

a guilty look on his face which caused me to lose my temper completely. I exploded in denunciation of the police, of the authorities
of Bukhara, of the so-called hospitality of the Soviet Union, and demanded to know whether it was customary to treat distinguished
guests with this kind of courtesy in Soviet Asia.

Kruban dissolved in embarrassment in the face of this denunciation. He hurriedly interviewed his militiamen and came back in a
moment, wringing his hands and smiling in sickly fashion. "It's all a
mistake," he said. "They want to apologize."

The two militiamen then presented themselves in turn. Each drew
himself up, saluted, murmured: "*Izvinitye* . . . excuse me," and
hurried away.

The crowd of spectators was still gathered outside the hotel so
the diplomat and I picked up our cameras and walked out into the
street. We strolled slowly up to the place where we had been arrested
and back again, pausing now and then to take a picture. I think we
made our point.

There were two things I was particularly interested in seeing in
Bukhara—one was the ancient colony of Bukhara Jews and the other
was in seeing how the famous carpets of Bukhara, those lovely fine-
knotted, wine-red rugs which have been the glory of the East for a
thousand years, are woven.

Kruban was strongly disinclined to show me either of these things.
He flatly declared that no carpets were woven in Bukhara (although
several residents had offered to show me rug-weaving artels) and he
said the Jews were "not interesting." However, by questioning a small
boy I found that the ancient Street of Jews where the Jewish community of Bukhara had lived for more centuries than I could count
was just a block up Lenin Street from the hotel. So I walked down
the Street of Jews beside the reluctant Kruban and even went into the
small and ancient Bukhara synagogue, a mud-walled building like
the rest, bearing no outer inscription to denote its use.

However, when I wanted to walk further down the street Kruban
flatly refused. When it became obvious that I could go further only
at the cost of an outright incident I gave up. But the next morning I
got up when the sun was still slanting over the white walls, the
minaret towers and the flat roofs of Bukhara and walked down the

Street of Jews. I quickly discovered the reason for Kruban's agitation. Not far from the synagogue there was a low-ceilinged building, dark and gloomy, with the front open to the street. There in the murky half light I saw a hundred women, seated cross-legged on low wooden platforms before their looms—the rug weavers of Bukhara, hard at work an hour after sun-up, laboring in the semidarkness, haggard and worn, old before their time, destroying with each tiny infinitesimal knot one infinitesimal part of their eyesight, headed as surely toward blindness as these rugs were to the Moscow market.

The night before we left, Kruban dined with us. It was a rather ceremonial meal and he had ordered the hotel to cook a special kind of pilaf of saffron rice and raisins and mutton in the Bukhara style. He drank a good deal, both vodka and sweet red wine and fell to talking about a subject which was obviously close to his heart— Uzbek marriage customs.

He said that, in accordance with Uzbek custom, he had never seen his bride before he was married to her. Because he was poor they had tried to marry him off to an old hag. Somehow, he managed to escape this fate, and his wife turned out to be not bad looking and, what was much more important, she was a virgin. That is most important to the Uzbeks. It is a terrible scandal if the bride is not a virgin. If a girl marries and the morning after the ceremony her shoes are sent back to her parents this means that she was not a virgin and she is cast out of her husband's house and she cannot come back to her parents. It is a great disgrace for the parents.

Of course, he said, all that is changed now. Young people see each other before getting married. They even go to dances together. They go walking and they go to the movies. Still, it is a worry for the parents. He had a daughter and he would be glad when she was safely married. He had a son, too, who was going to the institute and who, he hoped, would go to Moscow to study.

His wife, he said, was very "advanced." She no longer wore the *paranja*, or veil, and she no longer lived a harem life. She had been to Tashkent and to Moscow. It was the Uzbek custom, he said, for women to remove all hair from their body, either by shaving or by using a depilatory. It was also the Uzbek custom for man and wife to sleep together only twice a week. After making love to his wife a man stayed indoors. He didn't know why. But now, he said, things are much different. He can sleep with his wife any time he wants to.

Later that night I went for a stroll down Lenin Street, through the Toki Zargaon cupola where they used to trade in precious gems and ornaments of gold and silver. There was a full moon, dazzling white in its brilliance, and it led me imperceptibly but inevitably to that glory of the sultans of Bukhara, the incredible minaret of Kalyan. It loomed against the purple sky like a tower of gray Castilian lace and its loveliness came into my throat like cool wine from a crystal goblet.

So beautiful was the minaret that for some moments I forgot that it had served a most practical purpose, first for the Caliphs, then for the Czars and now? I wondered whether, sometimes, the Communists, too, didn't lead their prisoners, in chains, to the high balcony of the minaret and shove them, screaming and clutching, off to the street 150 feet below.

If Bukhara was an ideological backwater where, as I could see by the fly-specked posters, Stalin never quite supplanted Lenin as the symbol to an illiterate people of the Revolution, I found that Stalinabad, down near the Persian frontier, was a "little Moscow." Everything was up to date in Stalinabad. The Bukhara hotel had no running water and outdoor toilets. There was a yellowing portrait of Andrei Andreyevich Andreyev on the wall of the office. It had been years since Andreyev had been a first-rank political figure.

But in Stalinabad the hotel's toilets were cleaner than Moscow's. There was not only running water. There was hot running water. There was a fresh new portrait of Malenkov in the lobby, the first I had seen in Central Asia. And in the Park of Rest and Culture there was a display of portraits of Russia's military leaders, the first layout I had ever seen of the leading generals of the Zhukov group.

There was an atmosphere of efficiency and cleanliness about Stalinabad which you could almost smell. It was so pronounced and so obvious that when I was walking from the airplane to a taxi I said to myself: "I'll bet there are Germans here." I said it over again when I saw the well-run, flyless hotel restaurant and the fussy way the pillows were tucked into lace pillowcases.

And, of course, I was right.

A few hours after arriving in Stalinabad I hailed a taxicab on the street and climbed into the front seat beside the driver, a good-look-ing young blond boy. I told him I was a stranger in town and I wanted to see the sights. We started off and I noticed him eying me curiously. Finally, he could resist no longer.

"You aren't a Russian, are you?" he said.

Here we go again, I thought.

"No," I replied, "I'm not."

"Are you from the Baltic States?" he asked. I shook my head. "Poland? Czechoslovakia?"

"No," I said. "I'm an American. I'm from the United States."

The boy looked at me with pure wonder as though the words hadn't quite penetrated his mind.

"An American?" he said. "An American! Why, I'm a German!"

With a simultaneous gesture he reached into his pocket and whipped out his Soviet residence passport, flipped it open and said: "See? It says right there. I'm a German."

And he was all right. One of 100,000 or possibly 200,000 Germans, the so-called Volga Deutsch, who had been packed up in 1941 at the beginning of the war and shipped off to forced residence in remote Tadjikstan.

This youngster was a *spets*. That is, there was stamped on his pass-port not only the designation of his German nationality but a restric-tion which specified that he was only permitted to live in the city of Stalinabad and was not permitted to go beyond the city limits.

He himself had not actually come from the Volga. He had been living in one of the larger cities of the Ukraine with his parents at the outbreak of war. The family had been there since the time of Cath-erine II, who had brought so many of the German settlers into Russia hoping that their superior skills would serve to fertilize the backward Russian peasants.

The scheme, like so many schemes for changing the character of the Russian peasants, had not worked well. The Germans stayed aloof and despised the clumsy, dirty, ignorant Russians. A few mo-ments' conversation with the youngster showed me that not much had changed in the German attitude since Catherine's time except that aversion had changed to hatred. I couldn't help feeling as I listened to this boy that, perhaps, the Kremlin had been right in not placing too much trust in its German citizens. Not that this excused the Government for the harsh treatment and needless brutality which it had shown in uprooting the Germans and shipping them east.

First, the youngster said, they had been sent east along the Trans-Siberian. They were in freight cars. It was crowded and cold and food was given out erratically. Still, it wasn't too bad, principally because while it was cold it was not yet freezing cold. When they got halfway across Siberia the convoy halted for some time. The Germans were being split up, some to be sent further east, some to go south. His father persuaded the authorities to send them south which, as it turned out, meant Stalinabad. That had been a good thing because they had heard since that conditions in the east and north where many Germans were sent were even worse than in Tadjikstan.

"When we Germans," said the boy, "came here, things were terrible, too. You wouldn't have known the town. We have changed it all, we Germans. We have built new buildings, new roads. We have made the city clean and beautiful."

The pride that came into his voice as he said, "we Germans (*mye nemtsi*)" was unmistakable.

There had been much disease when "we Germans" arrived, he said. Many of the older people died. Especially those who were sent to the "interior"—deep into Tadjikstan—to live on collective farms. Even in Stalinabad it was not good. He had had malaria three times and once he had almost died.

Were things better now?

"*Chort*," he said, spitting out the window. "The devil."

While "we Germans" built good buildings—and this I could see myself—and fine roads they benefited very little from their labors. The fine apartment houses went to the Russians and the Germans lived, my young friend said with scorn, "like the ignorant Tadjiks." He showed me where he lived himself—a mud house with a mud courtyard. Clean and neat but poverty-stricken. Across the street was a new, gleaming white block of apartments, built by Germans and inhabited by Russians.

"We Germans" were so numerous that a whole quarter of the city was filled with them. They lived together. They did not mix with the

Russians. They had their own park—a botanical park, devoid of the propaganda and amusement features of the usual Park of Rest and Culture (the Germans had also built a fine park for the Komsomols, or Communist Youth, complete with an artificial lake—but they never went there)—and in their homes they spoke nothing but German.

"They are afraid to let us have German books," the boy said, "but we teach each other to read German and write German and we never use a word of Russian when we are by ourselves."

The Germans are not the only *spetsi* in Tadjikstan. But they are the most numerous.

An official of the local City Council looked me up in Stalinabad. I think the hotelkeeper told him I was there. He took me for a walk around town to show me the sights.

"This is a very progressive city," he said. "We do everything here just like in Moscow."

He peppered his conversation with quotations from *Pravda* and started every other sentence with "As Comrade Stalin said," or "As Comrade Malenkov says."

A couple of weeks previously the Government had put all offices and institutions on a strict eight-hour day and had abolished night work, so beloved by Stalin. Regular office hours in the daytime and rest and relaxation afterward was the new Party line. The time of setting-up exercises on the radio had been changed in the morning and the hours of theater performances advanced in the evening in conformity with the new edict.

As we walked through the evening dusk my companion commented on this change. "We have a new order," he said. "As Comrade Malenkov says—no more night work."

"Yes, indeed," I replied. "No more night work."

We walked in silence a bit and from somewhere I heard the radio announcing the time. It was nine o'clock.

"What," I asked my companion, pointing to a great building, ablaze from top to bottom with lights, "is that beautiful structure?"

"That," he said, "is the offices of the Tadjik Council of Ministers."

The new order . . . The new order in Central Asia . . .

Well, I thought to myself, perhaps it was wrong to go back to

Samarkand. Perhaps it would have been better to let it linger on as a kind of romantic dream.

But if I had, as the poet said, been driven to take the golden road to Samarkand by a "lust of knowing what should not be known" certainly I had satisfied that lust most thoroughly. For, indeed, it had been no accident that the road to Samarkand led through Karaganda. In a figurative sense Karaganda was Samarkand and almost every place I had gone to, from remote villages on the route of Genghis Khan to modern Stalinabad, bore the unmistakable mark of that pervasive force which obviously had ruled so much of Central Asia before Stalin's death and which, so far as I could determine, was still ruling with undiminished force. I mean, of course, the MVD.

XIII

A Walk in the Red Square

THE first thing I did when I returned to Moscow in late February, 1954, was to go for a walk in the Red Square. And I took my camera with me, the new Contax I had just bought in Berlin rather than the battered Lubitel which I had bought the fall before on my trip to Central Asia.

Almost immediately after the Central Asian expedition I had gone home to the United States on leave. So it was with eyes freshened by many weeks in America and a perspective sharpened by observing the new Soviet diplomacy at work in Berlin that I now looked again on the Moscow scene.

I had hoped when I went back to the United States that I would not have to return to Russia, but the editors of the *Times* wanted me to carry on until a replacement correspondent could obtain a visa and relieve me. So, my spirits lightened by the knowledge that my Russian assignment would be coming to an end within a few months at most, I had come back for a final look at post-Stalin Russia and, perhaps, something like a reassessment of the country to which I was surprised to find I had devoted the better part of the last decade.

While in the United States I had been bombarded with questions as to what had been happening in Russia in the months before and since Stalin's death. And I had found myself in some embarrassment because while the persons in New York and Washington who make a career of "analyzing" Russia all had very precise and pat answers

214

to what was going on in the Soviet Union, I myself was by no means certain.

Everyone asked me what had happened to Beriya. I said that beyond his arrest I really didn't know. Everyone asked me who was going to win out in the great duel between Malenkov and Khrushchev. I said I didn't know and, moreover, I wasn't sure there was a duel. Quite a few people asked me, rather anxiously: You don't really think anything has changed, do you? From the way they asked the question I knew they rather hoped that I would say, No, I didn't. But my answer on that was rather unsatisfactory, too. I said that it seemed to me that quite a few things had changed but I didn't know, yet, how fundamental they would turn out to be.

Now that I was back I hoped that I could get some more definite answers to the questions which I was asking myself as well as those I was being asked. When I had left Moscow in October certain trends, of course, were quite evident. But they were not well enough established so that I felt justified in basing any sweeping generalizations on them.

It had been apparent from the first days after Stalin died that the new Government wished to present itself as a clean break from the Stalin tradition. It had emphasized the backing and participation of the military. It had emphasized its "collective" nature. While the Beriya affair seemed to provide a notable exception, it had sought to give an impression of liberalism at home and good manners and reasonableness abroad.

Malenkov in his very first speech had promised the people "peace and plenty" but up to the time I had gone back to the States the plenty was just on paper. And I had seen enough in the back country during my swing through Central Asia to know that nothing fundamental had changed in the provinces. The heavy hand of the police and the dead hand of the bureaucracy were still supreme.

First things first, I thought. Let's see how well the Government is doing with its policy of "plenty" and let's see if these "liberal" words are more than paper deep. I felt that the new Government's initial preoccupation, like that of a government anywhere, must be to assure itself of popular acceptance and support. It had made some "campaign" promises but, unless I was mistaken, the people were acting as if they came from Missouri. They wanted to see before they bought.

These were the thoughts which brought me to the Red Square because that was where it had all started and that was where any real change must first be disclosed. For the Red Square was Russia's real heart. It was not red of course. Nor was it square. Its name, Krasnaya Ploshad, really meant "Beautiful Place," and it had been given to it centuries before there had been any Communists or "Reds." The word "red" in Russian simply happened to mean "beautiful" as well, and so the Russians had long called this central market area beside the Kremlin the "Beautiful Place." And it was by no means square but rather a long, irregularly shaped oblong, bounded at the lower edge by the Moscow River and at the upper by the old State Historical Museum.

It had been in the Red Square on the morning after Stalin's death was announced that I had seen the first unusual phenomenon, a freely assembled crowd of Russian citizens. And it was no accident that the very first rumor to run through Moscow had been that the gates of the Kremlin would once more be unbarred and the public would be free to come and go as in the times of the Czar. Within a week of Stalin's death I had heard this report from my cook and from my chauffeur, but unlike most widely circulated Moscow rumors this one so far had not come true, although many rigid rules by which Stalin had turned the fairytale castles of the Kremlin into a symbol of sinister secrecy were being lifted.

I myself, as long ago as the previous June, had won permission to take my camera inside the Kremlin to take tourist's snapshots of such sights as the great Tsar Kolokol, the biggest bell ever founded (it crashed to earth and broke before it could peal a single chime), and the great Tsar Pushka, the biggest cannon ever founded (it had never fired a shot for fear the powder charge might burst it).

I took these pictures, so symbolic of Old Russia if not of New, and a good many others. There was nothing unusual about any of them except that never in the Stalin regime had anyone but special guests been given the great honor of snapping these penny-postcard scenes.

Certainly I had not been allowed to take pictures in the great

Kremlin Armory where the most precious of Russian treasures, a nation's ransom of diamonds and rubies and emeralds and sapphires and pearls and gold are kept. I imagined it would be a long time before any correspondent tried on the sable-trimmed cap of Monamach, the ancient symbol of Russian sovereignty, as Walter Duranty did in the twenties.

Still, picture taking marked some progress. What was more important was that recently the Kremlin had become a kind of combination Russian town hall and junior assembly rooms. At New Year's the most beautiful of the Kremlin halls, the Georgievsky, a dream of white marble, gold and crystal, had been opened up for a young folks' ball. And this was followed by *yelka* or Christmas-tree parties for younger children at which Dedya Moroz (Grandfather Frost), who bears a startling resemblance to Santa Claus, and that lovely lady, Sneguritchka, the Snow Maiden, handed out gifts and entertained the children with games and stories.

Now, a series of meetings which would run on for months was in progress. It seemed as though the new Government was going right down the list of every important social and economic group in the country and inviting them to come to the Kremlin for two- or three-day sessions of speeches and festivities. Sometimes longer. The railroad men had come. The river and steamboat workers. The collective farmers. The Communist youth. One group was hardly out of town before another arrived. It was pretty obvious what lay behind it all. The new Government was engaged in lining up political support, in trying to rally the various social and economic groups behind it. And one of the symbolic appeals it was using was the Kremlin. It was trying to show that this traditional heart of Muscovy belonged to all the people and not just to one fearsome old man.

The Red Square . . . As I walked out into it on this February afternoon when the sun shone with a yellow deceptiveness which soon was to disappear in a light flurry of snow it occurred to me that just a year previously I had strolled into the Red Square, then, as now, bent on observing the scene to see what I might learn by keeping my eyes and ears open.

What had it been like a year ago? It was the end of February, 1953. Stalin was still alive then, or so I supposed. Certainly the thought of his death had not crossed my mind at that time. The day, I remembered, had been unusual for Moscow in February. Clear, with a cold sun shining, and before I had finished my walk I was chilled through and through. It had been a Sunday and I had left the Metropole Hotel a little after noon, walking through Sverdlov Square, past the Lenin Museum and into the Red Square.

I remembered noticing that they had taken down the sign in English which had always hung beside the entrance of the Museum which said: "Lenin Museum, Open 11 A.M. to 8 P.M. Closed Mondays." And thinking that here was one more little evidence of the tightening of relations and strengthening of Russian chauvinism.

That day I had passed through the Red Square and noticed that there were several groups of sightseers and tourists being escorted to the Lenin Mausoleum and St. Basil's Cathedral with guides who spoke their spiel with the traditional, bored singsong of guides around the world.

I had walked out of the lower square through Stepan Razin Street, an old, old medieval lane which was once known as All Saints' Street. I had been interested to see whether in the clearing away of old buildings and the excavation of the foundations for the great forty-six-story skyscraper with which Stalin proposed to ornament the Zaradiya area of the lower square it had been necessary to disturb one of Moscow's most ancient and historic relics, the gloomy old house where the Romanovs lived in the sixteenth century before mounting the Russian throne. I found the house undisturbed and gloomy as ever behind its iron shutters. Years before it had been open as a museum—the "boyars' museum" it was called. But never since I had known Moscow had it been anything but closed and shuttered. I remembered that some youngsters were sliding down an icy path across the Romanovs' courtyard and that a line of washing, stiff and frozen, was attached to a corner of the house.

There wasn't much else about that walk which had stayed in my memory except the recollection that in an hour's stroll from the Red Square, through the Arbat Square and finally emerging at the Crimean Bridge near the Gorky Park of Rest and Culture no one had spoken to me nor had I the slightest impulse to speak to anyone. And this, in the time, was completely normal. I had walked along the street tight-lipped and probably looking rather grim and, if I could trust my impression, that was the way the people had looked also—silent, somber, each going about his business and the less he had to do with anyone else the better—and probably the safer—it was. For those were the days of the deepening terror that had followed the announcement of the Doctors' Plot and it was almost on the eve of the announcement of Stalin's death. Not a time for idle talk. Certainly not a time for street-corner talk with a foreigner like myself.

I remembered writing a little sketch of that stroll for the *Times* and my amazement when the editor cabled back and asked me to include some "typical conversations" with Russians I had met en route. By this time it had become so entirely and completely customary for me to walk the Moscow streets for days at a time without ever exchanging a single word with a passerby that it struck me as nothing less than extraordinary that my editor would even ask such a question.

But, on second thought, I could only realize that this was a measure of the enormous gap which the censorship had widened—between the reality of conditions in Moscow and the perception of them abroad.

I remembered one other detail—the sudden swish and vacuum in the air which had set the snow flying two stories high in narrow Arbat Street when a convoy of Government cars passed through as I walked there. There were four cars in the convoy, two escort cars ahead, the usual big bullet-proofed Zis limousine, and one escort car behind. They slashed through the street much too fast for me or anyone to see who was riding in the Zis and there was the usual frantic flagging down of all traffic and scurrying of pedestrians as the cavalcade passed.

The Arbat was the famous "Route"—the route which Stalin followed almost every day in going from the Kremlin to his house in the country out the Mozhaisk Chaussee. Everyone in Moscow knew that it was the best-policed half mile in Russia, and probably the world. There was a traffic officer every twenty yards or so down the center line of the narrow two-lane street and no one was permitted to live in the old apartments above the busy shops without a special stamp on his passport, given after a rigorous security check. It was said with only a little exaggeration that the reason so many shoppers had to walk in the street was that the sidewalks were so full of plainclothes men.

I had not thought of it before but I supposed that the cavalcade might well have been one of Stalin's last passages through the Arbat.

One of the very first things the new government had done after Stalin died was to withdraw these great police details from the Arbat. The first time I had driven down the street and seen no more militiamen than the usual traffic details at each corner I had hardly believed my eyes. And I knew that the Government could hardly have chosen a more dramatic way of telling the people of Moscow that this was a "new deal."

Much the same thing had happened in the Red Square. Long before I had left Russia on leave I had noted a fundamental change in the character of the square. Under Stalin strollers were few indeed. Casual strollers, I mean. Of course, sometimes, on hot summer nights when all of Moscow was baking, you found young people walking through the square, usually en route to the river embankment which provided quiet and secluded nooks for holding hands. And as long as the American Embassy was located on Mokhovaya Street, across from the Kremlin, some of our people made a habit of taking a daily stroll around the Kremlin for their exercise.

But the Red Square itself, except for organized groups of tourists, peasants in for the day from the Moscow oblast, groups of visiting Rumanian technicians, or students from China, was not a popular gathering place. People assembled in the square on formal occasions decreed by the government, such as the evenings of May 1 and November 7, when the parade guns of the Kremlin fired a skyrocket salute, and a fantastic transparency of Stalin, illuminated by airplane searchlights, was suspended over the square from a blimp.

Immediately after Stalin died the square regained its old character as a meeting place and strolling place for Muscovites. The militia who had strictly forbidden walking in the open square so long as Stalin was alive now paid no attention whatever, except to keep people out of the stream of motor traffic.

Now, further and even more significant changes had occurred. The great gray block of buildings which lined the side of the square opposite the Kremlin had been restored to its original purpose, which was trade. This block of buildings, known as the Upper Row, the Middle Row and the Lower Row, had been built in the 1890's as Europe's greatest shopping center. They formed a series of long arcades with glassed-over passages in the French style, decorated inside with fussy statuary and even a big indoor fountain. The buildings were erected on the site of old wooden trading rows which in turn occupied the area which from time immemorial had been that of the Moscow traders, the merchants, the caravan men from the East—the typical Russian bazaar.

The idea of trade in the Red Square apparently had gone counter to Stalin's notions of the proprieties. Or, perhaps, it simply made him nervous to look out from behind his walls and see so many people coming and going in the Red Square. In any event, more than twenty years ago the stores had been closed up and the space turned over to Government departments, offices, and even small artels, such as watchmakers and umbrella menders.

Now, as the first and most impressive earnest of the Government's promise of plenty the old trading rows had been cleaned out, refurbished, stocked with the greatest agglomeration of consumer goods which had been seen in Moscow since the Revolution and reopened under the aegis of Minister of Trade Anastas Mikoyan as the State Department Store, or GUM, as it was familiarly known in Moscow from its Russian initials.

This, indeed, had changed the character of the Red Square. On the day that I stood there, my camera in hand, there were thousands of people flowing in and out of the GUM buildings. I had been told that on an ordinary day from 150,000 to 200,000 people visited GUM, and judging from the throngs this seemed a reasonable estimate. It was also apparent that GUM was drawing customers not just from Moscow alone but from all over the country. There were hundreds of peasants with their frost-rosy faces, their gray and beige scarfs and shawls over their heads, their quilted cotton jackets and warm *valenki*. There were Orientals, the men with *tybitekas* on their heads and the women with long black pigtails. There were Caucasians in their fierce caps of sheepskin and their flaring brown sheep's-hide coats.

On the other side of the square around the famous Mausoleum, two or three mechanized snow loaders were at work, clearing away the remains of the snowfall of the night before. And here was further evidence of the "new look." For several hundred people, mostly men, boys and children, stood around the snow machines, watching and gaping, unhindered by the police.

I snapped a few pictures—another evidence of relaxation. This was a privilege which had previously been reserved to visiting delegates. But, while I had been absent from Moscow, a formal circular had been sent to the foreign embassies by the Ministry of Foreign Affairs, announcing that ordinary photographs of street scenes, historic and picturesque buildings and places, and, in general, anything which was not a military objective, such as a bridge, a harbor installation or, perhaps, a factory, were now permitted.

This was why, in Berlin, I had equipped myself with a better camera. I had never been a camera fan and until the previous year when I went to Soviet Asia had hardly ever taken a picture in Russia (with the exception of the Kremlin snapshots). In fact, I had made it a strict personal rule not to take pictures because I regarded it as entirely too dangerous. Regardless of the innocence of the photographer's intentions he was almost certainly bound to get into trouble with the police. I had taken pictures in Central Asia in defiance of my personal rule simply because I felt the opportunity was too great to let pass. And, of course, my experience there had shown that my premonition about police interference was only too well founded.

I had started my Asian trip with an ordinary Kodak but I ran out of film in Samarkand and not being able to buy more for my own camera I had purchased the cheapest kind of Russian machine, called a Lubitel or "Amateur." The Lubitel, a reflex lens camera made of plastic, something like a very cheap Rolleiflex, had given me surprisingly good results, probably because of its simplicity. However, I had a typical experience with it at the start. The very first day the little red glass film window fell out. The second day the film winder jammed (because the film fitted so badly that it bound the winder).

The third day I managed to get the winder working again, although it was half stripped. And the fourth day when I reached for the camera to show someone the troubles I'd had I knocked it on the floor and dented the focusing gear.

Despite all these difficulties, which typified to me the run-of-the-mill quality standards of Soviet consumer goods, the little Lubitel took very respectable pictures, and it was a good long time before I was able to achieve comparable results with the complicated Contax.

I had bought the Contax in East Berlin during the Foreign Ministers' conference when, by special permission of the East German authorities, conference personnel were allowed to make purchases in the East Berlin stores. I had been most fortunate to get the camera because at the prevailing exchange rate for East marks it was a fantastic bargain, costing only about $60, and I was eager to see if, under the new policy of "abundance," it was possible to buy a Contax camera in Moscow and what it cost.

Crossing the street I allowed myself to be carried by the flow of the crowd into the big GUM store. I was frankly astonished by the variety and wealth of consumer goods which was displayed. The prices were high and quality remained low but in quantity and selection the improvement was obvious. This was especially true in the textiles and dress-goods departments where despite prices which would have put an American housewife into a faint peasants and city women were buying hand over fist.

However, there were still many notable shortages. Only twenty to forty television sets per day were available at prices running up to 2,800 rubles ($700 at the official exchange rate) and it was obvious from the queues that there were three hundred to five hundred potential purchasers for each set—maybe a thousand, for such things are hard to judge. The Russians have a way of "organizing" their queues which makes it difficult to know how many people are really waiting to buy a given article if it is a big item, like a television set or an automobile for which they must wait many months. The purchaser gets in line on a given day and when he gets to the top of the line, which may take many hours, he registers his name in the queue. This gives him a right to a given place, but he must turn up at regular intervals and stand in line for several hours, or perhaps all day, in order to preserve his place. He may have to stand one day a month or one day a week—whatever is the rule of the given organized queue. Then, as he gradually works his way up toward the top of the line the matter becomes more urgent. Now he will go every day and stand all day in line, just in case something unexpected should happen. An unusual supply of television sets might arrive and he might not be there to pick up his order, in which case he would lose it as well as the months of time and trouble. Or other members of the queue may have dropped out in the months of waiting and he may be closer to the top of the list than it appears from the record. The last weeks on a big important queue are a tense and nervous time.

I hunted out the photographic department to see what the situation was there. I found they had no Contax cameras and no imported cameras of any make. The best camera on sale was one called the Kiev, which is a Russian version of the Leica. I have been told that the Russians simply moved a Leica factory bodily from Germany to Kiev after the war. In any event this camera is identical with the German apparatus, although some camera experts say the lenses are not up to the German standards. Others say it is just as good as the German camera and that the lenses still come from Germany. I don't know the truth of the matter. I do know that the camera was selling at prices of 2,750 to 3,100 rubles, depending on the lens you preferred, which works out at $687 to $775. At the official rate this is two or three times more than the price in Germany or the United States.

A month or so later there was the customary spring Soviet price cut. Every spring since 1947 the Russians have been cutting their retail prices and it is a measure of how high they were at the start (as well as the ridiculous four-to-one exchange rate) that only now are some of them beginning to come down to American levels, despite the fact that during the comparable period most U.S. prices have been rising.

One of the things on which prices were sharply cut this time was cameras. They were reduced well below the officially stated level. The Kiev came down to about 2,000 rubles and my little Lubitel, which cost me 163 rubles or more than $40 in Bukhara, dropped to

123 or about $30. Finally, in the summer of 1954 the East German Contax D made its appearance in the Moscow shops. It was priced at about 2,400 rubles—$600 at our exchange rate, or just ten times what I paid in Berlin. A dramatic but by no means unusual contrast.

The real purchasing value of the ruble is something which I prefer to let the economic experts argue about. But I do know a few things about it. I know, for instance, that the ruble's value varies drastically, depending on what you are buying, and that, in part at least, this stems from the Government's use of prices as a kind of rationing device. Thus, prices of some scarce articles are deliberately fixed high above the cost of manufacturing just to discourage buying. Other things are arbitrarily cheapened to push consumption. And one mechanism which the Government uses for this purpose is a sales or turnover tax which is built into the price of every commodity and which is one of the main sources of revenue.

For instance, the Zim automobile, which is comparable in some ways to a Pontiac or Buick, sells in Moscow for about 24,500 rubles or $6,000 at the going exchange rate. But recently the Ministry of Foreign Trade has been selling those same cars to foreigners for hard currency for export at about $2,450, which would seem to indicate an exchange rate of ten to one instead of the official four to one. I know of some other minor Soviet export items which have been offered at similar prices.

It is true that Soviet economy has been deflationary since 1947 and that prices have been materially lowered (after a currency revaluation which wiped out about 90 per cent of the savings of the city dwellers and 95 per cent of the very large peasant hoardings of cash). But at the same time wages have remained static and in many cases have actually decreased on a piecework basis. A very great deal of Russian industry is operated on a piecework, bonus-for-production-above-norm basis. It is not unlike the Bedeaux system which American labor unions have so bitterly and persistently fought. And with the pressure on Soviet factory directors to "make the planned profit" the temptation to sweat labor is irresistible. I was told once by a man named Victor who worked in a shoe factory that several times he managed to raise his wages to a very respectable level, say eighteen hundred to two thousand rubles a month, by producing above the norm for his job. But after a month or two of such production the factory supervisor came along, revalued his norm (always upward) and he found himself cut back to the eight or nine hundred he was making before. Or even lower if he was unable to maintain the high new production level.

Victor with his eight hundred rubles a month was earning about the average wage for the Moscow area, and in thinking about the prices which I have quoted it is best, I believe, to calculate them in terms of hours worked. Victor and the others like him received their eight hundred rubles for a forty-eight-hour week, a six-day eight-hour shift (which they often worked in the form of two twenty-four-hour shifts, a highly uneconomic and inefficient procedure but one which enables many workers to hold down two jobs, sleeping half the time on both of them). Thus, Victor earned a little more than four rubles an hour.

While Victor was subjected to constant sweating under the Stalin regime and while not much change has occurred under the new regime he has gotten one financial benefit in addition to the annual price cuts (which in the April immediately after Stalin died were very sharp). His payroll deduction for "voluntary" subscriptions to the state savings loans has been halved from 10 per cent of his wages to 5 per cent. Thus he has had what amounts to a straight across the board 5 per cent pay boost—his first and only since the war. Victor never regarded the bonds as savings. He regarded them as a contribution. The bonds, in theory, run fifteen years. They carry no interest but participate in drawings for lottery prizes in which a sum equal to 3 per cent interest on the whole loan is given away. One-third of the bonds are supposed to win prizes running up to 100,000 rubles, one-third are supposed to be cashed ahead of due date and one-third are cashable at the end of fifteen years. Unless he should happen to win a prize Victor never expected to see this money.

He was greatly interested in the lottery drawings and read the monthly table which the newspapers print of the winning bonds. It is very much like a monthly Irish sweepstakes and the Government even issues a second series of demand bonds which are almost solely for gambling purposes. Victor sometimes bought these, paying a premium of 3 to 5 per cent over their face. If his bond didn't win he could turn it in at face value the next day for a cash refund or, if he wished, hold it until the next quarterly drawing. The most Victor ever won was two hundred rubles, but he knew a man who had won ten thousand. Victor limited his gambling to bonds. He was full of scorn for the State Race Track with its parimutuels and said that only persons who had an "in" with the track ring which controlled the racing could win. I think he was right because one of the American correspondents used to go to the track. So long as he bet the tips his chauffeur got for him he won. But when he lost his chauffeur and tried to bet on his own he always lost.

I went back to GUM time and again until I finally left Moscow because it was such a good barometer of the consumer-goods drive. GUM always had the best and the most but, unevenly, more was flowing out to the provinces, too.

Certainly not the giant amber topazes which GUM's jewelry store offered, big as ducks' eggs, at 2,742 to 3,327 rubles (roughly $700 to $830), nor diamond brooches at 5,410 and lavalieres at 4,775, nor a rajah's sapphire at 45,000 ($11,250), nor ruby earrings at 38,000 ($9,500), nor emerald pendants at 33,000 ($8,250). Nor, even, Chinese brocades at 300 rubles a meter ($75 a yard) or men's good winter overcoats at 1,750 rubles ($437.50). And nowhere but Moscow could be found mink coats at 11,000 to 20,000 ($2,750 to $5,000).

I would not say that any of these items was selling like hot cakes although I saw in GUM many men buying overcoats at prices of more than $400 at our exchange rate and suits at $300 and $350.

And the price which GUM charged for Chinese brocades gave me a good clue to the kind of markups which Mr. Mikoyan was pinning on imported goods because I had seen the same silks in East Berlin, selling at the fancy Stalin Allee stores at prices that worked out at $3 and $4 a yard. This increased my already considerable respect for Mr. Mikoyan's business acumen, as did my calculations which showed that he was selling oranges which he bought from Israel at about two and a half cents apiece for prices ranging between 43 and 52 cents. And he was selling little medallions of gold, supposedly for use in dental fillings, at 90 rubles a gram or almost $700 an ounce.

Later he cut his price 10 per cent but I still thought that for a
Communist Party leader, theoretically most strongly opposed to any
form of capitalist profit-making enterprises, Mr. Mikoyan was not
doing so bad.

I jotted down the prices of half the goods in GUM. And this, too,
was new and another evidence of the lighter hand of the new
regime. Because in all the years I had been in Moscow the censorship had never allowed me to cable back a single price of anything
to New York. With one notable exception. Once I had been allowed
to cable the price of penicillin drugs, apparently because the censor
thought they were cheap enough to make good propaganda.

But one of the initial discoveries I made on returning to Moscow
was that the censorship on prices had suddenly been lifted. Moreover, I was allowed to make a number of comments on the quality
of goods and to compare the Russian products with those in the
United States. This provided another change because a fundamental
of the Soviet censor's rule book was to permit no comparisons of
conditions in Russia with conditions anywhere else (apparently on
the well-grounded conviction that nine out of ten such comparisons
would be invidious).

Now, at a stroke, that barrier was lifted and I had a field day. I
cabled back the prices of practically every item in the Moscow
stores. Then I went to the Central Market and priced the vegetables
(not much on sale at this time of the year) and fruits (only dried
ones available) and meats and dairy goods and sent so many prices
to New York that finally the novelty wore off and the *Times* got
tired of printing dispatches which at any other time in the past ten
years (or twenty years) would have been sensations.

I even explored the cosmetics field and wrote a story about some
of the scents whose names had long been my private joy, such as
"Jubilee of the Red Army," "Await Me," "Kreml," "Spirit of Red
Moscow" and "Fly Away." I looked in vain for another favorite,
"Svetlana's Breath," named for Stalin's daughter. I thought it had
been discontinued, but later on in the summer I spotted this brand
on sale in a Gorky Street shop. Apparently the ban had only been
temporary.

In the course of my explorations I tried to do a little shopping for my household. I needed an ironing board and expected to have no trouble in getting one as I had often seen them in the household-goods stores, selling for about 40 rubles—$10. Expensive for the U.S.A. but not too bad by Moscow standards. However, I could find no ironing boards in GUM. Later on my housekeeper looked, too. She found some made of steel and priced at 160 rubles but I was not going to pay $40 for an ironing board, Moscow or no Moscow. Mariya Ivanovna could go on ironing my shirts on the dining-room table. As weeks went by and no ironing boards appeared in the stores I grew puzzled about the mystery. But, finally, I managed to solve it. It was simply a by-product of the Government's new policy of "plenty." The supply of electric irons had been radically increased and the prices radically cut. Thousands of Moscow housewives for the first time were buying irons. Naturally, they needed ironing boards as well. But the plenty planners hadn't thought about that and the handful of ironing boards provided by ordinary co-operative artel production had quickly been exhausted and there was no plan for any more.

A little more foresight was invoked in the case of another planned shortage. This was the meat shortage. Moscow and all other Russian cities suffered a sharp meat shortage in the spring and summer of 1954. And it actually was planned that way. That is, the Government didn't want to run short on meat but it was willing to accept the shortage for the sake, it hoped, of better supplies in the future.

This arose because of a program to encourage the peasants to increase their own home-owned livestock by relieving them of certain taxes and making it more profitable for them to hold the livestock for fattening and breeding rather than rushing the animals to market. Inevitably, the program cut down on the supply of meat to the cities, beginning about April, 1954, and the effects were not expected to be overcome much before the end of the year. But, in this instance, Mikoyan warned consumers of what was to occur and tried, at least on paper, to increase the supply of substitutes, such as fish. He also went into the foreign market and bought fairly substantial supplies of meat in the Argentine, Denmark and elsewhere. I think the Russians were planning to buy a good deal of meat from Australia but they gave up the idea when they broke off diplomatic relations as a protest against the Petrov case.

I returned to the Red Square often during the spring and summer, sometimes to visit GUM, other times to take pictures. I quickly found that it was not only in the field of consumers' goods that discrepancies occurred between plan and practice. I found that it was one thing for the Ministry of Foreign Affairs to issue a circular on the subject of photography and it was another thing to take pictures on the Moscow streets.

In the Red Square there was one advantage. The militiamen regularly assigned to traffic and police duty there had been briefed on picture taking. They knew it was permitted and they never interfered. But that did not stop the busybodies. I don't believe I ever visited the square without at least one individual stepping up to me, usually politely but sometimes roughly and rudely, and telling me: "Comrade, it is not permitted to take pictures here." Or, "Comrade, do you have permission to take photographs? Permit me to see your *dokumenti*."

Sometimes it was civilians. Sometimes it was military men. Sometimes they went away when I said: "I have permission to take photos." Sometimes they stayed and argued. Sometimes they would call a militiaman, who would solemnly examine my documents, hand them back and say: "Please."

It was annoying but not so annoying as the trouble I encountered in other parts of Moscow or in other parts of the Soviet Union.

And here I think was an interesting phenomenon. I have no doubt that the Foreign Office was quite sincere in its desire to remove a restriction from the lives of foreigners and that this motivated its circulation of the circular on photography. But the prohibition against photographs was so ingrained in the people; the suspicion of the photographer was so strong; and the basic xenophobia so active that it was literally impossible to expect to take pictures in Russia unless you were prepared to have endless trouble with interfering civilians and officious police. American Embassy personnel and other diplomats often got into trouble and not a few angry protests were made.

In the ensuing months I lost all count of the number of times I was arrested or taken into custody. I even succeeded in getting arrested taking a picture of the street just half a block away from my apartment.

But I do not want to give the impression that all my photographic experiences were difficult. My camera led to many a talk with Russian camera lovers. One thing was very evident as the time of Stalin's death faded further into the distance and that was that the old fear of people about talking to strangers and to foreigners, at least on the street, was breaking down. Not to a great extent. And newcomers would still find Moscow street crowds rather more grim than those of Paris or even Berlin. But to one who had seen them in the February days before Stalin's death the change was obvious. Small but measurable.

One day while I was taking pictures in the Red Square a pleasant young man in a windbreaker came up to me.

"Pardon me," he said, "but I am a camera lover myself. Could you tell me what kind of a camera you have and what lens you are using?"

I showed him my Contax and we got into a very pleasant conversation that lasted fifteen minutes or so. He told me all about his camera and I told him about mine.

He thanked me profusely and then asked one more question. "Tell me," he said, "is it now permitted for Russians, also, to take pictures in Moscow?"

Yes, I said, I believed it was. At least I had seen many Russians taking pictures in the Red Square.

"Excuse me for having asked," he said. "I don't get very often into the center. Thank you again for your professional consultation."

Russians, also . . . The phrase still sticks in my mind because it is so important. It is one thing to remove stupid harassments from the lives of foreigners. But if Russians, too, are being given even these small freedoms, it is worth thinking about. Not a matter big enough for sweeping conclusions. But worth remembering.

XIV

The Rule of the Junta

ONE of the most astonishing things I have ever seen was the disappearance of Josef Stalin as a public figure in Russia. I don't mean the death of the old Generalissimo. That may or may not have been natural. I mean the way his name simply vanished from public sight. One moment it was there. The next time you looked at *Pravda* it was gone. Literally and completely.

This banishing of the name of Stalin occurred within two weeks of the coming to power of his successors. Beginning about March 23, 1953, Stalin's name, which I had often counted as many as 150 or 160 times on *Pravda's* front page began to disappear and by April 1 I was able to write a dispatch (which the censorship killed) saying that Stalin was no longer being quoted or mentioned in Soviet publications.

There were, of course, exceptions to that rule and it took a little time for word to get around. After all, the Soviet is a big place and the habit of speaking of the Stalin era, the Stalin Constitution, or the Great Construction Projects of the Stalin Era is hard to break.

But within a reasonable period the Russian editors all got in line. This was probably the first and most dramatic means by which the new group sought to disassociate themselves from the old regime. It did not seem that they placed a very high value on Stalin's name. Frankly, I thought they carried the disassociation considerably further than was called for by the psychology of the situation. In fact, it seemed to me that the vigor with which the new junta,

232

as the group came to be called, leaped to the task of eradicating Stalin's name could spring only from the strongest kind of personal feelings and the bitterest vindictiveness—the kind of feelings, in fact, which men would experience if they were dealing with their worst and most treacherous enemy.

Alongside this blotting out of the name of Stalin there was conducted a new glorification of Lenin, who had been allowed by Stalin to sink to a rather secondary position in the iconostasy. And it was repeatedly insisted that "collective leadership" and *colleagialnost* or "colleaguality" was the guiding principle of the Communist Party.

In the first week after Stalin's death, however, a few missteps or miscues occurred. On successive days *Pravda* published three varied pictures of Malenkov. One showed him addressing the Nineteenth Party Congress with Stalin apparently peering over his shoulder. I called this one "The wise old leader and the brilliant young disciple." The next showed Malenkov on the podium of the Red Square tribunal with a little girl presenting him with a bouquet of flowers— "the kindhearted statesman shows his love of children." And the third pictured Malenkov and the Chinese Communist leader, Mao Tse-tung—"solidarity of leadership, Russia and China, now and forever."

The Mao picture was the most curious of the sequence, for it instantly struck a familiar chord in my memory. And when I thumbed back through *Pravda* I saw why. The last time the picture had been published it had been a group photo, showing Stalin, Mao, Molotov, Chou En-lai, Malenkov and several others.

The picture had been cut in two and refitted together to eliminate all but Malenkov and Mao. It demonstrated that the Russians also can crop photographs.

I don't know whether this picture caused a row within the junta or not but something must have happened because no more appeared. And from that day to this the Soviet press has published no individual photographs of any of the top leaders except for Khrushchev's picture on his sixtieth birthday and a picture of Marshal Zhukov which *Red Star* printed during a Supreme Soviet meeting. Both of these were in a slightly different category.

Instead of building up Malenkov in the Stalin manner the Communist Party propaganda machine was turned loose on the popularization of the idea of committee rule. I thought it particularly significant that this line was continued unchanged after the Beriya affair because I had suspected that with Beriya out of the way the pendulum might swing back to personalities.

Apparently it was not thought practical or, perhaps, proper to take down the hundreds of thousands of statues and pictures of the Generalissimo which dotted the Russian landscape like the smallpox. Perhaps it was realized that the plaster images will crumble away before too long, and perhaps it was beyond the means of the Committee on Art to supply replacement paintings necessary to cover so huge a wall space in so short a time.

But it was obviously felt that Stalin should be cut down in size so far as the printed page was concerned. So by the middle of 1953 theoretical works and treatises had shifted over to Lenin rather than Stalin as their principal source of quotation. And *Pravda* even advanced the heterodoxical thought that it was possible to write articles without citing a quotation from the founding fathers in each paragraph.

I saw these tendencies before I left Russia for leave in October, 1953, but I could not decide how permanent they might prove because I felt the whole situation might still be a good deal more fluid than it appeared. After all, Beriya had, then, not yet been executed and Khrushchev only recently had emerged as the principal secretary of the Communist Party.

My feeling in the winter of 1953–54 was very much one of wait and see. I felt that the junta still lacked stability and that it was quite possible that Beriya's ouster was not the last of the changes which we might see before the situation steadied down.

However, almost the first thing I was told on arriving back in Russia when I checked with those persons in whose judgment I had the most trust was that "collectivity" and "group leadership" were still very much the phrases of the moment and that, so far as could be judged from Moscow, all members of the junta were seriously and deliberately seeking to make the committee system work.

Another factor which had led me to reserve judgment on the

stability of the junta was my own complete lack of any kind of first-hand or even secondhand impressions as to the personalities of these men.

I had seen Malenkov and Khrushchev only from a distance when they appeared at meetings of the Supreme Soviet in the Great Kremlin Palace. I had heard Malenkov speak twice and was favorably impressed by two things—his pleasant oratorical delivery and the purity of his Russian diction. He was by no means as lumpy and pasty as he appeared in his pictures. But I knew little more of him than this. I had heard some gossip about Khrushchev because he had been the Party boss of the Ukraine during the UNRRA days and our people had had a few dealings with him. But I hadn't heard enough about him to detach his personality from that of the run-of-the-mill Communist Party chief.

Molotov, of course, I had known for many, many years. I had seen him both close up and far away. I had studied him at press conferences, at receptions for the diplomatic corps and in debate at the United Nations. I had even had personal business dealings with him back in 1944 and had been the object of a very stiff lecture indeed on the subject of the vagaries of the American press. I thought I knew Molotov pretty well and I had no doubt that he was a much happier and much freer man now that Stalin was dead. But while I was confident that Molotov was running Russia's foreign affairs, under a delegation of broad authority from his colleagues, it was obviously Malenkov and Khrushchev who counted most in the general direction of the country.

Soon, however, the top leaders started a series of public appearances and I had a chance to see them at close hand and collect information about them from diplomats who talked with them. Even before this I heard that Malenkov had moved out of the Kremlin into an old Moscow merchant's palace on Pomerentzov Street, only a few blocks from Spaso House where the American Ambassador had long resided. And I heard, too, that Khrushchev had moved in next door.

So it came as no surprise when I learned, late in the summer, that Khrushchev had told the British that the Government was planning to give up the Kremlin as its principal offices and open up the grim old fortress just as had been rumored since Stalin's death. None of the Government people lived there any more and it would not be difficult to transfer the remaining offices with the possible exception of that of the Presidium of the Supreme Soviet, whose functions, after all, are almost entirely ceremonial.

When I heard the report about Malenkov's new house I went around to Pomerentzov Street to see for myself. I found it a quiet little *pereulok*, or lane, running between Metrostroi and Kropotkin streets in a quarter of the city which used to be known as the "Old Stables," about seven or eight minutes' drive from the Kremlin in an area next door to the Arbat quarter.

The site is only about a hundred yards distant from the modernistic Finnish Legation and the adjoining Chinese Embassy. The upper windows of the Finnish Legation overlook the Premier's courtyard. The block of houses which he occupies runs from No. 2 to No. 6 Pomerentzov and extends through the block to Yeropkinsky Street. In front of the site some ugly old barns and sheds have been torn down and replaced with a small park. About two hundred feet of frontage is occupied, in all, including at least two good-sized houses, which supports the idea that Khrushchev and Malenkov live side by side. One house is a four-story mansion in late nineteenth-century pseudo-Russian style. The other is set back from the street and has been surrounded by a massive fifteen-foot wall, topped with a light steel-and-wire barricade, with two heavy steel doors which may well be armor plate.

I found that I could not see the house in which the Premier probably lives from the street. All I could see, front or rear, were the tops of ornamental frosted street lamps which illuminate the grounds. The back is also protected by a fifteen-foot wall into which a single steel door has been set.

Big, full-grown poplar and lime trees were transplanted into the grounds. The Finns reported that the restoration work went on day and night under floodlights. The Premier apparently moved in about January 1, 1954.

New traffic rules were put into effect, barring bicycles from Kropotkin and Metrostroi streets, prohibiting passing and left turns, and I saw inconspicuous little police posts at both ends of Pomerentzov Street. However, and this was obviously no accident, there are no police details outside the Premier's house. All I saw were two plainclothes men idling across the street.

The unostentatiousness of the residence and arrangements was in calculated contrast to Stalin's police pomp and ceremony. The houses were typical homes of wealthy merchants of the nineteenth century, differing very little from dozens of others. The whole quarter at the end of the eighteenth century and the beginning of the nineteenth was perhaps the most aristocratic in Moscow. There were on Kropotkin Street, then known as Prechistensky Street, forty-nine Palaces in the 1850's, eleven of them belonging to princes, counts and generals. And, by 1914, there were fifty-one, only two of them belonging to princes and some sixteen to middle gentry and thirteen to merchants.

Malenkov is using as his summer house the beautiful old Morozov estate at Barvika, thirty-six kilometers out of Moscow on the same Mozhaisk highway as was Stalin's and in the immediate vicinity of many other datchas of Government people. This is the estate which was occupied by the famous Russian writer, Maxim Gorky, when he returned to Russia from abroad, and which, with some changes of locale, is described in Gouzenko's book *The Fall of a Titan* as being the estate of the writer, "Gorin."

Malenkov, Khrushchev and Molotov all have villas also on the Black Sea in the resort of Matzesta, just south of Sochi not far from where Stalin used to vacation, and one of the "collective" acts of the new junta is to take a "collective" vacation for a month toward the latter part of August and early September in the south.

The first sustained public appearance in the company of foreigners which Russia's new rulers gave occurred on the occasion of the visit of the Attlee delegation of British Labour Party members in August, 1954. There had been a number of previous contacts but nothing so long and so intimate.

It was this occasion which demonstrated so clearly to me that the man who gives the signal nowadays in Moscow that the party is over is Georgi Malenkov, regardless of the fact that Nikita Khrushchev usually lingers behind for one last word.

On the night when the Soviet Premier and the Party Secretary went to the British Embassy to a dinner in honor of Attlee it was nearly 1:30 A.M. before Malenkov finally rose and moved toward the door.

Molotov and Mikoyan got up, too, and began to make their farewells. But Khrushchev, deep in discussion with Aneurin Bevan, went on talking.

"*Znachit* . . . that means . . ." said the compact little Party Secretary, repeating the word *znatchit*, as is his habit, two or three times in every sentence, "*znatchit* . . ."

By now Malenkov was standing at the door. He smiled a little tiredly as he watched Khrushchev jabbing a pudgy finger in Bevan's chest to drive home his points. "*Po'yekali*," Malenkov said, quietly. "Let's go."

Bidding his hosts a courteous good-by, Malenkov went down the stairs. Mikoyan had already left and Molotov followed closely. A moment later, still talking, Khrushchev hurried after them.

Down below huddled under the portico of the old sugar king's mansion which serves as the British Embassy I and several other correspondents were waiting. We stood at arm's length as Malenkov, Mikoyan and Molotov came out the door, nodded to us and got in the car. By the time Khrushchev got down his colleagues had taken their places in the waiting Zis with its three-eighths-inch bullet-proof windows and heavy bomb-proof steel body. Mikoyan and Malenkov were sitting in the rear and Molotov on the jump. Khrushchev hesitated a moment and I thought he was, like a good politician, going to shake hands with all of us. But he didn't. He pulled down the second jump seat, a security colonel popped into the front beside the driver, and the new Soviet junta, complete in one car, pulled off down the Sofiskaya Embankment across the Moskva River from the Great Kremlin Palace.

I thought that scene typified pretty well the way the junta acts in public in Moscow and the kind of impression it seeks to give. The junta, as I use the term, really means Malenkov, Khrushchev and Molotov as a first-string trio, strongly supported by the Zhukov group of the Army. I regard Bulganin, Kaganovich and Mikoyan as the second string but I feel sure they deliberate in common. Their manners among themselves are free and easy. And there seems to be an absence of signs of strain or concern about primacy. For instance, when Malenkov, Khrushchev and Molotov went south in August, 1954, leaving Bulganin as the top man in Moscow he jokingly remarked when a toast was offered at a diplomatic party to the "Soviet Government": "That is a toast I can drink. At this time I am the Soviet Government." Not the kind of remark anyone but Stalin would have made while Stalin was alive.

Regardless of the powers they still exercise, particularly in such MVD areas as Siberia and Central Asia, the secret police with the elimination of Beriya seems no longer to have any direct voice in Government policy. Sergei Kruglov, the new MVD chief, is a man who is known to some Americans from the time when he headed Molotov's bodyguard in San Francisco during the United Nations conference. He and Serov, the security chief, seem to be old-line police officers whose chief duties for many years were in the so-called "industrial" section of the MVD. They were not involved in political affairs, which is probably the reason they survived Beriya's downfall when so many of their companions did not. One American who saw a good bit of Kruglov calls him "a typical flatfoot."

It may be only a coincidence but it was not until after speculation concerning rivalry between Malenkov and Khrushchev had become quite widespread in the West that the junta began to show itself more intimately to foreigners in Moscow.

Watching the spreading activities of Khrushchev, particularly in the sphere of agriculture, some Western specialists wondered whether the Party chief might be making a bid to supplant Malenkov. This kind of speculation was accentuated after a meeting of the Supreme Soviet at which Malenkov and Khrushchev made parallel speeches, covering almost identical ground, both in foreign and domestic policy, and saying much the same things. The only real difference between the speeches was that Malenkov's language was considerably more restrained in dealing with East-West relations than Khrushchev's. Since Khrushchev had no technical reason, as Secretary of the Party, to be making a policy declaration before the body which Malenkov was addressing by right of his office as "Chairman of the Council of Ministers" there was some reason for lifting of eyebrows.

But the twin speeches might equally well have been interpreted as evidence of the unity of Party and Government, as an effort to show that the two men were in complete harmony.

Spurred, perhaps, by wishful thinking and a hope that personal rivalries might be disrupting the junta a good many "experts" in the United States and in Europe increased their speculation regarding a possible Malenkov-Khrushchev rift. I doubted this as did other men in Moscow whose judgment I felt was reliable and conservative.

However, it was a photograph in *Pravda* which really brought this ill-guided speculation to a climax. This photograph was published the morning after the big May Day parade and it showed the government leaders standing on the podium of the Mausoleum. There was nothing notable about the picture beyond the fact that Khrushchev was standing a bit forward of his colleagues and was shown with his hat off, acknowledging the plaudits of the crowd. Malenkov, beside him, stood seemingly diffident and dwarfed by Khrushchev's sweeping gesture.

In view of the great importance which has always been given by the Russians to this kind of picture I suppose it was not surprising that this was seized upon as evidence, as symbolic evidence, that Khrushchev was now No. 1. And the fact that papers, such as *Izvestiya*, the Government organ, and *Red Star*, the Army paper, used other photos in which Khrushchev had no special prominence did not seem to make any impression on the backers of the Khrushchev theory.

Somehow, I could feel nothing but skepticism for this idea because it just didn't seem to fit the "feel" of things in Moscow. About a month later *Pravda* published another photograph of the Government leaders, again on the Red Square platform, this time for a celebration of the three-hundredth anniversary of the uniting of the Ukraine to Russia. It was a holiday to which Khrushchev with his long and intimate Ukrainian associations had devoted special time and attention, if he had not originated the whole idea as one in a series of steps designed to improve relations between the two Slav cousin peoples.

The photograph which *Pravda* published on this occasion showed both Malenkov and Khrushchev waving their hats to the multitude.

This time the men were standing toe-to-toe but Malenkov's hat, plainly, was two inches higher than Khrushchev's. In a somewhat sarcastic mood I reported this fact in my dispatch to *The New York Times*. It seemed to me that if Khrushchev's hat waving on May Day was significant, this picture was even more significant. It showed, didn't it, that Malenkov had now put himself out in front by a two-inch margin? And at Khrushchev's own party.

Needless to say none of the energetic commentators of May Day thought fit to speculate about the second picture.

The fact is that the more the junta has come in contact with Westerners the stronger has grown the impression among those who have met them that the most significant fact about the group is how well it works together (now that Beriya has been done away with) rather than any question of rivalry. Of course, events may prove these impressions mistaken but, so far, every foreigner who has met both Malenkov and Khrushchev or has seen them both together will give you odds that Malenkov is top dog and that, in any showdown, he would take Khrushchev.

I have not spoken to either man but I have watched them together for several hours at a time and my impression is that Malenkov is the leader of the Government group and that all of them, including Khrushchev, regard him as their leading member. Of course, temperamentally, Malenkov and Khrushchev are dissimilar. One experienced Western diplomat who spent a good many hours in the company of each of them put it like this: "Both of them are shrewd, able men but there is this difference. When Khrushchev starts a sentence he doesn't know how it is going to end and he doesn't care too much. But Malenkov never starts a sentence without knowing exactly how it is going to come out."

The Premier is eight years younger than the Party Secretary, and in the company of a small group he has a grace and charm which belie the impression given by his photographs of a fat, gross man. A Western diplomat once told me some years ago that no matter who succeeded Stalin it never could be Malenkov because his physical appearance would repel the artistic sensibilities of the Russian people. Without regard to the artistic sensibilities which in the Russian masses cannot be said to be very high, this judgment was founded on complete ignorance of Malenkov's personal manner. He has a winning smile and just a touch of Little Lord Fauntleroy about him which startles Westerners.

Malenkov, for instance, captivated Dr. Edith Summerskill, a rather prim English Labourite, first, by picking her a bouquet of lovely posies from his own garden, second, by the warmth of the feminist sentiments which he expressed and, third, by the fact that when he proposed an old-fashioned toast, "To the Ladies!" he rose and walked to one end of the table to clink glasses with the wife of the British Ambassador, Lady Hayter, and then to the other to clink glasses with her.

At a reception in the Polish Embassy Malenkov interrupted the drinking of toasts while he saw, personally, to a waiter bringing a chair for the eighty-two-year-old Dr. Olga Lepeshinskaya, whose soda-bath technique was supposed to keep Stalin eternally youthful. And when Malenkov and his colleagues paid a surprise backstage visit to the Comédie-Française during its appearance at the Maly Theater in the spring of 1954 it was the Premier who was the hit among the somewhat more sophisticated ladies of the Paris theater and who quickly put them at their ease by assuring them that they needn't worry at being surrounded by Communists because, after all, Communist was just an old French word.

"Malenkov has a very attractive personality," one Englishman who has seen a good bit of the Premier told me. "In fact he worries me rather more than the rest because he is so pleasant."

The impression which Malenkov makes on people inevitably reminds me somewhat of the impression which the late Hermann Goering used to make on visitors to Hitler's Germany. Goering was quite a different sort of man—that is obvious. But he, too, while not photogenic, had a way of ingratiating himself.

One reason why Malenkov makes such a good impression is that he does not push himself forward in conversation. But when the discussion begins to get tense or sharp he is the one who cuts in with a little joke or a deft change of subject which clears the air.

During a meeting with the English Labourites Khrushchev started to hammer away on the subject of British support for the entry of Communist China into the United Nations. Although it was obvious that the Labour Party people resented what Khrushchev was saying he plodded ahead, unheedingly, repeating himself and insisting on his points. Just as the discussion was about to get heated Malenkov intervened with a joke about Mikoyan's grandchildren and everyone relaxed.

Neither Malenkov nor Khrushchev knows English. Malenkov knows a little French, Khrushchev a little German. But Malenkov's Russian is perfect and his pronunciation and literary style are what the Russians call "cultured." This has strengthened my belief that he comes from a family of middle-class origin and that he learned to speak and use good language at his home in Orenburg before the Revolution. This impression of middle-class, rather than worker or peasant origin, is borne out by his official biography, which is as severe and restrained as Stalin's was florid and ornate. It merely says that he comes from an "employee family." This certainly means he was not of proletarian origin and, in all probability, his father was a Czarist civil servant. I have been unable to obtain any further reliable information as to Malenkov's early years.

The Soviet Premier has good table manners and so do his associates. He eats in the European rather than the American style, wielding his knife with the right hand and the fork with the left and not transferring the fork from hand to hand as we do.

His clothes are well tailored of excellent material and his light summer suits of tropical worsted stood up well under Moscow's record heat of 1954. For many years during the life of Stalin Malenkov wore the old-fashioned Party tunic, a loose Russian-style blouse of khaki or worsted, olive drab in color, and belted with a wide leather belt. With this blouse he wore military breeches and the usual Russian pull-on high boots. Presumably, as do other Russians who affect this type of boot, he wrapped his feet in strips of cotton fabric rather than wearing socks.

Malenkov continued to wear his old Party tunic for nearly a year after Stalin died. He was the only member of the present Government group who still affected this old-fashioned dress and I had always thought he had adopted it as kind of a trademark, like Al Smith's brown derby or Herbert Hoover's stiff collars.

But in the spring of 1954 Malenkov gave up the old Party tunic in favor of the plain sack suit. He also put away his old Russian-style cap with the stiff visor and crown in favor of a light dove-colored fedora.

I suppose I could draw some profound deductions from Malenkov's change of garb but I confess I can't think of any unless, perhaps, he wanted to show to the public that it was "time for a change." Something like Peter the Great did when he came back from abroad and, with his own hands, scissored off the beards of the boyars.

Malenkov and Khrushchev are of identical height, about five feet, four inches. The first time I saw the whole junta walk into a room, one man behind the other, my eyes bugged out in astonishment. They are so close to being the same height that you could run a yardstick over their heads, each of them a rather short, rather chunky man, broad of beam, broad in the shoulders. One thing it made plain: Stalin was a short man himself and he refused to allow any tall men to be around him. A little support for the theory I tentatively evolved in Georgia so long ago that Stalin's smallness was a major factor in the drive that took him to the top in Russia.

Malenkov has been married for many years but not to a sister of Khrushchev as has sometimes been reported in the West. His wife, a pleasant, plain woman of about his age, has not as yet appeared with the Premier at any public social event, although she was shown on the Soviet newsreel last spring at election time, accompanying her husband to the Soviet polling booth. The Malenkovs have two children, a boy and a girl.

While none of the wives of the Chief Government members have, as yet, accompanied them to big formal social functions, with the exception of Mme. Molotov, most of them were shown with their husbands in the Election Day newsreel.

How different from Stalin's haremlike policy of concealment and suspicion! Never after the death of his second wife, Nadezhda Alliluyeva, who probably committed suicide in the early thirties in a mood of despair brought on by Stalin's purge of his old comrades, did the dictator show himself in public with any member of his family.

In fact he developed such a mania for secrecy that to the end of his days no foreigner was able to ascertain for certain whether Stalin had, as was rumored, taken as his third wife Rosa Kaganovich, sister of the Politburo member.

He erected a monument of simplicity and dignity out of white marble to Mme. Alliluyeva in a corner of the Novo Devichye cemetery and cut a special gate in the wall so that he could visit the spot. Police guarded the grave night and day to keep spectators away and a big floodlight was installed. Countless times, late at night, Stalin left his Kremlin quarters and, swiftly gliding through the silent streets in his big Zis limousine, made a pilgrimage to his wife's tomb.

I often thought that in this one case, at least, Stalin suffered from a guilty conscience and perhaps it was this guilt which caused him to persecute so mercilessly anyone who, in one way or other, seemed to violate the veil of secrecy which he cast about his family.

Stalin had three children, a son Jacob by his first wife, who was captured early in the war by the Germans and died on the barbed wire of a Nazi camp in Czechoslovakia during an escape attempt; Vassily, an unpleasant, hard-drinking young man who rose to the rank of lieutenant general of aviation before vanishing in some curious manner about six months before his father's death; and Svetlana, from all reports her father's favorite and apparently a not unattractive young woman.

Contact with any members of the Stalin family almost invariably proved unfortunate. Air Marshal Alexander A. Novikov, leader of the Soviet Air Force during World War II, was a victim of one of the numerous intrigues that revolved around Vassily during his aviation career. Novikov was disgraced and spent nearly eight years in one of the far northern political prisoners' camps near the coal-mining center of Vorkuta before the new regime released him and restored him to rank.

Meantime, what has happened to Vassily himself is a mystery. He vanished from Moscow after leading the Air Show in August, 1952, and has not been seen or heard from since. The censorship, mistakenly, passed a report which I sent saying that he had turned up for his father's funeral. However, examination of photographs of the funeral cortege conclusively shows that the young man I mistook for Vassily is merely one of the Red Army stalwarts whose shoulders relieved Malenkov, Molotov, Beriya & Co. of the real weight of the coffin.

Svetlana is probably still living quietly in Moscow. She was married in her last year at Moscow University to a young scientist but I was told that she had been divorced and was living alone with two young children. I believe Stalin had five grandchildren in all, two by Svetlana, one by Jacob and two by Vassily.

At least one of the persons who got into trouble by associating with Svetlana has also recently been released from prison camp by the new regime. He is a film scenarist named A. Kapler whose sin was to become acquainted with Svetlana when she and Vassily were evacuated to Kuibyshev in the autumn of 1941 at the time when Moscow's capture was threatened.

Kapler and Svetlana, Vassily and a couple of young actresses ran around together in Kuibyshev for several months. Apparently Papa Stalin was too busy fighting the Germans to notice what was happening to his offspring. But eventually his spies told him. Svetlana was removed to Moscow and sent back to school. Vassily was packed off to the Air Force. Kapler was sent to a concentration camp and the actresses to remote provincial theaters.

Now Kapler has been given his old job back at the studio where he was working in 1941. It will be interesting to see what effect twelve years at "corrective labor" have had on his creative talents.

The new regime has given no special publicity to cases like those of Novikov and Kapler. But it has seen to it that their names have been mentioned in the papers so that the citizens of Moscow know which way the wind is blowing.

For here again the new regime wants to stress the point that it has broken with the old Stalin regime.

So far as personalities go it is very difficult to imagine a contrast more sharp and more complete than the secretive, suspicious and sly Secretary of the Communist Party who was Stalin and the Secretary of the Communist Party who is Khrushchev.

It should be remembered that for many, many years—in fact until just before the outbreak of World War II—the only post which Stalin formally occupied was that of Secretary of the Communist Party, and that, basically, is Khrushchev's position. For while he was named a member of the Presidium of the Supreme Soviet he is not, formally, a member of the Council of Ministers which, on paper, is the body which runs Russia. He is the Party Secretary and that is all.

It also should not be forgotten that Malenkov held the secretaryship at the time he was made Chairman of the Council of Ministers. He resigned the job and it went unfilled until after Beriya was dealt with. Then Khrushchev was named to it. This sequence of events should be kept in mind in considering who is senior to whom in the Soviet hierarchy.

In contrast to Malenkov's suavity Khrushchev presents himself as a diamond in the rough. He is the bluff, open, frank one-time miner who blurts out the things which Malenkov is too tactful to mention. Khrushchev is the kind of man who would (and did) tell the British Labourites that all they represented was the working class of one small country, England, while his Party, the Communists, represented not only the workers of Russia but of all countries. And he it was whom I heard tell the British Ambassador, Sir William Hayter, that if England wanted to take a tip from him she would model her relations with Moscow upon those which exist between Russia and China because Russo-Chinese relations are the best in the world.

Malenkov proposes few toasts and drinks most of them in white wine. Khrushchev proposes many and drinks them in vodka. He likes to indulge in the old Russian custom of drinking *do adna* or bottoms-up, and the more he drinks the more he talks. At one diplomatic reception in the summer of 1954 I watched Khrushchev while he talked on and on to Hayter. The British Ambassador smiled thinly, standing first on one foot and then the other. But Khrushchev's words flowed on. Finally Malenkov left and Khrushchev was still talking. At this point Kaganovich, who over the years had come to drink more and more at such public occasions, took Khrushchev by the elbow and gently and firmly, if somewhat unsteadily, steered him along in Malenkov's wake.

Khrushchev's language is rough and ready, often marked by verbs that don't agree with subjects, full of dangling clauses and uncompleted ideas. He is a buttonhole talker. He likes to put his hands on the man he is talking with, not infrequently grasping a lapel with one hand and gesticulating with forefinger jabs to the chest with the other. He looks his listener straight in the face with eyes so wide open and baby blue that one diplomat frankly said he had to look away because "in another moment he would have had me believing he was just as honest and open-hearted as he looked."

After seeing the members of the junta in public on several occasions I agreed with the impression of others that they often interrupted, corrected and contradicted each other. Mikoyan and Kaganovich within my hearing repeatedly broke into Khrushchev's statements to challenge or deny something he had said. I could see no evidence of fear or restraint on their part.

It should not be thought that Khrushchev is dull-witted or stupid. He simply has an ebullient personality and he expresses himself in a free and easy Ukrainian manner. On the other hand it is plain to see that he is a man who is forceful, energetic and dynamic. He is obviously capable of wielding power and used to it. He has come up the hard way on the Soviet political ladder from his start as a coal miner and each time he takes a step up he plants his feet firmly and he is not lightly to be pushed off.

In this company Molotov is the most quiet, most reserved and dignified. As always he looks rather like a retired headmaster of an English boys' school, and while he has thawed considerably he will never be the life of any party. In this circle Kaganovich and Mikoyan move freely and familiarly. Curiously, both Malenkov and Khrushchev were in their time political protégés of Kaganovich, but he does not impress me as the *éminence gris* of the regime. Instead, it seems to me he drinks too much.

Junior members of the junta like Saburov and Pervukhin sit quietly and say little. Watching them I thought of the ancient admonition: "Children are to be seen, not heard." They sit with straight backs and alert ears, watching their elders. Saburov is the only member of the leading group who speaks English. He spent some time in the United States in the thirties, studying engineering.

I have noticed that at big public events Marshal Georgi Zhukov almost always is present, sometimes at the head table and sometimes not. But he is never far away and his public conduct permits some inferences to be drawn.

Sometimes Zhukov sits with the junta and expresses his opinions forcefully and bluntly, as on the occasion of the November 7th reception in 1953. At other times I have watched him spending the evening in the room adjoining that in which the guest of honor is being entertained.

On the night Molotov gave a party for Chou En-lai I happened to be in the room next to the innermost room myself. Marshal Zhukov was there, too, and between peeking at the honored guests I kept an eye on the famous marshal. He chatted quietly most of the evening with the Navy chief, Admiral Kuznetzov. I saw him munching new Crimean apples. After he had eaten four he switched to green cucumbers and ate two large ones.

Occasionally he glanced into the room where the junta was entertaining Chou, as though to satisfy himself that all was in good order. Then he returned to his conversation and his cucumbers. He gave me the impression of a man who is confident that his affairs are in good hands and going well.

And, so far as I could find out in Moscow, he has every reason for such confidence. He doesn't have to be a member of the junta himself so long as he knows that his opinions will receive the consideration they merit.

XV

Cold Minds and Warm Hearts

IN THE late winter and spring of 1954, that is in the first weeks of my return to Moscow after leave in America, it was almost impossible to escape the impression that a fundamental change had occurred in the Party line toward the arts, the humanities, science and even possibly toward human beings.

I was not exactly certain of the nature of this change since I had seen no ideological directives pointing in the direction of greater freedom of expression up to the time I had departed in the previous October.

And it was not until I had the extraordinary good fortune a month or so later to spend an afternoon discussing and arguing questions of art and culture, politics and party lines, with the composer Dmitri Shostakovich that I was given a clue to what had produced the creative revival I found in progress.

It is virtually impossible to spend any length of time with Shostakovich without being convinced of his sincerity and earnestness. You may disagree with him strongly—as I did. You may regard him as naïve—as I did. You may believe him to be mistaken—as I did. But you are in no doubt about one thing. He is completely honest and completely sincere and his mistakes come from the heart and not from the mind.

The central question which Shostakovich and I were discussing was that of the role of the artist in Communist society as opposed to the role of the artist in capitalist society. And, inevitably, the

250

discussion carried us right to the key question, that of freedom . . . freedom of the artist . . . freedom to create.

I expected Shostakovich to defend the role of the Soviet artist and he did so. Naturally, I challenged his contention that the Soviet artist was more free to create than the Western artist. I said that we of the West felt that there could not be freedom for an artist in a society like the Soviet where the role and objective of the artist was defined by a single source, the Communist Party, which laid down a "line" which the artist must follow. To us, I said, this was the same as having all artists working for a single boss.

Our conversation was taking place in a gloomy room—the secretary's office of the Composers' Union. I do not remember ever seeing so many overstuffed black and brown leather chairs crowded together in a single office. There were heavy velour drapes of some dark mahogany shade at the windows and as we talked Shostakovich took one Kazbek cigarette after another out of a cardboard box, toying with each for five or ten minutes, then lighting it and smoking it in four or five strong puffs. But if the setting was gloomy the talk was lively.

The essence of Shostakovich's reply to me was familiar. He said the Party held the interest of the artist foremost and was inspired by wholly unselfish motives. It only wanted the best possible creative work and, having no personal considerations, was able to achieve this.

Then, Shostakovich, who is blond, trim and fit and looks you directly in the eyes from behind fairly strong spectacles, made a point which surprised me. He said the Party not only was engaged in inspiring differences of opinion. It was demanding a conflict of opinion. He said that the common idea in the West that the Party insisted on rigidity of doctrine was quite wrong.

In support of his statement Shostakovich referred me to an article which *Pravda* had published the previous November at a time when I was in New York.

"It has to do with the theater," Shostakovich said, tamping out his cigarette. "But the same thing goes for music. You must read it."

Read it I promptly did and I found there the key to what was going on in Moscow. The article was cast in the form of a review

of a new and original production of an old Ostrovsky play called
Thunderstorm which had been presented by a director named
Okhlopkov at the Moscow Drama Theater, making considerable use
of symbolism and other theatrical devices alien to the Russian stage
in recent years.

What *Pravda* had to say certainly bore out Shotakovich's statement. It said that "the more bold the search for the solution of
artistic problems then the sharper the arguments, the discussions,
the disagreements and the more alive the struggle of opinion and the
greater its value."

Pravda went on to denounce mediocrity and stereotypy.

One of the most terrible things in art [it said] is the leveler who
adjusts even the best to a single standard. Such an approach irons
out individuality, impedes the development of creative personality
and deprives art of the joy of new discoveries.

The theater has a right to experiment, to express its views. But
not to experiment just for the sake of experiment. Art cannot suffer
stagnation. It demands inspiration—cold minds but warm hearts.

Then it will live.

Here was an expression of artistic and critical doctrine with which
I myself could find little to disagree. Perhaps I would not have included the stricture against experimentation for the sake of experiment. But for the rest almost anyone in the West would subscribe
to *Pravda's* words.

The only thing I would have said in rebuttal to Shostakovich was
what I had known already before I read *Pravda*—that *Pravda* had
not always spoken in such terms and might not speak that way in
the future and that if the freedom of the artist to experiment depended upon the word of the Party then true freedom did not exist.

For, if today *Pravda* demands a "struggle of opinions" tomorrow
it may call for "unanimity of opinion" and the writer who was
"struggling" only yesterday may find himself read out of the Party.

It was unfortunate that my conversation with Shostakovich did
not occur two or three weeks later because events quickly provided
a cogent footnote to this very point.

However, before this turn of events came about something like a
creative renaissance had already gotten under way in Russia and

may, to some extent, still be proceeding. Eloquent testimony, it seemed to me, of the enormous creative resources which existed in Russia and which had been so suppressed in the last years of the Stalin regime. Only a tiny amount of encouragement was needed to set the catalytic forces in motion.

Shostakovich, himself, had completed in late 1953 and early 1954 his Tenth Symphony, certainly one of his best works and quite probably the best since his Fifth and Sixth. The symphony aroused ideological as well as musical interest in Russia because one group of critics contended that Shostakovich had created a "pessimistic" tragedy rather than the ideologically correct "optimistic" tragedy. In an "optimistic" tragedy man's sacrifice is shown not to have been in vain. The critics of Shostakovich contended that his symphony was the tragedy of a "deeply lonely individual" who goes down to defeat against the forces of evil, unaided by his comrades and terrified by the mighty powers arrayed against him.

While Shostakovich vigorously denied this charge it seemed to me that, in fact, the composer, possibly subconsciously, had set to music the fundamental tragedy of Russian life in the epoch in which he lived—the defeat of the little lonely man by the overwhelming forces of evil.

Regardless of whether I was correct in my reading of the significance of the Shostakovich symphony one thing was certain. The composer for the first time in some years had been able to produce a great piece of music instead of winding up with a self-tortured collection of notes which only revealed the intensity of the conflict between his own native talent and his sincere effort to write music which would be in conformity with Stalin's provincial tastes.

And what was true of Shostakovich was true of a variety of creative talents. The Bolshoi Theater ballet company had been struggling for nearly four years with the problem of presenting Sergei Prokofiev's final ballet, "The Stone Flower." It was plain as the nose on your face what the trouble had been. The company was simply frightened. They knew that if Stalin didn't like the production they probably would all lose their jobs. Some of them would wind up in provincial theaters. Some, perhaps, cutting wood.

Now, with Stalin dead, the "technical problems" which had so long perplexed these theatrical geniuses were quickly solved and the ballet was staged with Galina Ulanova in the leading role. The music was sheer delight, the staging was that of wizards, Ulanova danced like a dream and I found it the finest contemporary ballet I had ever seen. My opinion, I might say, was not shared by some of the more sophisticated balletomanes of the Moscow diplomatic colony nor by some of the Soviet ballet experts. But *Pravda* liked the show. It was one of the rare occasions when *Pravda* and I agreed.

I saw the same tendencies at work in literature, the drama and the movies.

For years I had been cynically amused at the conduct of Russia's greatest writer, Mikhail Sholokhov, the author of *And Quiet Flows the Don* and *Virgin Soil Upturned*. Here was the only real novelist of talent whom the Revolution might be said to have produced. And he had not published a work since the mid-thirties. He lived on a farm down in his beloved Don country, drank vodka with the peasants and came to Moscow as rarely as possible. Once, I had covered a big "peace" meeting at the Hall of Columns. One morning Sholokhov was supposed to be present and make a speech. But when the chairman called his name there was no answer. A snicker ran through the hall. The chairman called the name again. No Sholokhov. That evening the writer showed up and made a five-minute speech. You only had to look at him to know why he hadn't been able to arrive at the morning meeting. His eyes were bloodshot and his face was flushed. It was obvious that he had spent a night on the town.

Sholokhov from time to time was reported to be working on a great new novel. It was said to be about the war years. Each year I read some report about this great project. But it never seemed to get any closer to completion. And the reason for this was well known, too. Stalin had liked *And Quiet Flowed the Don* and *Virgin Soil Upturned*, but in addition to being a literary genius Sholokhov was a canny peasant. He knew how great a gamble it was to write a new novel. Stalin might or might not like it. And surely it was impossible to expect to improve on the standing he already enjoyed in the Kremlin. In anything new there was an element of risk. So Sholokhov

puttered and puttered and put off from one year to the next the
dangerous task of trying to satisfy the literary opinion of the cranky
old man of the Kremlin.

But, now that Stalin was dead, it seemed that Sholokhov had
gone back to work. Excerpts from his forthcoming novel began to
be published in the magazine *Ogonek* and it was quite apparent
that Sholokhov's robust talents had not suffered irreparable harm
in the long years of virtual idleness.

In the theater many interesting things were happening. In April
there occurred an event which excited Moscow's intelligentsia more
than anything in many, many years. This was the visit paid to Russia
by France's Comédie-Française. The French company spent about
three weeks in Moscow and Leningrad and no one in Moscow could
remember such a sensation in the theater.

People offered 200 or 300 rubles for tickets ($50 to $75). Little
shopgirls quit their jobs to wait in line for days, literally, in the
vain hope that they might be able to buy one of the handful of
tickets which were not distributed to the favored few, largely
through theatrical organizations. The plays were televised and taxi
drivers who didn't know a word of French would park their machines
outside a friend's home in order to watch a scene or two of Molière's
Tartufe.

The whole thing took on a kind of hysterical atmosphere. Not
within the memory of the present generation of Muscovites had a
foreign company from the West played in Moscow and it was
obvious that the Muscovites were reading more than a theatrical
significance into the event. It was equally obvious that no one need
wonder any longer whether the Russians were eager for a breath
of air from beyond the iron curtain. You only had to see the bright-
eyed audiences, the thousands of citizens who lined up every day
outside the Maly Theater, just to watch the French actors come and
go, to realize how exciting even a whiff of fresh air is to people
so long confined to a cultural dungeon.

It was exciting, too, to go to the Maly Theater on those evenings.
It was exciting because the Russian audiences were acting just like
children who had been told repeatedly that Santa Claus does not

exist and then, in a moment of profound despair, have gone to a party and found Santa, hale and hearty and even more wonderful than they had ever visualized him in their imagination.

I only hope, I said to myself one night coming out into the cool Moscow evening air and walking past the softly lighted white columns of the Bolshoi Theater and up through the narrow alleys leading toward Art Theater Lane and the Central Telegraph Office, I only hope they don't wake up in the cold early morning and find out it was all just a dream.

Probably the talk was just stimulated by all the excitement of the visit of the Comédie-Française. Or maybe it had more substance to it. But in the next few weeks I heard one rumor after another. The La Scala Opera Company was coming from Milan for perform-ances at the Bolshoi Theater. A Shakespearean company was coming from Stratford-on-Avon to perform at the Moscow Art Theater during the summer. The Sadler's Wells Ballet Company was coming for a series of outdoor spectacles later on.

I don't know whether the authorities were considering such attractions or not. Perhaps they may have been a little frightened by the enormous enthusiasm which greeted the Comédie-Française. Stalin and his suspicions might be dead but no Russian government had ever felt too comfortable at the sight of Russian citizens show-ing great enthusiasm for anything non-Russian.

Perhaps the discourteous treatment meted out to the Bolshoi ballet company when it went to Paris to repay the visit of the Comédie-Française may have had something to do with it. Because, aside from a few second-rate English concert artists, no more im-portant foreign attractions came to Moscow. Not in 1954 at least.

But I could see no great dampening of Russian spirits. I went to a concert given by Leonid Utuesov, the famous leader of the All Union State Variety Orchestra. Utuesov was a true curiosity. A genuine survival of the past.

Utuesov was an Odessa Jew and for many, many years had been a leading ornament of the Russian variety or vaudeville stage— which is called in Russia the *estradny* theater. He was a talented musician, a great mimic, a singer of personality if limited technical ability, a great stage performer. When I saw him I invariably was reminded of Eddie Cantor, George Jessel and Al Jolson. He was that kind of man with that kind of appeal.

Before the war Utuesov had organized and led the best jazz band in Russia. There was no ban on jazz in those days and his orchestra was officially called the All Union State Jazz Band. But one unhappy day the band was invited to the Kremlin on a New Year's Eve and gave a concert for Stalin. Stalin didn't like the band. He didn't like jazz. He didn't like Utuesov.

Perhaps if the war hadn't come along Utuesov would not have survived at all. Perhaps he might have wound up his days leading a four-man string band in some provincial hotel in Khabarovsk or Magadan. But the war did come along and diverted Stalin from such minor matters as jazz. So Utuesov and his band survived. True, they had to change their name to the All Union State Variety Orchestra. And they had to change their style of playing a good deal. And they had to pretend that they never had played jazz. Jazz was a dirty word and at almost every concert Utuesov had to make a little speech or a series of snide remarks, denouncing jazz and denouncing people who slandered him and his orchestra by saying they played jazz.

Somehow, however, Utuesov survived. After all, he was from Odessa and the people of Odessa are smart. They know a good deal about problems of survival.

I liked Utuesov and had gone regularly to listen to him play all during my stay in Moscow. Often it was rather pathetic but I enjoyed the way he would manage to play a rattling good jazz tune, in the guise of denouncing America and the horrible "music of the fat men"—which was the party tag for jazz, a phrase borrowed from Maxim Gorky.

Sometimes, Utuesov managed to get over five or ten minutes of good Dixieland jazz in this fashion. Of course, his audience knew what he was doing and applauded repeatedly for encores. For the undeniable fact was that Russian audiences liked jazz. I never will forget a concert which Paul Robeson gave in the great Tchaikovsky Concert Hall in 1949, at the height (or depth) of the ideological drive against jazz and Western music.

Robeson's program consisted of a potpourri of songs from various

Communist countries—a Russian number, a Rumanian number, a Polish number, etc. He sang each one and each was politely applauded by the jammed hall. Then came the intermission and a storm of applause that went on and on. Suddenly, above the sound of the applause I heard shouts from the upper gallery. At first it was impossible to determine what the spectators were calling for. Then they took it up as a chant. It was: "St. Louis Blues . . . St. Louis Blues . . . St. Louis Blues."

Over and over again they called. Robeson tried to ignore it. Obviously he had planned his program to meet the current ideological demands of the Party. Finally he had to raise his hand and stop the shouting. He apologized and said his accompanist had not rehearsed "St. Louis Blues" but that he would try and sing it on a later concert. Reluctantly the audience quieted down. Needless to say Robeson never sang the song at any other concert.

Utuesov, however, was a man of different character from Robeson. One way or another he had tried to keep his beloved jazz alive all through the worst times. And they really were bad. I never was able to find out for certain whether Utuesov was among the Jews who were arrested in the grim days of the Doctors' Plot. But Moscow rumor said that he was. He may very well have been seized at that time. And, perhaps, like Mme. Molotov he was among those who were sent east. If so he was among the first to return to Moscow. Mme. Molotov was back in the capital within a month or six weeks after Stalin died. And Utuesov was too.

Not only was Utuesov back but the long years of persecution had not broken his spirit. I knew from an article which he had written for the magazine *Soviet Music* that he had already begun a public campaign for the recognition of jazz as an acceptable Soviet art form. The only concession he was willing to make to the old Party propaganda was that it would be "Soviet" jazz, as distinguished in some hair-splitting manner from that bad old bogeyman, "American jazz."

And it did my heart good to listen to Utuesov at his concert. He certainly wasn't singing any better. And I really didn't notice any great improvement in the quality of his music, although he was obviously trying to get back in the old Dixieland groove. But what was good to see was his spirit. He had bounced back like a rubber ball and half of his wisecracks were nasty remarks about his old enemies on the Committee on Arts who had tried for so long to get him to stop playing jazz. He even had a crack or two about "informers."

An indestructible man and a real performer—Utuesov.

In the legitimate Russian theater the same heady yeast was at work. In addition to its experimental production of *Thunderstorm* the Moscow Drama Theater staged another unusual production, a dramatic presentation of an old Persian love tale, written by the Turkish poet, Nazim Hikmet, which was unique in that it was little more than pure romantic poetry with only a whisper of ideology dragged in at the finish.

I thought the production, actually, was a little clumsy, as though it was done by a group of actors who had been laying bricks for so many years that when they began to handle the gossamer fabric of a Persian love legend their calluses got in the way. But as a step away from so-called "Soviet realism" I was all for it.

And what seemed even more encouraging was the gossip that the director of the Moscow Drama Theater, the same experiment-minded Okhlopkov whose ideas had won *Pravda's* approval, had been named by the new Minister of Culture, Alexandrov, to run the famous Committee on Arts. This committee was the apparatus by which the Party directed the cultural life of the country. To put an experimenter like Okhlopkov in such a position was a break with precedent, indeed, and made me think a bit more about Alexandrov himself.

Alexandrov was not an ordinary Party bureaucrat and in the forties had been the victim of a particularly slashing attack which was directed against his work, *History of Western European Philosophy*. Alexandrov was accused of being soft on capitalism, of propagandizing Western European philosophy under the guise of describing it, a familiar old Communist bogey line.

Rightly or wrongly, Alexandrov had lost some of his Party jobs but not, as I had personal reason to know, his courage. Because when I had first come to Moscow I had noticed an advertisement announcing that he was giving a series of public lectures. I attended several of his talks and I found his head neither bloody nor bowed. He spoke with vigor and confidence and when members of the audience asked him heckling questions about his book he snapped back at them as though he had every reason for believing in his own complete vindication and the annihilation of his enemies.

Okhlopkov and Alexandrov . . . an interesting combination, I thought.

There were other signs of regeneration in the badly stultified Moscow theater. The Vakhtangov Theater, an offshoot of the famous Art Theater, had already presented one lively, if rather pedestrian, satire on contemporary Soviet life, a work by Mikhail-kov, called *Raki* or *The Crabs*. It was a frank adaptation of Gogol's *Inspector General* to modern times and good for laughs. I found it amusing enough to go several times in order, by repetition, to understand all the wisecracks, and it was a hit with the general public.

However, I was really more excited by word that at long last Chekhov's *Chaika*, the famous *Seagull*, on which the Art Theater practically had been founded, was at long last returning to the repertoire of a Moscow theater, the Vakhtangov, in fact. It had seemed to me something of a scandal that this Chekhov classic was no longer given by the Art Theater and had, in fact, seldom been on the Art Theater repertoire since its original presentation at the turn of the century.

I felt sure that even though this was the fiftieth anniversary of Chekhov's death the Vakhtangov a year earlier would not have been able to spare the energy between productions of new dramas of "Soviet life" and new dramas of the "People's Democracies," stories about the Korean War, etc., to devote any attention to a restaging of this most difficult of Chekhov dramas.

And when I attended the premiere of *Chaika* I was sure I was right. For here was no mere revival. Here was a performance of beautiful sensitivity with a glorious young actress named Galina Pashkova giving life to the role of Nina which I doubted that it had ever had before, even in the original production of Stanislavsky. There were fourteen curtain calls for Galina Pashkova at the finish and I would have gladly given her fourteen more.

Even the Soviet film industry revived. The old dictator insisted on seeing every picture before it was released and his edicts were stern and terrible. He broke Eisenstein, Russia's real film genius, with his carping criticisms of the great director's effort to transfer to the screen the new Bolshevik line on Ivan the Terrible. Excuse me. Ivan "the dread." Or, better yet, in the new Party terminology, simply "Ivan."

The only safe kind of film to make was one which was a long panegyric of Stalin, his wisdom and genius. Something like *The Fall of Berlin* or *Stalingrad Battle*, Parts I and II. That ground was fairly safe, although even here a director had to be careful because the old man's concept of himself and his role in these great events changed from time to time.

But this was ruinous to film production. The industry was half paralyzed. It took two years to bring out a picture which easily could be filmed in two months. And the public stayed away in droves. Only occasionally when a semi-musical like *Kuban Cossack* was sneaked through the projection room did the thousands of film houses in Russia have anything that would draw. And each of those houses had a "profit plan" to fulfill. It drove the managers crazy. They were so frantic for pictures that three times negotiations were opened up with Hollywood to buy American pictures, no matter what the state of the cold war. But each time Stalin himself had killed the deal.

So they bought "proletarian" Italian pictures. "Arty" French pictures. An occasional solid British film. And the incredibly mediocre film output of Poland, of Czechoslovakia and China. They reran and reran old Soviet films until the prints were in tatters. Anything to keep the screen busy.

But only one thing drew the public. The Red Army had captured a library of one or two hundred old American pictures in Berlin. Each year a few of these oldies, Hollywood products of the thirties, were fed out to the Soviet houses with the original English sound tracks and Russian subtitles. They were announced only as "new foreign pictures." But the public learned that this meant "old American picture." The titles were often changed but these pictures the public patronized. The sensation of Moscow in the summer of 1954, for instance, was Greta Garbo, in *Camille*.

Of all the American pictures the one which was the record hit—
and this, of course, is a criterion of the Russian need for "escape"
media—was Johnny Weismuller in *Tarzan*. In the Red Army's captured film bag there were four old Weismuller *Tarzans*. They were
fed out, one at a time, into the Soviet houses over a two-year period.
People lined up for blocks to get in. Youngsters saw them again and
again. Children often sat through a whole day's showing in a movie
house. Nine and ten performances per picture was a common score.
And everyone from baby to babushka was delighted and charmed
by Tarzan. Many a taxi driver and even schoolchildren asked me
whether Tarzan really lived.

So great was the Tarzan fad that teen-age boys took to wearing
"Tarzan haircuts"—a horrible kind of long bob. And I have walked
up Gorky Street on early summer evenings when the boys and girls
were promenading and heard boys shouting to girls: "Eh . . .
Zhane . . ." Because Jane was Tarzan's girl friend in the movies.

The Tarzan fad became so widespread that the Party got
alarmed and started a propaganda campaign against it, particularly
against Tarzan haircuts and Tarzan war cries, which were said to
be so piercing that they disturbed the cattle on collective farms and
kept cows from giving milk.

In this situation the appearance of a film like *Anna on His Neck*
was a sensation because here was the first genuine hit which the
Russian film industry had produced in the nearly six years I had
spent in Moscow.

Here, again, an assist to Chekhov must be credited, for the film was
based on one of his short stories. It was a beautiful picture, I thought,
and what made it popular was worth thinking about. Here was a
story without a suspicion of ideology or politics. It was a story about
pre-revolutionary Russia. It was filled with the symbols of pre-
revolutionary times. There was a beautiful Orthodox Church wedding. There were troikas racing through the snowy streets of St.
Petersburg. There were borzoi dogs with their lean aristocratic
Romanov faces. There were court balls, officers, dancing. There
were gypsy parties and singing. It was a picture that transported
you straight out of 1954 and back to 1880.

It delighted not only my heart but the heart of all Moscow. For the first time since Tarzan queues of two and three blocks turned up around the twenty Moscow houses where *Anna on His Neck* was being shown.

I thought to myself that if I were a member of the new junta I would take a good long look at those queues and indulge in a little serious thought.

I've told enough to set the mood of Moscow as I found it in the early months of 1954. And there were other straws in the same wind. A famous Russian satirist, Mikhail Zoshchenko, who had been denounced by Andrei Zhdanov in the literary purge of 1946, came back into the limelight. He had not been heard of since being read out of the Writers Union and blacklisted by the Central Committee of the Party. But one day I picked up the allegedly satirical journal, *Krokodil*, and found Zoshchenko denouncing current Soviet literature as scandalously mediocre. He also took a crack at the "oleaginous tone" in which the reviews of favored authors were written and said, sarcastically, that "to write a novel is not the same thing as sewing a pair of pants."

If I had picked up *Pravda* one day and found an article by Tito criticizing Stalin's economic theories I would have been little more surprised than to see Zoshchenko emerge as a literary critic.

In almost the same vein was the publication by one of the magazines of a series of lovely, lyric, nonpolitical poems by Boris Pasternak, who had been condemned to the same critical Siberia as Zoshchenko in the same edict of the Party in 1946.

Times, indeed, seemed to have changed.

For the next thing I read was a series of denunciations of two of the nastiest of the crew of Stalinist ink slingers, a pair of Party red hots named Anatoly Surov and Nikolai Virta. Surov wrote the play, *The Mad Haberdasher*, which even the censors apparently were ashamed of. Virta wrote a couple of almost equally slanderous works, called *The Conspiracy of the Doomed* and *In a Certain Country*.

Surov was accused of being a drunkard and Virta was said to be living the life of a petty nobleman on an estate in his native Tambov province. His wife was described as dressing in English riding habit and riding through the cabbage patches where peasant women were at work.

I had heard gossip about both these unsavory characters. Many of Surov's plays were said, actually, to have been written by one of the Jewish critics who lost his job during the anti-cosmopolitanism drive of 1949 in which Surov took a leading part. A series of scandalous stories were told about Virta and his wife.

The upshot was that Surov and Virta were expelled from the Union of Soviet Writers. Good riddance, I thought, and I was surprised when I came back to the United States to find some people who thought they were martyrs. Their martyrdom was fashioned of the same Party fabric as Beriya's.

On top of this came the fall from grace of the most perfect creature of the Communist ideology, the incarnation of its most dogmatic and least dynamic phase, Trofim D. Lysenko.

If there is anyone in America who is still ignorant of the true nature of the real Communist threat to freedom and to liberty I recommend that he read one of the most incriminating pieces of self-evidence which I have ever seen. I mean the published *Proceedings of the Discussion in the All Union Agricultural Academy Named for Lenin,* carried out under Lysenko's leadership in August, 1948.

This was the famous Soviet discussion on genetics at which Lysenko provoked his opponents to state their objections to the theory he had compounded on the basis of the empirical teachings of the Russian Burbank, Ivan Mitchurin.

Once Lysenko had succeeded in getting most of the better-known Russian geneticists, botanists and biologists publicly committed against him he quietly rose at the end of one of the sessions to say he had a brief announcement. He was authorized to say, he declared, that his views had received the full support of the Central Committee of the Communist Party and, he was authorized to add, "of Comrade Stalin, personally."

It was one of the most sinister proceedings of state since the time of Torquemada. Lysenko needed no iron or forge to break his victims' bones. He did it with a few words read from a slip of paper, as casually as if he were announcing that after the morning session all those interested would be permitted to visit the experimental laboratory where he was grafting yellow tomatoes onto red tomato plants.

Now, this sinister man whose baneful influence had spread like a disease from one Soviet science to another, from biology into medicine, from medicine into mathematics, into chemistry, into physics, into astronomy, was suddenly toppled from the pedestal where Stalin installed him and a whole series of little Lysenkos came crashing down as well.

It only took a few words from Party Secretary Khrushchev, an editorial or two in *Pravda*, and the metamorphosis was accomplished. It was just as easy as that. Of course, that was where the whole trouble lay. The power of life and death, or good or evil, lay concentrated in the Party and in *Pravda*.

And, as I had thought after reading *Pravda*'s call for critical discussions and freedom of opinion, this cannot be real freedom so long as it is founded upon *Pravda*'s dictate.

For now came the evidence from *Pravda*'s own pages to prove how right I was. After four or five months of this atmosphere of increasing liberty and creative inspiration the brakes suddenly were slammed on—hard. I picked up *Pravda* one morning to read a vitriolic denuciation of an obscure Leningrad critic named Pomerentzev who, under the obvious inspiration of *Pravda*'s own words had had had the temerity to publish an essay in the magazine *Znamya*, praising the virtues of "sincerity" in writing. Pomerentzev also had the effrontery to attack several of the best-established of the Soviet hack writers, men who had fed at the Kremlin trough for fifteen or twenty years.

But this was only a beginning. *Pravda* went on to denounce Zoshchenko and Pasternak and the editors who had permitted such views to be circulated. No more of this said *Pravda*.

And, as *Pravda* said, so it would be. The Union of Soviet Writers met and denounced the new "liberal" tendency. Several editors who had published offending articles were fired and first-rank sycophants like Konstantin Simonov were put in their place. It looked, on the surface at least, as though there had been a complete return to the hard line of the Stalin era.

But after I had watched developments a bit longer I became aware that it was not quite so simple as that. Here we had, I thought, an excellent example of thesis and antithesis at work. First, there was the hard Stalin line (thesis). Then, the new November line of *Pravda* (antithesis). Now, an effort was under way at synthesis, or a mixture of the two.

In theory that was how these conflicts were supposed to be resolved. But whether it would come out that way in practice I could not be sure.

There seemed to be some indication that the Lysenko case was designed as a kind of "pilot" project in this direction. For, somewhat to his own surprise, Lysenko was not shorn of all his government perquisites. He was simply denounced for bad theory and faking evidence. But he was allowed to go on functioning as a kind of glorified county agent, doing just what he had done before he was made Dictator of Science by Stalin. He was permitted to continue to lecture to Russian farmers on practical problems, such as the relative virtues of horse manure and chemical fertilizer. There was no one, it appeared, in Russia who had a more intimate knowledge of this subject than Lysenko.

In other words, it seemed to me that the Government was trying to demonstrate that it was possible to have an argument and disagree without one side or the other being sent to Siberia. Whether I was right or not in this reading of the Government line I could not yet be certain. And, of course, I well knew that the attitude of the Government toward the artist had by no means, in the past, been the controlling factor in the production of great works of art. Russia had been persecuting her best sons for a good many scores of years. The Czar undoubtedly acquiesced, if nothing more, in Pushkin's death by duel. The Czar personally censored Lermontov. The Czar personally sentenced Dostoievsky to death—and then reprieved him on the execution scene. Some of Tolstoy's works had fallen afoul of the Czar's disapproval and even Chekhov and Turgenev had their troubles with the regime.

I remembered how the time finally came when Chekhov to satisfy a deep instinct of his duty to himself and the society in which he lived felt that he must make the long pilgrimage to Sakhalin to investigate at first hand how the Czar's prisoners were being kept in that most remote of all the places of exile in his time.

And, despite his tuberculosis, despite his many writing projects and his comfortable life, Chekhov had started out on the long, long journey east.

It seemed to me that it was time, too, for me to make a journey east. Time that I had a look at Siberia. I had read enough, I had heard enough, I had talked enough about Siberia. But I had not been to Siberia. And by now it was perfectly plain to me that the real answer to the question of whether the new government had genuine intentions of liberalizing its rule of Russia could be found only in Siberia.

For it was one thing to give a little encouragement to the well-fed and well-cared-for intelligentsia of Moscow. It was fine to speak of "cold minds and warm hearts" and it was good to see *Chaika* and listen to Shostakovich's Tenth Symphony.

But, as I well knew, Moscow was not Russia. The great literary flowering of the late nineteenth century in Russia occurred in the same years as the horrible prison-camp conditions exposed by George Kennan's uncle after his famous trip across Siberia.

It was time, I decided, to go to Siberia myself. Perhaps there I might better learn whether in all truth the Soviet Government actually was carrying out a policy of "cold minds and warm hearts."

XVI

The Nether World

So FAR as I can recall, the sense of fear which I had so
often felt in Moscow before the death of Stalin and particularly in
the final weeks of his life came to an end with the Generalissimo's
death.

I do not know whether fear disappeared to the same extent from
the life of Russians. Probably not. But with the exception of occasional incidents with the MVD, such as I encountered on my trip to
Central Asia, my life in Russia in the first year after Stalin had been
marked by an absence of terror.

And, as I prepared to leave Moscow at the end of May, 1954,
on a very long journey which was to take me from one end of Siberia
to another, all the way to the Maritime Provinces and the approaches
to the Pacific and far into the sub-Arctic I was easy in my mind.

Not that I looked forward to this expedition. I well knew that I
was going to penetrate some of the most desolate and backward
regions in the whole of the U.S.S.R. I was going to visit a number
of points where neither Americans nor any other foreigners had
been for many years. I was prepared for difficulties and hardships
but there was nothing in the easy atmosphere of Moscow to suggest
that the trip might involve any kind of danger.

My plane left Moscow at twenty-five minutes after midnight on
June 1. It was a warm, star-lighted night in that season of the year
when darkness lasts only two or three hours in the latitude of
Moscow. By the time we touched down at the sleepy old city of

Kazan on the Volga where once the Tartars reigned, it was only twenty minutes of three but it was fully daylight.

The plane was a DC-3, the work horse of the Soviet airways. Russia received several thousand DC-3's from us during the war and she built many thousand of her own under license from the Douglas people. It was comfortable and clean with regular seats, no seat belts, fussy embroidered Ukrainian curtains at the windows and a mass-produced Soviet "Oriental" carpet on the floor.

The stewardess was a determined young woman. She obviously had been briefed to see that the "comrades" had rest and relaxation and she was determined to obey her superiors. She passed out books and old magazines and when she caught me idly looking out the window she said severely: "Comrade! Why are you not reading? Rest! Relax! Please!" It was an order.

It was typical of the internal airways, however, that neither I nor any passenger had the slightest idea when we left Moscow at what time we would arrive at our destination, which was Yakutsk. This was one of the three weekly planes from Moscow to Yakutsk but not even the crew seemed to know when we might arrive.

I, actually, had only a meager idea of where Yakutsk was. I knew it was up close to the Arctic Circle, that it had been visited in wartime by both Wendell Willkie and Henry Wallace, since it was on the great-circle route to Alaska, that it was a site of one of Russia's most notorious prison camps and that it was located on the famous Lena River.

Nor did I learn much more from my seat mate, a big bosomy Russian woman who had clambered aboard the plane, laden with more packages than a suburban housewife at Christmastime. She was, it seemed, a mining engineer, as was her husband. They had worked all over Russia and for the past three or four years had been stationed in Yakutsk while carrying out various surveying and exploratory operations in the countryside.

It quickly developed that this woman liked Yakutsk and she liked the north country. Her feeling was genuine enough, if unique. She was the only person I was to meet who I think actually liked the *taiga*. But she didn't like the country as a place for her small son to live, and after I saw it I understood why. Her son, seven years old, was living with his grandmother in Minsk and she was returning to her husband after a visit to the boy and a vacation in Moscow. Her parcels provided a commentary on the kind of consumers' goods available in Yakutsk. She had a huge bag of oranges—the kind Mr. Mikoyan was selling at two and a half rubles this season. She set the bag on the floor and the oranges kept rolling all over the airplane. But the amused passengers returned them to her. She also had a big cream cake. I guess it weighed about six or eight pounds anyway, and I knew the shop in the Stoleshnikov where she had bought it. It must have cost at least 100 rubles, or $25. And she had three bottles of Staleshny (Capitol) brand vodka, the very best Moscow kind. No doubt there was going to be a celebration when she got to Yakutsk. No doubt, also, I thought, there must be a few shortages in Yakutsk.

I was right. After nearly forty hours of travel (including a ten-hour layover in Novosibirsk) we arrived in Yakutsk. The plane had hardly touched down and we had not yet gotten off when a terrific wind, dust and rain storm struck. It literally blotted out the landscape. This was a *purga*, the dread storm of the Arctic. The sun disappeared, the buildings vanished, everything went black.

The storm lasted not more than half an hour but when it was over the whole city was drenched in mud. It did not seem like a pleasant omen, and when I got to the primitive Yakutsk hotel I was sure that it was not, for I discovered that a most unpleasant thing had occurred.

Someone had jimmied open the Yale lock of my bag and searched it with ruthless thoroughness. The linen lining had been slit, presumably to make certain that I was carrying no subversive leaflets. And a good many rolls of fresh unused film had been taken out and exposed.

While I presumed that my possessions had been searched many times by the agents of the MVD this was the first time it had ever been done in so crude a manner. In forcing the lock they sprang it and, unable to close the bag, simply left it open. In other words they didn't care whether I knew they had gone through the suitcase or not.

This did not frighten me so much as it angered me. I wrote out a notice to MVD agents, telling them in future when they wanted to search my bag to please ask me for the key. I pinned it to the bag. For several days I kept it there, but eventually it struck me as silly, and I took it off.

Yakutsk was a flat wooden town built on the low-lying marshy banks of the River Lena, which at this point was more than ten miles wide, flowing in numerous channels toward the sea. The land was permafrost, which meant it never thawed more than six inches, and, therefore, sewers and water mains or other underground facilities were impossible.

I arrived there June 2. This was almost the first day of "spring." Ice had gone out in the River Lena only two days before. The first steamboats of the year, coming down river, were expected soon. Steamboats and the airplane provided the city with its only communications. A long "highway" along the Lena which was supposed to be passable for gold caravans could be used only as a trail in the frozen winter.

As almost always proved true in any Russian city I met a few admirable people in Yakutsk. There was a fine, intelligent man directing the branch of the Academy of Science, a biologist named Efrim Yegor, who was specializing in some of the problems of permafrost agriculture, problems very similar to those of Alaska and Canada. The mayor, a Yakut woman named Elizaveta Tomskaya, a former teacher, also impressed me. She asked me questions about Alaska and wanted to know whether many Russians still lived there. She was proud of Yakutsk's schools and I thought she had a right to be. The teachers seemed well qualified and the buildings were the only ones of brick and concrete in town.

But I found nothing else good in Yakutsk. In fact I was shocked by the city.

There was only a lunchroom in my hotel so I ate most of my meals in the Severny or Northern restaurant, Yakutsk's best. It was a four-block walk from hotel to restaurant. The main street of town was "paved" with round slices of pine wood, about four inches thick. The sidewalks were of wood. Most of the side streets were mud.

At seven in the evening when I walked over to dinner the streets were fairly crowded. This was the hour at which many men from mines and forest operations around the city got back to town. Now, in their muddy clothes, sometimes wearing military breeches but often heavy, wide, blue miners' pants, which are very much like Dutch-boy bloomers, they were headed for the small vodka shops and restaurants.

Here and there on the streets I passed a young woman, cheeks rouged like the side of a barn door, and of an unmistakable profession—the first and only time I had seen open solicitation by prostitutes in Russia. Before the *zabegolvki*, or so-called drink-and-run establishments, that is sidewalk stands where vodka was sold, there already were long queues.

At the head of each line an argument was in progress between the queue and the drinker who wanted to hold his spot long enough to down more than one *poltarasta y krushka*. A *poltarasta y krushka* is Russian slang for a one-and-a-half-ton truck and a trailer. In drinking terms it means 150 grams, about half a water glass, of vodka and a beer chaser.

As among Moscow factory workers, this seemed to be the favorite drink in Yakutsk. But many men preferred straight spirits, raw alcohol, which was sold by the drink or by the bottle. And some drank what was called Severny Napitok which literally means "Northern tipple." I don't know what it was exactly. Apparently some strong spirits flavored with a red northern berry of the cranberry family.

There were not only quarrels at the heads of these drinking queues. Some men had already achieved their purpose and were staggering off, drunk, into the night. I had seen drinking enough in Moscow. But never such hard and such determined drinking.

My path to the restaurant took me past two building sites. One of these, I had been told by the Yakut assistant editor of the local paper, was a new printing plant. What he did not tell me but what I saw from the tommygunners in little wooden watchtowers at the corners was that these buildings were being put up by convict labor.

Here was my first sight in Siberia of Russia's famous "corrective labor" system. Here, if you would believe the propaganda, Soviet citizens were rehabilitating themselves and getting rid of any taint of criminality by honest, productive labor. And if any question should arise about their rehabilitation, a tommygunner was at hand to remove the doubts with a quick burst from his gun.

After the first night I could hardly bring myself to return to the Severny restaurant. By the hour I arrived it was jammed with men, either sitting at tables or queued up at the counter where a harassed, big-breasted young blonde girl sold vodka by the gram.

Drinking can be a pleasant and convivial sight. But the scene in the Severny chilled me. Almost every customer in the restaurant was a youngster. Many of them were not more than seventeen or eighteen. The men were not drinking together. There was hardly a woman in the place but they were drinking singly. They came in alone and sat down alone, even if there were four to a table. And there was not much conversation. Each man waited in sullen silence for the waitress to take his order. He sat quietly with his eyes turned to the table, looking neither to the left nor to the right.

When the waitress finally came he gave his order quickly, in a rush of half-whispered words, as though he were afraid he might be interrupted or overheard before he got them out. And he did not order a single drink. He ordered all he wanted. Enough, in other words, to get drunk on.

When the drinks were brought, a carafe of vodka, perhaps, and four bottles of beer, he hardly waited for the traditional Russian *zakuski*, the sausage and bread, or cheese or fish, to eat with his drink. He simply poured out a shot of vodka and rocked it back. He swallowed his bottle of beer almost at a draught. Then he poured the second slug of vodka and went on downing vodka and beer as though his body could not bear a moment longer without the blessed analgesia of alcohol.

In a few moments if you looked at him again his eyes had begun to glaze and his hands, which had been so tense, were beginning to relax. Soon he would stagger up and out into the night.

And these were not hardened old bums whom you might see on Skid Row. These were fine-looking youngsters with good faces and shoulders and mannerisms which told you plainly that they were not peasants and they were not born and bred in the sub-Arctic. These were city boys and almost certainly educated youngsters. Somewhere something had gone wrong. They had said a hasty, ill-considered word. Some girl had tattled on them to the Komsomol. Or perhaps nothing at all had happened. More hands were just

needed for work in the *taiga* and they were co-opted. "Directed"—
that was the Party word. They had been "directed." Or perhaps they
had "volunteered." What did the word matter once they were here?

You only had to look at their eyes to know something had happened to kill all hope in them. Something was dead in their eyes.
Something would never again be alive in them. So here they sat,
night after night, night after night. Racing between reality and
drunkenness, pouring alcohol into themselves because it was the only
ticket which existed to take them out of the horrible reality of the
present.

By the time I had eaten it would be well after 9 P.M., but broad
daylight still, in this far northern land. Walking back to the hotel it
was chilly and you could feel that there would be at least a thin
crust of ice over the water-filled mudholes by morning.

There were not so many people on the street now. A few late
shoppers coming out of the dreary general store. A handful of people
returning from the movies. The loudspeaker system attached to the
local radio transmitter was still blaring out cheap waltzes, inter-
spersed with occasional speeches in Yakut. And across the north-
western sky there was a blaze of red and orange where the sun had
briefly set.

At each corner a Soviet policeman was on duty, but what his duties
might be I could not exactly understand. There was no traffic to
direct and the officers paid no attention to the drunken miners who
weaved up and down the street. Even when the men fell in a drunken
stupor and lay unconscious on the sidewalk in the chilly night the
officers paid no heed to them, although once I saw an MVD man
drag one of these bodies away from a busy corner and hurl it up
against a wall.

I told the Yakut editor that I wanted to take a picture of the River
Lena. Apparently he must have thought the river was a prime military and strategic objective. At any rate he took me about ten miles
out of town before he could find a place where he would permit me
to point my camera out across the wastes of water. I didn't care too
much because on the way to the Lena I took another picture which
will always be with me. It is the picture which I have in my mind of
the famous Yakutsk prison, the one where Radek is supposed to have

died and where his friend Grigori Sokolnikov, the famous Soviet diplomat, was also sent after they were convicted in the purge trials.

Probably the editor had seen the prison so many times that it no longer registered in his consciousness. Or perhaps he thought I would not notice it. At any rate we drove past it twice. I had seen in the Yakutsk museum photographs of the old wooden prisons which the Czarist police used in Siberia. The Communists hadn't changed the architecture much but they had made a few improvements.

The Yakutsk prison was a long building of log construction about two and a half stories high and surrounded by fences and barbed-wire barricades. There were big offices and barracks for the MVD within the barbed-wire enclosure. The walls of the building had no windows and it looked like a pioneer fort or a warehouse or possibly a place for storing ice.

The Czarist police built their prisons exactly the same. But they put windows in them. The Communists have improved on that. There are narrow, long slits, near the roof, which may let in an hour or two of light in summer but none at all in winter, which is practically a permanent season in Yakutsk.

I didn't have to see the inside of that prison to know what life must be like behind those walls.

Seldom have I been so glad to put a city behind me as I was Yakutsk. As my airplane carried me back up the great Lena River I thought over what I had seen. One thing puzzled me a good deal. In wartime both Willkie and Wallace had seen Yakutsk and had come away with good impressions of it. How could this have been? Surely if the city had changed at all it must have improved a bit since then. And to me it had been the most chilling spectacle I had yet seen in Russia.

How uncertain and unreliable, I thought, are the quick, subjective impressions of the hasty travelers. And I contrasted them with the great novel of Siberia, possibly the finest product of Russian literature of the last two decades, Shishkov's *Ugrim Reka* or *Grim River*. There was a man who had lived most of his life in Siberia, much of it along this great Lena River over which I was now flying. What was it that the old river man, Farkov, had said about the Lena? I

had brought the book along as my traveling companion and now I
opened it and hunted for the passage which I had in mind.

Here it was. Here was what Farkov said of the Lena:

"It is the river of the devil. And fierce as well. So God created it.
And human life is just the same. That is why we call it the Grim
River. It is grim—just as is the life of the people. *Da.*"

And what Farkov had said of the Lena could be said as well for
the whole of Siberia, I thought. At least that part of the north and
east which I had been looking at.

Beside me on the plane this time sat a good-looking Russian girl.
She had a sweet, rather animated face which was only spoiled when
she opened her mouth and you saw her two big gold incisor teeth. I
had watched her from the plane window before she got on at
Yakutsk. Two MVD officers saw her off—a colonel whom I guessed
was probably her father and a young lieutenant who might have
been her sweetheart.

We got into a little conversation as the plane flew over the endless
miles and she asked me how I had liked Yakutsk. I made a few polite
remarks. I never believed in deliberately saying nasty things to
people about their home cities. However, I could not resist one
statement.

"You know," I said, "I think the people in Yakutsk drink a great
deal."

"*Da,*" she said. "Yes. S*ever* . . . The north, you know."

"Of course, it's the north," I persisted. "But why do they drink so
much?"

She looked at me with wide-open eyes as though I had asked a
question almost too stupid to require an answer.

"But what else is there for them to do?" she replied.

"*Da,*" I said. "*Da.*"

She was so right. And it had been a stupid question.

I turned back to *Grim River.* I thought there was more to be found
out from Shishkov than from looking out the window at the endless,
endless forest.

It was several days later and I had finally gotten to Khabarovsk,
a great gray city on the gray Amur, when I began to be afraid. Since
the suitcase incident in Yakutsk I had had no more serious encounters

with the secret police. From time to time I was aware of their presence and twice, in Chita, I had had trouble with the military over taking photographs. But, outside of losing some film, I had suffered no damage, except to my feelings.

But in Khabarovsk it was different. Actually, I had no particular interest in this city but had been forced to come there in order to get a train to Birobidjan, the former Jewish settlement region. Although at first sight Khabarovsk seemed a pleasant enough place I quickly revised my judgment.

I asked the hotel to get me a taxi to show me the places of interest. There was a long delay and when the cab finally appeared the driver was surly. He asked me where I wanted to go. I said for him to show me what was interesting in Khabarovsk. He said he didn't know what was interesting. We stuck at that point and, in order to get going, I suggested that he drive up the main street. We did that and he asked where next? I said let's go down the main street. We did that and he asked for more instructions. We played this game for an hour or so. Meantime, I had noticed that while he was wearing a dirty old jacket he hadn't bothered to change his uniform trousers. He was wearing the telltale blue-and-red-piping breeches of the MVD.

Finally, I suggested that we try one of the principal cross streets. Just off the main street we passed a huge gray office building, a block long and six stories high.

"What's that building?" I asked brightly.

Mumble . . . mumble . . . from the driver.

"What did you say?" I asked.

Mumble . . . mumble . . .

My curiosity was now aroused and I was pretty sure what that mumble was designed to conceal.

"I don't understand you," I said.

"It's an administration," he said finally.

"What administration?" I asked (I was sure now).

"An administration."

"What?"

"Mummmmmmm."

"What?"

In an almost inaudible whisper: "M . . . V . . . D . . ."

"Oh," I said. "Fine-looking building."

After that I released the taxi after paying the hundred rubles which he had the nerve to charge me, and started out to explore the city on foot. Immediately, I discovered that I was under close surveillance. There were at least two plainclothes men following me and it was evident they didn't care two kopeks whether I knew they were following me or not. It was in the same blatant, careless style of the suitcase business.

This I did not like at all. I went back to the hotel and sat outside on a park bench in the sunshine. I saw then that there was a detail of four men assigned to me and that they had made their headquarters behind a small tobacco kiosk just beyond the hotel.

I sat on the bench and thought. Here I was a good many thousand miles away from Moscow. There was no doubt that what I had once heard about Khabarovsk was correct. That it was the capital of MVD-land. General Headquarters of Slave Labor, Unlimited. The size of the office buildings on Volochayevskaya Street was a tip-off if nothing else and so was the character of the city. I had been back and forth on Karl Marx Street with my MVD taxi driver several times. In six blocks five new buildings were going up. Each was an MVD job with forced labor and tommygunners. One was being built largely by women.

I had seen forty to fifty buildings going up in Khabarovsk. Not all MVD jobs, to be sure. A few were being built with Army labor. But not one was being built by free labor.

No, I thought, this is not a healthy place for an American correspondent. Particularly not a correspondent with a camera. And I decided to forgo the dubious pleasure of picture taking in Khabarovsk. Because while old General Sergei Goglidze, who had been Wallace's host up and down Siberia and Central Asia, was no longer bossing the headquarters on Volochayevskaya Street (because he had been shot with Beriya the previous December) it was plain that another general sat in Goglidze's place.

And, so far as I could tell, this new general and the rest of the setup in Volochayevskaya Street were running things according to the old pattern. No sign of any such nonsense as freedom out this way.

I took one more walk up Karl Marx Street and stopped near the addition which the MVD was building to a hospital in Lenin Square. It was a busy corner and the wooden gates were open. A tommy-gunner stood right on the sidewalk, guarding the labor crew inside.

What I was interested in seeing was whether I could detect in the faces of the passersby any sign that their eyes had seen the tommy-gunner or the prisoners. As I watched, the plain citizens of Khabarovsk streamed past the place steadily. Not one of them averted his eyes. Not one of them looked away. But not one, by any movement of eyes or facial muscle, displayed a single sign that he had seen anything unusual.

It was a good lesson about the psychology of people who live in a prison country and one which I saw over and over again in the great gray land which is ruled by the generals and officers who inhabit the great gray building on Volochayevskaya Street.

That night, after midnight, I left by train for Birobidjan. Two plainclothes agents occupied the compartment next to mine. One stayed awake with his eye on the open door all the way to Birobidjan. It was about 4 A.M. when we got there, and I was startled to see, as I picked my way through the gloomy streets to the dimly lighted hotel, an armed rifleman with a gun strapped across his back suddenly spring up out of a dark alley. But later I realized he was merely a watchman guarding the rear of a row of shops.

I was too tired and too glad to get away from Khabarovsk to be much concerned about the hotel and the hotelkeeper. Not that I had stopped worrying. In fact, before leaving Khabarovsk I had sent off one of those "I am mailing this at 8 P.M. Tuesday and you should receive it by 10 A.M. Thursday" letters to a colleague in Moscow which was designed to test whether I would be permitted to communicate with him and to put someone on guard if I should be unaccountably "delayed" in Birobidjan or elsewhere on my way.

I was concerned and seriously concerned about the openness of the police work which I was encountering. Always, in the past, when the police dropped their mask and openly started to follow a man or search his possessions it was only because a definite denouement had been determined upon and there was no further need for concealment.

What I was afraid of was a provocation. I was afraid that the police had decided to arrest me at some previously determined point in my travels and that they would "discover" in my baggage an incriminating document or photograph which they had taken the trouble to plant there.

For this reason I spent a good deal of time packing and repacking my bag, checking it closely each time I had to leave it alone to make sure that it had not again been opened and that some "secret spy document" had not been concealed in it by the very agents who would then "find" it.

While I was alert enough to notice that the Birobidjan hotel manager behaved a little peculiarly (before he could say whether or not he had a room for me he went out on the street to confer, I suppose, with the agents who had accompanied me), I was content to go to my hotel room and collapse on the clean but lumpy bed I found there.

I would, perhaps, have rested less well had I known that except for those moments when I was inside that hotel room I would never be out of the sight of MVD agents during my entire stay in Birobidjan. They even followed me to the wooden toilet, outside the hotel, and occupied one of the two booths every time nature called.

Never, in my stay in Russia, had I experienced such surveillance. Nor could I recall any other foreigner having such an experience. I estimated that there were a minimum of twenty agents assigned to my visit. The hotel manager as I quickly discovered was the local secret police chief, just as the manager had been in Bukhara. He showed no signs of embarrassment when I walked in on him one day and found two uniformed militiamen reporting to him on their arrest of some black marketeers in the local bazaar that day.

The only thing that frightened the agents was my camera. They were deathly afraid of having their picture taken. I could only imagine that there must be some strict rule in the MVD that a man who allows his picture to be taken is dropped back five grades.

At any rate I found that if I emerged from the Birobidjan hotel at a quick pace, holding my Contax up as though I were about to snap a picture, I could create amazing animation in the otherwise quiet and sleepy street. Because idle loafers who had been leaning on telegraph poles or conversing by twos and threes suddenly sprinted in all directions to get behind fences, trees, bushes or any other photograph-proof barrier.

This was a dubious pleasure, at best. I did not find the situation funny. I think the incident which made me most angry occurred one day when I visited a children's home. I wanted to take pictures of the youngsters, but the director, a bright and pretty young woman, asked me to wait a bit. The children were not dressed for the street. In an hour or so they would be going to the park to play. Would I meet them there and take my pictures then? I agreed and went to the park in accordance with the appointment.

But when I saw two plainclothes men skulking in the underbrush —literally skulking and threading their way under and through the bushes—I blew up. I chased one of the men and snapped his picture as he sat in a summer house with his head buried in his hands to protect it from the danger of the lens. Then I went to the deputy mayor of Birobidjan who had been acting as my official guide and complained to him. I said it was a *bolshoi skandal!* which means big scandal, only it has a stronger sound in Russian. But it was a waste of breath although perhaps it restored my temper a bit. Because the surveillance continued undiminished.

I was unable to take a single step in the streets of Birobidjan without the company of the agents. The detail included a number of local MVD lads, youngsters from the Birobidjan headquarters. Their role was obvious. They were to make it evident to the local residents that I was being followed and that it was more healthy not to talk to me. The lesson was easily understood by the populace. No one talked to me on the street. Several times I was spoken to while eating in the restaurant. But, conversation on a normal human level was out of the question.

Nonetheless I learned a great deal about Birobidjan. I was the first outsider to come there in many years, probably since before World War II. Established originally as a Jewish settlement colony in an obvious move to provide a counterweight to Palestine in the early thirties it was plain that Birobidjan had lost its significance as a Jewish center a long time ago.

To be sure the street signs were still posted in Yiddish as well as

Russian. And the name was officially the "Jewish Autonomous Oblast."

But, beyond this, as I told Lev Vingkevich, a Communist of Jewish descent who is the chairman of the executive committee of the Oblast Council, a position roughly comparable to that of governor, I could not see that the place had any special Jewish character. I said I thought it should be called the "Soviet Autonomous Oblast" because it was, outside of its special history and a certain percentage of Jews in its population, merely an ordinary Soviet administrative region. He was inclined to agree with me.

I suppose that about half the residents of this region, which has a population of about 200,000, are Jews. In the city, which has 40,000 residents, the percentage may be somewhat higher than in the country.

But no special effort was now being made to send Jews to Birobidjan. In fact, I doubted that any had been sent since 1948, the real watershed year in Birobidjan and Jewish history in Russia. That was the year of the "anti-cosmopolitan" drive.

Exactly what happened in Birobidjan that year no one would tell me. But part of the story came out. The Jewish theater was closed and turned into a Young Communist Club. I think the Jewish newspaper was suspended, but perhaps a vestigial edition remained. Now it was published three times a week in an edition of a thousand copies, but the twenty-three-year-old Jewish girl who had become editor only three weeks before admitted that circulation had been "less" in the past.

I think that in 1949 the oblast museum was closed but I could not find anyone to admit it. It was open now and was obviously brand new. It looked to me as though, perhaps, it had been open less than a year. There wasn't a word in the museum about Jewish culture or the Jewish language or the Jewish contribution to the oblast. The only indication that Jews had had any part in Birobidjan was three old copies of the Yiddish paper which I saw in one obscure cabinet along a side wall.

I embarrassed the black-eyed young Jewish woman who ran the local library by asking to see the latest books and literature in Yiddish. At first she said the director of the Yiddish book section was

away on vacation and had locked up the books before going away.
Then she and an assistant hastily pawed over a huge pile of books,
looking for Yiddish ones. They found Mark Twain's *Prince and the
Pauper* and a few others but none, of course, dated later than 1948
when the Yiddish Publishing House in Moscow was shut. In the local
bookstore I found they had a few volumes in Yiddish, two or three
by Sholem Aleichem, and copies of Stalin's *Problems of Leninism*
and a *Short History of the Communist Party,* translated into Yiddish.

I bought two of the Sholom Aleichem volumes, and apologized to
the book clerk for her trouble. She had had to climb a ladder and get
the books off the very topmost shelf of the section devoted to
foreign-language books. She in turn apologized to me for having
nothing but these dusty old copies. I assured her it made no difference whatsoever.

So, as the deputy mayor of Birobidjan assured me, Jewish culture
was not dead in Birobidjan. In addition, he recalled, they had sung
some Jewish songs at a festival which had been conducted recently
on the occasion of the twentieth anniversary of the establishment of
the oblast.

But what, I asked him, about the Jewish religion? Was there a
synagogue?

Assuredly, he said, and he would be glad to take me to visit it. We
had a little trouble finding the place because the deputy mayor, who
until a year previous had been in charge of highway construction
for the MVD, had never been there before. But, aided by the "hotelkeeper," who said he also had not been there before but who proved
astonishingly familiar with the neighborhood, we found the plain
barrackslike wooden building which served Birobidjan as a synagogue.

But it was a little harder to find the rabbi because he was off drinking wine with some friends. But finally we located him and he proved
to be a spry and egregious man of sixty-odd years named Solomon
Kaplan and he was not a rabbi but a cantor. However, he said he
had founded the synagogue in 1947. Before that, he said, there were
only illegal congregations and he appealed to the "hotelkeeper" for
confirmation of his words. His congregation numbered about fifty
persons, he said, "all of them older than me." He said no young peo-

ple came to the synagogue and that even on the high holidays not
more than sixty assembled.

It was plain enough that within a predictable number of years the
Jewish congregation of Birobidjan would simply die out. It was also
my very strong suspicion that Cantor Kaplan had founded the congregation in 1947 with the blessing if not at the inspiration of the
"hotelkeeper" or his predecessor in the MVD.

Deputy Mayor Zhelenov told me repeatedly that Yiddish was still
used in the schools, but when I asked the teachers and pupils in the
half-dozen schools which I visited whether any language besides
Russian was employed I got a uniformly negative answer.

So, I soon came to the conclusion that it was also merely a matter
of time before the Jewish aspect of the oblast faded out completely.
The name might be perpetuated for a while simply because the Foreign Office in Moscow might think that the day would again arise
when it would be of some value to have a Jewish Autonomous
Oblast for diplomatic or propaganda purposes.

But it was dead as a Jewish center and never had had too much
vitality. I knew from my visits to schools and talk with the Mayor of
Yakutsk that there was a large Jewish minority there. It was easy to
see that in the Jewish population transfers of 1948 and 1949 they had
been sent to places like Yakutia rather than to the "Jewish" oblast.
And it was no surprise to find that in Birobidjan there was a big Tar-
tar minority, the remnants of the Tartars who were transferred out of
the Crimea at the end of the war on charges they had been more
interested in sitting in the sun and drinking wine than in conducting
partisan war against the Germans. I didn't doubt that there was basis
for the charge. How could it make much difference to the Tartars
whether Russians or Germans were dictating to them? Just, I supposed, as there was truth in the charges made against the small
Caucasus tribes which were resettled in Central Asia.

What interested me was the plain evidence of the divisive policy
of the MVD. Don't send Jews to join their countrymen in Birobidjan.
Send them to Yakutia. Don't send Tartars to join their cousins in
Yakutia. Send them to Birobidjan. And so on. Mountain Caucasus
people to desert Kazakhstan. Divide—and rule more safely. An old
colonial motto.

And this, of course, was the heart of MVD-land. The telltale guard towers, ramshackle wooden ones but easily recognizable, were mounted at the construction sites in Birobidjan as well. Wherever I had traveled in these thousands and thousands of miles east of Novosibirsk, north to Yakutsk, east to Khabarovsk, I was traveling in MVD-land. Nor was this its end. I could go on for a thousand miles. To Magadan and the horrible Kolyma goldfields to the north. To Sakhalin where Chekhov had been. To the Kuriles.

It was truly an enormous country and being in its center gave me a pervasive sense of fear. It was not just the agents who watched me. It was the atmosphere that hung over the whole vast empire. It looked as though I was going to escape from it without arrest and without provocation, but not until I reached Moscow did I draw a free breath. There must have been secrets indeed in Khabarovsk and Birobidjan to justify the use of so many agents.

As I rode the train back to Khabarovsk and the airplane which would fly me west once more I watched from the window. Once in mid-morning we stopped at a small station. They were putting in a new siding and a crew of women was unloading stones from flat cars, tossing them out by hand and shovel. They were sunburned, husky and healthy and many wore bright cotton dresses. Two or three even wore straw sunbonnets, and it was a curious sight indeed to watch sunbonnet girls unloading carloads of building stone. But this was not what struck me so forcibly. What came into my mind was the sudden realization that in the West we had really missed the whole point about Siberia. We had been fascinated by the labor camps, by slave labor. But that wasn't the point of Siberia.

The real point of Siberia was that the whole country was a labor camp. It didn't make any difference whether you were a prisoner, or a *spets*, or a "free" citizen. These women unloading stone, for instance, were free labor. The women I had seen digging in a potato field outside Chita were slave labor. The women building the hospital addition in Khabarovsk were slave labor. The men working up the street were soldiers. And the labor that put up the new apartment buildings in Stalinabad were *spets*.

How did they differ, one from the other? Not much. They worked under much the same conditions and they lived under much the same conditions. True, there were guards and barbed wire outside the barracks where the prison laborers lived. And spotlights. But the *spets* lived in barracks, too. As did much of the "free" labor. And outside not a few of those barracks there were guards, as well.

No, I thought to myself. When we argue about statistics, about the number of prisoners in the slave labor camps, we are like the medieval scholastics worrying about the number of angels who can dance on the point of a needle. It is Siberia itself which is the scandal. It is Siberia which is the evil underbelly of the Soviet system.

And what has the new regime changed in Siberia? Surely, a few old Bolsheviks have been hunted up and released. Surely, some common criminals have been set free. And maybe even a few political offenders, like the English-speaking Russian in Alma-Ata who got too fond of Western life while he was attached to the Soviet High Command in Tokyo.

Some little changes had occurred. And perhaps others would come about, but could anyone, having seen Siberia, write with a clear conscience that Russia's new rulers were displaying a tendency toward liberalism.

Indeed, not.

I could only wish for the sake of the Russian people that it was a correspondent of *Pravda* who was making this trip and not a correspondent of *The New York Times.*

I would be able to put down on paper what I had seen. It would be published and the people of America and the free world would be able to learn what it really looked like behind the iron curtain within the iron curtain.

That picture could not be drawn from Moscow, I knew, but soon I would be back in New York, free to write exactly what I had seen. Freedom to see and freedom to write were rare privileges in Russia and even more rare in Siberia.

So rare, in fact, that often the most revealing pictures of conditions in that vast land were those set down privately by the jailers themselves. I wondered whether in that vast gray building on Volochayevskaya Street there was anyone like the famous Siberian Governor General, Count M. M. Speransky, who something more than a hun-

Samples of Censorship

Following are deletions typical of those made by Soviet censors in dispatches recounting a trip to Siberia and the Soviet Far East last summer.

The deleted material was varied—sometimes economic, sometimes political, sometimes quasi-military, sometimes sociological. The deleted sections are printed in bold-face type.

From a dispatch date-lined Novosibirsk: "The mighty Novosibirsk dam **which is scheduled to produce upward of 700,000 or 800,000 kilowatts of** power is the first effort to turn its [the River Ob's] vast energy to a useful purpose. * * *"

From dispatches from Yakutsk:
"They drink a special kind of brown vodka called hunter's vodka and also straight spirits with or without a beer chaser. **Drunkenness is a real problem. And not all residents of Yakutia are happy with their lot. To many this is an alien countryside and they would much prefer their native Kiev or Odessa or Tiflis. As is inevitable when a considerable fraction of the population has been directed to a particular region, not everyone adapts himself. And, there is plenty to adapt one's self to in Yakutia.**

"Housing is another problem. **Even miners get tired of barracks life and it is not suitable housing over the long term for families, especially with children. In work camps, of which Yakutia has many, of course this form of housing is normal.** But in Yakutsk a big drive is now being launched to provide better building * * *."

From a dispatch from Kirensk:
"This country virtually provided its own punishment although if the climate and living conditions were not enough the police were handy to make things worse for the prisoners. **It is easy to see why this region has an inevitable attraction for a police administration looking for a place to send persons from more civilized areas. While it seems doubtful that camps would hold any particular terror for local residents accustomed to a grim life already it would be a different matter to persons from Russia's more effete west.**"

From a dispatch from Chita (the introductory sentence):
"Perhaps every third person you meet in the street in Chita is in uniform—the uniforms of the Soviet land forces, of the air force and civil air service and of the railroad enterprises and mining enterprises. **This is natural because Chita is one of Russia's eastern 'watchdogs.' * * *.**"

From a dispatch from Khabarovsk:
" 'Of course we are a very young city and things are not as well fixed up as they will be later on.' This kind of remark is designed of course as an excuse for **all sorts of bad conditions and abuses—huts and barracks for housing, unpaved dirty streets, poor municipal facilities, inadequate sewers, almost any evil you can name.**"

By deleting unfavorable material and leaving the favorable material, the whole impression of the article often is changed and distorted.

From *The New York Times*, October 2, 1954

dred years previously had made an inspection trip through much of the area in which I had been traveling.

While I had been in Chita I had chanced on a little book which quoted some of Speransky's impressions. As the plane flew westward over Siberia, over endless forests, here and there idly burning by the million or two-million-acre patch, I dipped into Speransky's reminiscences and found that he had described the prison area of Siberia as a "nether world" in which he had found "the last stage of human distress and endurance" where the prisoners were forgotten by God and man.

How little, I thought, has Siberia changed and how little, except perhaps for the airplanes, there was which I had seen which would not have been completely familiar to Speransky's eyes.

XVII

Volga Matushka

I DON'T know what kind of trips small boys dream
about nowadays but when I was a kid in Minnesota my favorite
pastime was to imagine myself drifting down the Mississippi on a log
raft like Huck Finn and Tom Sawyer.

Nowadays, I presume, log rafts and the Mississippi have gone out
of style in favor of rocket ships and Mars or Venus. But I guess I
would still settle for the Mississippi.

Perhaps that is why ever since I had first gone to Russia I had
hoped, someday, to take the steamboat trip down the Volga. I had
always been certain that if I really wanted to know Russia the way
to find out was to float down the Volga. Now I was returning to New
York within a few weeks and there was little time left. So the moment
I got back from Siberia I booked steamboat passage from Moscow,
through the Moscow-Volga Canal, to the upper river and all the way
down through the Volga-Don Canal to Rostov-on-Don. A ten-day
trip through the heart of Russia.

My trip to Siberia had been frightening and strenuous. But it
taught me more about the Soviet Union than years spent in Moscow.
It had shown me the real price that was still being paid in human
suffering, in toil and hardship in what seemed to me an endless task
—the task of pulling Russia up abreast, industrially and technologi-
cally, with the West. It was the same problem Ivan had faced. And
Peter and Catherine. Always it was solved the same way—by force
and black toil. It seemed to me that here was the real significance of

the millions of mobilized laborers in the East, the "slave" and the "free." I could not see that the death of Stalin had made much difference east of Novosibirsk and I wondered whether it had along the Volga. I wondered what was happening in Russia proper. Mother Russia, the eternal land of the Slavs.

I had gotten just a taste of old Russia at the tag end of my Siberian trip when I stopped off at Barnaul, a very old Russian town in southwest Siberia. In Barnaul it seemed to me that very little had changed since Stalin's death or since 1917 for that matter. The favorite sport of the city was horse racing just as it had been, I was sure, even before the Revolution.

In the old city market on Sunday I found sideshow barkers, jugglers, magicians and a circus, all in the tradition of old Russia, and a couple of thousand people, engaged in "hand" trading, selling anything from a pair of shoelaces to a dining-room suite. It was all legal, too. Anyone who wanted to engage in trade merely had to buy a two-ruble ticket.

Nor, so far as I could see, had collective farming transformed the life of the peasant.

I had come to Barnaul because it was supposed to be a center for the great new drive to plant grain on virgin soil to which Khrushchev was devoting so much time. And I was eager to see how the thousands of "volunteer" youths from Moscow and Leningrad were faring.

An accommodating city official said he would arrange this for me and on a Monday morning a man named Dimitrov called for me at my hotel and we set off for the country in a Pobeda car. It had rained rather hard during the night and we soon bogged down in the clay gumbo as did almost everything else on wheels, including jeeps and six-wheeled trucks.

After we got pulled out we returned to town, commandeered a four-wheel-drive command car and set off again.

Mile after mile we rolled over the flat, open country of Pavlovsk County. I thought we were never going to get to our destination when finally Dimitrov asked me if I wouldn't like to see the collective farm we were now passing. Why not, I said.

We drove in and asked a man where we could find the chairman of the farm but he didn't seem to know. We asked another man and he gave some vague answer and wandered away. The farm office and village store were both closed. It seemed peculiar but I didn't quite understand until a group of men and women came up to us. One of them had a bottle of vodka in his hand and they were all drunk.

"*Pyedem-tse*," one woman said. "Come to us and let's drink. Come."

My companion seemed to hesitate but I was in a sterner mood. "Where is the *predsidatel*, the chairman?" I asked.

Half an hour passed before the chairman put in an appearance. He was a tall, good-looking man but he was so drunk he could hardly talk.

By this time I knew what was going on. It was the Monday after Troitsa, Trinity Sunday, the great traditional summer church holiday of the peasants.

Finally, I made out what the chairman was trying to tell me.

"The *kokhozniki* came to me," he said. "They said, Comrade Chairman, what about a holiday? We have worked very hard. We have done all the seeding. The work is finished. So, what could I say? It was true they had worked hard and it was true the seeding was all done. So. We are having a little holiday. A sports holiday you might call it. Just for two or three days."

I had read in the Moscow papers frequent diatribes against the celebration of religious holidays in the countryside and how it interfered with farm work. Now I was prepared to believe there was something in what *Pravda* had said. For as we walked among the little thatched cottages of the collective farm, which obviously had been a peasant village long before anyone in Pavlovsk County had heard about communism, I saw, lying here and there in the sunny fields, a good many collective farmers who were spending this "sporting" holiday at rest, oblivious to the world.

As it turned out I never did find any of the Communist youths who were tilling the virgin soil nor did I manage to get to the virgin lands. But for once it was not an iron curtain that stood in the way.

When we left the collective farm Dimitrov said to me: "Why did you want to visit this farm when there weren't any youths there?"

"I didn't want to visit the farm," I said. "You suggested that we go there."

"Well," he said, "where do you want to go?"

"I don't know," I said. "I've never been here before. Where do you propose?"

"So," he said. "Very strange. I've never been in Pavlovsk County either. I thought you knew where you wanted to go."

He was not, it transpired, the farm specialist of the city council but merely a council worker who had Monday off and had been persuaded to go out with a "correspondent from Moscow who wants to see collective farms in Pavlovsk County."

We spent the day visiting farms and found plenty of Troitsa celebrations but the virgin land always seemed to be just over the horizon.

I had an idea that the spirit which I had encountered in Barnaul would prove not much different from that down the Volga. The old-fashioned race track at Barnaul with its bookmakers openly violating the strict law against what the notices called "*bookmakerstvo*" reminded me of what I had once been told by the "Penguin." The Penguin was at that time the maître d'hôtel of the famous Georgian restaurant in Moscow, the Arogvy. We called him the Penguin because, in his black tails, white shirt and tie and pince-nez he looked like a penguin. He said one night that he was leaving the next day on his vacation.

What will you do? we asked him.

The Penguin smiled.

"I have a friend," he said. "Every year we spend our vacation together on the Volga. We get on the boat at Moscow and ride all the way. And all the way we play cards. Then we turn around and ride back. And we play all the way back. Sometimes we make as much money on our vacation as we do in a year of work."

The Penguin smiled cryptically and when he did so I was astonished at how much he resembled a picture I once saw of an old Mississippi River gambler.

So it did not surprise me much on the first morning out of Moscow as I was circling the deck of the S.S. *Lermontov*, which had, by then, just entered the upper Volga, to find on the rear deck two tables of cardplayers, eight earnest gentlemen appropriately clad in the Russian traveling and lounging costume, that is to say, in pajamas.

And all day long and into the early evening the games went on throughout the ten-day trip. The Penguin was not among the players but I am sure some members of his fraternity were. The game only stopped when it was no longer light enough to see. Then the rear deck was taken over by the young people, a dozen boys and girls of college age. Some of the boys were cadets, learning navigation on the S.S. *Lermontov.* The girls were university students. They plugged in the radio loudspeaker or played records on a portable hand-wind phonograph. And danced. The boys with boys and the girls with girls. I asked them why the boys didn't dance with the girls. They said the boys were too bashful because they didn't dance well enough to have girls for partners.

It was a quiet, lazy life on the *Lermontov.* One of the passengers was an eighty-two-year-old Moscow professor who was making the Volga trip for the fortieth time. He was an irascible old man with a tweaky goatee. His wife and a sister accompanied him, waiting on him hand and foot. They spent most of their time reading a new Volga River guidebook and looking at the sights of the river through opera glasses.

From what I was able to observe of life on shipboard it had not changed much in the professor's forty years of travel. Outside of the two tables of cardplayers the passengers amused themselves by reading, playing dominoes, chess and checkers, writing letters, looking at the scenery and conversation. I saw one game of parchesi and one jig-saw puzzle.

Another pastime much indulged in by the ladies was to get off the boat at every landing (we stopped five or six times a day) and rush to the market, usually located close to the stage, and buy some local product—eggs, sour cream, fresh cucumbers, radishes, strawberries, raspberries, plums and apricots (as we got further south) or tomatoes.

But most of the time was spent in talk, talk of the old-fashioned summer-boardinghouse variety. Gossip about the handsome bearded mathematics professor from Rostov and the slightly faded Moscow lady, with a half-grown son, whose cheeks were just a bit too pink and whose smile was just a bit too bright.

She took possession of the professor on the second day out and from that time on he could not appear on deck without her joining him. But, said the ladies, she won't get him. He is a sly old one, that professor. He has a wife who is vacationing in the Caucasus at Piatigorsk and he is going to meet her.

I am afraid the gossips were right. Because on the last two days of the trip the professor and the Moscow lady seemed very sad and very quiet. And the professor spent a lot of time taking pictures of her and her son with the new Kiev camera which he had bought in Moscow. It looked to me as though Rostov was the end of the line, so far as romance was concerned, and it made me a little melancholy.

I felt transported back in time on the S.S. *Lermontov.* The people and the atmosphere and the way of life were not twentieth-century Communist, they were nineteenth-century bourgeois.

The *Lermontov* had four classes. First class and second class occupied the top deck and there was little difference between the two except that first-class cabins were forward and second-class were to the rear, where they got the soot from the steamer's crude oil smoke. The *Lermontov* was not one of the new Czech-built, all-steel Diesel steamers. She was an old rebuilt pre-revolutionary wooden-hulled steamer but in fine trim. Her paint was fresh, her brasswork bright and her toilets clean. The showers worked. There were two pleasant restaurants, fore and aft, where you could get not bad food. Lunch or dinner took about an hour and a half because there were only four waitresses for sixty passengers but since we had nothing but time to waste it made no difference.

The women on this deck were "ladies," and you knew they were ladies by the way they dressed and acted. They carried parasols and fans and, often, white gloves. They wore big picture hats, usually of straw and decorated with bunches of artificial cherries or clusters of daisies. They carried pearl-handled opera glasses with which to look at the scenery and they made appropriate expressions of "oh" and "ah" at such picturesque sights as the Stepan Razin cliffs. Their dresses tended to be long and rather frilly, of flowered organdy or crepe de Chine. And when they went ashore to bargain at the markets they often donned linen dusters. Two or three ladies even had veils which they tucked up in their hats, and I'm sure that when I passed them, sitting on the deck, I caught a whiff of mothballs.

The ladies were mostly married and accompanied by their husbands, but some were maiden ladies, obviously schoolteachers or elderly bookkeepers, and they traveled, for the most part, with companions.

It was one of these maiden ladies who inadvertently gave the passengers of the S.S. *Lermontov* the biggest sensation of the trip. On the day after we passed Ulyanovsk it occurred to one of the stewardesses late in the afternoon that she had not seen this old lady all day and when she knocked at her cabin door, Cabin No. 13 as it happened, she got no answer. The old lady, it transpired, was dead. She had apparently suffered a heart attack in her sleep.

I thought the tongues would never cease wagging about this. It was nearly twelve hours before Captain Yertakhov, a fine Scots-looking man with sandy hair and red sideburns, was able to put the body ashore, because there were no rail connections at any of the little river ports until we came to Volsk.

Many of the ladies felt certain that their fellow passenger had suffered the heart attack because she had climbed the long flight of steps at Ulyanovsk the day before—a quarter mile of steps leading up a steep embankment. They said it was a *skandal* that such a thing should have happened, and at Ulyanovsk of all places because Ulyanovsk, of course, was Lenin's birthplace.

Ulyanovsk was Simbirsk when Lenin was born there. New revolutionary names have been given to many of the big Volga towns—Shcherbakov which used to be Rybinsk, Gorky which was Nizhni Novgorod, Kuibyshev which was Samara, Stalingrad which was Tsaritzyn and, of course, Ulyanovsk which was given Lenin's family name, Ulyanov.

Whether or not our passenger's death might properly be attributed to the staircase at Ulyanovsk this was not the only *skandal* about Lenin's birthplace which aroused the passengers. There was almost an indignation meeting on the forward deck of the ship after we had visited the city.

"What a *skandal!*" one passenger, a Moscow doctor, said. "To treat Lenin's birthplace like this."

"Yes," chimed in a young instructor from the Moscow University. "They have spent millions on Gori. But here for Lenin's city not a kopek. It is a second-rate provincial town, no less."

"And Gori has been turned into a modern city with paved streets and factories," said one of the schoolteachers. "Here they haven't even the culture to pave the streets. What a shame!"

The passengers were absolutely right, of course. Practically nothing had been spent on Ulyanovsk in comparison with the vast sums invested by Beriya in Stalin's home town of Gori. But while I was astonished to hear Soviet citizens criticizing their government so openly (this was one of the few occasions when I ever heard critical talk like this in public) I completely disagreed with them.

To me the great charm of Ulyanovsk was that it was so completely unchanged. I liked the fact that only a few of the streets had been asphalted and that you could see droshkies on the main avenue of town. I liked the spreading old beech trees and the absence of new "Gorky Street" buildings. Most of all I liked the provincial intellectual atmosphere of the old Ulyanov home. It was easy to see that very little had touched that house since the Ulyanovs lived there in the seventies and eighties, the father a small-town teacher, the mother alert and courageous, and the three bright children, the ill-fated Alexander, Lenin himself and his fine-looking sister.

You could see it was a family where books and learning were important. There were books in every room and in every language— English, French, German, Spanish and Italian, as well as Russian. And the old photographs . . . Lenin at eighteen, very young and very fierce. His brother Alexander, with something of a touch of fanaticism in his eyes (he was executed for an attempt on the life of the Czar). And the sister with eyes so clear and cool and honest that they seemed to stare right out of the photograph and into your soul.

The Ulyanov house was a lived-in house. You could still feel the life and breath of the family. Out in the backyard there was a croquet court and a "giant swing," where the family played, and a big apple orchard with summer seats and nooks.

Next door a little museum had been set up and there among the Lenin relics I saw the report cards of the Ulyanov boys. Alexander's erratic and brilliant, spotted with 5's (the Russian equivalent of A) but spotted, too, with blanks for the subjects he had skipped. No mark at all in logic; and Lenin's complete and precise and marked in every grade—all 5's except in one subject—logic. In that Lenin too was a little weak. He only got a 4.

I thought as I walked back to the steamboat from Lenin's home that I understood, now, a good deal better the chief factor that turned him into a revolutionary. I could sense very vividly the tragedy of Alexander and the terrible impact his fate must have had on this bookish and idealistic family here in a backwater city on the Volga. For Lenin was Alexander's younger brother, and looking at these exhibits you could almost see young Vladimir Ulyanov quietly biting his lip half through and swearing to himself an oath to which he alone would be answerable that from the moment his brother died on the execution platform at St. Petersburg he would not deviate from one fixed goal—the destruction of the system which had produced this tragedy and the overturn of the regime in which such tragedies were commonplace. The single-mindedness of an idealist. Nothing is more ruthless.

Yes. I hoped, indeed, that the new regime would not think it necessary and appropriate to turn Ulyanovsk into another Gori, garish with monuments. Let it remain drowsing in the nineteenth century so that, occasionally, someone might visit it and understand a little better how 1917 had come about.

It would be good to keep at least one of the Volga cities unchanged because slowly, but perhaps with increasing rapidity, the river was beginning to change. It was not only the names of the cities. It was the cities themselves.

Take Nizhni Novgorod, for example. Now it was a bustling industrial center with a population of one million, a kind of Russian Detroit with the Soviet's biggest auto plant, employing sixty thousand men and women, and huge jet-motor and jet-plane works as well as a rapidly expanding machine-tool industry. All day long over Gorky there was the roar of single- and twin-jets from the test-

ing shops, and where the great Nizhni Novgorod fair used to be held
with thousands of buyers from the far ends of Europe and Asia there
now stood a shipbuilding works.

To be sure, there were slums along the waterfront which still
looked as though they had come straight out of the pages of Gorky's
The Lower Depths, but in a few years, no doubt, they would be
razed and something monumental in bad concrete and plaster would
be erected in their place. There would remain, of course, the Peshkov
house where Gorky was said to have spent his childhood years with
his uncle. But even the citizens of Gorky admitted that they really
couldn't be sure that it actually was the Peshkov house or just one
that looked somewhat like it. For myself I thought it was much too
well preserved to fit Gorky's description.

The day of the *burlaki* and the mournful chant of the Volga boat-
men, the "yo heave, ho" was gone. No longer did human beasts of
burden trudge the tow paths, pulling the great Volga barges against
the slow current. Human labor had become a little too costly for that.
Perhaps it still might be so used on the Lena or in Siberia. But no
longer on the Volga. Here the day of the push-button river was at
hand.

I saw evidences of it all along the river. Not just in the fine new
Diesel boats. But in the canals and locks. Soon the whole river would
be a chain of great lakes. For twenty miles above Kuibyshev we
threaded our way through construction works for this enormous dam,
the biggest hydroelectric project in the world. And upriver as far
distant as Gorky they were busy building new wharfs and new ware-
houses high up on the river bank, against the day in 1955 when the
Kuibyshev locks would close and the water would begin to back up.

It was the same up and down the river. The huge new Stalingrad
Dam, the only rival of Kuibyshev. The Gorky Dam. The Molotov
Dam on the Kama. The dams already installed in the upper Volga
and the great Volga-Don Canal.

The old order was changing on the Volga, if slowly. The machine
was replacing the man even on the projects being built by the Ministry of the Interior. For many of these huge tasks were being carried
out by the MVD. It had been the MVD and slave labor which built
the Moscow-Volga Canal just as earlier it had been the MVD and

slave labor which built the White Sea Canal. But now a change had come about. The MVD with its enormous crew of engineers and its vast experience in waterworks and dams was still building, but even the MVD had turned to the machine. It had built the Volga-Don Canal, for instance. But it had used more excavating machines than men, and it was said, while it was participating in such jobs as the Kuibyshev and Stalingrad dams, that they were being erected with hardly any prison labor.

Times were changing on the Volga. That was true. But the pace was not breath-taking. If at Kazan there was a continuous belt conveyor to unload the rubber tires we had taken aboard at Gorky there were Volga stevedores at every other port to haul the hundred- and two-hundred-kilo sacks of potatoes, the heavy farm machinery and the weighty boxes from the hold.

Even the first-class passengers on the *Lermontov* were shocked at the way the peasants were treated. The peasants came aboard at every landing stage. Usually they traveled only two or three stops but sometimes they stayed aboard for two or three days. They staggered up the gangplank, women for the most part, their backs bent under the weight of the long curved carrying poles which fitted around their necks and shoulders and to which they attached their burdens.

They were carrying almost anything you could think of—a side of beef, half a veal, a whole fat sheep, a pig, two hundred pounds of potatoes, a hundred pounds of flour, an iron bed and mattress. They wore white kerchiefs on their heads and cotton dresses and even though it was hot July many of them still had on their padded jackets. Sweat streamed down their faces and soaked through their clothes. Some wore the bark shoes I had often read about but never seen before.

When they got aboard they disappeared into the murky depths of the freight hold. These were the fourth-class passengers and they were sold nothing but passage on the boat. It was up to them to find some corner of the hold, atop a packing box, in a corner under a field cultivator, or on the dirty deck where they could sit or stand or lie for the duration of the journey. Once or twice, dirty-faced, whiskered men appeared at the first-class restaurant, up from these Lower

Depths, trying to buy beer or vodka. Natasha, the blonde buxom first-class waitress, chased them out with a torrent of swift-spoken invective and they slunk out of the first-class restaurant with its bright lights, white tablecloths and sparkling crystal glasses, cursing under their breaths. I could almost imagine them saying: "Comes the Revolution . . ."

So bad were the conditions in the hold that the first-class passengers got to talking about it one night. This, too, they called a *skandal*. They said the shipping company should not be permitted to sell space to people unless it was prepared to give them a place to ride. One knowing man whom I took to be a director of some small factory shook his head cynically.

"It is all because of their profits plan," he said. "They are interested only in making the plan. They don't care how they do it."

As we plodded down the Volga, day after day, I became more and more struck by one circumstance. Here I was completely surrounded by Russians, talking with them and listening to them talk, and day after day went by with hardly a word about politics. I could understand that they might show some tact in speaking to me about political matters since, after all, they knew I was an American. But what about themselves? Weren't they interested in politics?

I noticed that I was one of the few passengers who usually bought a paper when we stopped at one city or another and most of the people spent their time reading novels rather than current literature. One girl was reading a new Russian translation of Stendhal's *The Red and the Black*. Another was reading a collection of Chekhov short stories. One of the schoolteachers was rereading *Anna Karenina*. And I saw one of the younger boys with Cooper's *The Last of the Mohicans*, much dog-eared.

The evidence was strong that these people who, plainly, were a cross-section of Russia's upper middle class were simply disinterested in political matters. Nor did I think this disinterest was inspired by the fact that there was, as I quickly discovered, a detachment of four plainclothes men aboard the ship to keep an eye on me. Unlike the details in Siberia these men carried out their job quietly and inconspicuously. I never set foot ashore without two of them for company, and usually one of them had me under observation while I was on deck. But I doubted very much if the passengers had detected these agents, even though one of them made a habit of pretending to fall asleep in a deck chair outside my cabin window when I retired at night.

No, it was apparent that the disinterest of the passengers in politics was genuine. Not that they were disinterested in the United States. Whenever I got into conversation with one of them they wound up by asking questions about life in America, ordinary questions as to how the people lived, how much clothes cost, what kind of wages people earned. And often questions about American novels, plays and films.

Once or twice I was asked why the United States wanted to make war on Russia. This was a question I had been frequently asked by Russians in recent years. When I replied, as I invariably did, that the United States had no desire whatever to make war on Russia my questioner looked relieved. Occasionally, another question would follow. Why, if the United States didn't want to make war on Russia, did the Soviet papers say that she did? My reply to that was that I didn't know why the Soviet newspapers made this statement, that it was not correct and that, if I were my questioner, I would find that circumstance worth thinking about. From the look of puzzlement which usually appeared in the Russian's eyes I could see that this often started an unexpected train of thought—which was what I hoped it would do.

But even such questions were rare aboard the S.S. *Lermontov* where talk seemed eternally to revolve about the weather, the price of tomatoes in the local bazaar, and did you really think that thin little blonde Russian girl and that handsome dark Oriental-looking boy, a Kazakh or Uzbek, perhaps, were married as they said or had they just sneaked off on this trip to be together?

But what of the new regime? What of Stalin? I heard no talk about either, except for the discussion about Ulyanovsk, unless the constant conversation about new television sets, new automobiles and new refrigerators could be taken as a sign that the government was on the right track with its campaign to increase the supply of consumers' goods.

As for the goods themselves there was little evidence in the stores

of the Volga towns, except for Stalingrad and Gorky. Men and
women still came aboard the boat at almost every small stop, trying
to buy rare foods, such as white bread, bottled beer and sugar. There
seemed to be no shortage of bread anywhere but it was black or
brown bread in the country towns. Beer was scarce everywhere as
I had found in Siberia, as well. Sugar was to be had in all cities but
not in all landing stages at all times.

I could see from the cities and town that it was going to be a long
time before the impact of the new government would be felt very
strongly in this Volga region. Volga *matushka*, the Russians called it.
Volga, dear little mother. It was that all right and even the arrival
of the push-button river was not going to change some things—the
churches, for example.

For up and down the Volga it was still the churches which
dominated the scene, despite the new dams and locks. And I had an
idea that the domination was not just in the field of architecture,
either. I watched the women stream in and out of the great cathedral
at Saratov in the early-morning hours, making their way through
the dozens of beggars and the hundreds of pigeons on the portico.
And I saw them in the cathedral of Rostov's central square. Watching those strong Russian peasant faces as they knelt in prayer and
bowed their foreheads to the floor I thought to myself that it would
take a great deal more than revolution or communism or terror
or propaganda to shake the power of the Russian Church or the
simple faith of the Russian peasant in his God and his priest.

Back in Moscow now a new propaganda campaign had been
started against the Church and I could understand why. Because
since the crisis days of World War II when Stalin and the old
Patriarch Sergius had signed their virtual concordat the Church
had waxed and grown.

Now, for six years at Easter time I had been going out to Zagorsk,
the famous old monastery forty miles northeast of Moscow for this
greatest of Eastern Church holidays. Each year more believers came.
Now some twenty-five or thirty thousand gathered inside the ancient
monastery walls.

Only last Easter I had stood in the nave of the ancient cathedral
beside which Boris Godunov is buried. At midnight I had listened to

the great bells of the church peal out. I had heard the resounding iron knock at the church door as the holy procession with its golden icons, its gilded church banners, its incense and burning candles, completed the circuit of the cathedral. I had listened to the swelling chorus as the procession re-entered the church . . . "*Kristos voskres* . . . *Kristos voskres* . . . Christ is arisen." And with the multitude I had stood, small pink burning candle in hand, amid the smell of incense and sweet branches of balsam and spruce, as the Metropolitan read out his blessing and gave to each of us a red-dyed egg marked with the sacred initials "K.V."

It was impressive. But no more than the drive across the countryside from Moscow to the cathedral, through one village after another. The first time I made the pilgrimage only one village church was open. Now, each village but one along the whole highway had a church and on Saturday afternoon before Easter believers by the thousand streamed toward the churches, carrying their white linen bags with the *pashka,* the *kulitch* and the colored eggs, for the priest to bless.

Even in Moscow each year brought more and more people into the churches. Young people as well as old. For it had become fashionable to be married in church and, as I knew, the *babushki* never had stopped taking the children to be baptized regardless of what the parents pretended.

So it was not surprising that the Party had again decided to attack religion but what interested me was the fact that there was no direct assault on the Church. In fact, local authorities were warned against using any "administrative means." Which meant that priests were not to be arrested and churches were not to be closed. For the Church was valuable to the regime. It had supported the state in the desperate days of war. It had offered prayers for Stalin's life and it was a great bulwark of the "peace" campaign. It was no surprise to me when Party Secretary Khrushchev warned Communists against antireligious excesses and against antagonizing the believers.

The Party might campaign against religion but it needed the Church, too, and the people had come to realize this. It was obvious that along the Volga no one had been frightened by this campaign. In fact, I doubted if the believers in Kazan or Saratov or Cheboksari had even heard that *Pravda* was denouncing "religious superstition," And I was certain that it would make little difference to them if they did hear about it.

For, the plain truth was that the Party had never devised a means of replacing the Church in those great hours of a man's life—birth, marriage and death. The Zags office would never be a substitute for the marriage crowns of the Orthodox faith nor would the Party orator find words more comforting than the benediction of the priest.

Life was short but the Volga was long and the Church was eternal. Marx was dead and Lenin was dead and Stalin was dead but Christ lived on in the hearts of the simple people. And the simple people were still Russia. Always, century after century, there had been a man in the Kremlin who ruled them, who oppressed them. Now there were new men in Moscow. But the life of the people went on. It was like the Volga. I knew by the time I reached Rostov that the Soviet might install as many push buttons and conveyors as it wished along the course of the river. It could banish the *burlaki* and replace the chorus of the Volga boatman with a Party hymn. But the river would go on and the people would go on and Russia would go on. . . . Changing—of course. But slowly. Very slowly.

Volga *matushka! Matushka rossiya!*

XVIII

"X" Minus Stalin

BEFORE I left New York to return to Moscow in early 1954 I wrote out a brief memorandum in which I tried to summarize, largely for my own clarity in thinking, the Russian position on the eve of the Berlin conference.

In this I said that Russia's power potential might be now calculated by the formula "X minus Stalin" instead of "X plus Stalin." The X in the formula represented the sum total of resources, physical and human, available to Russia—her own and her allies'.

Now, after criss-crossing Siberia, penetrating the depths of Central Asia, voyaging down the Volga and motoring back up through the Ukraine I felt that I had as accurate a general idea of the strengths and weaknesses of the Soviet Union as any foreigner was likely to obtain, although I admit that the X in the formula still represented the traditional unknown quantity in many respects.

Having seen a little of Berlin and Poland and inquired of others who had seen much more I felt fairly competent to judge the value of the European satellites and East Germany. The Russian strength in all these countries and particularly in Germany, seemed to me to be primarily a military one. They provided a glacis, a *cordon sanitaire* in reverse—a military asset but a political weakness.

The great mystery of Russia's foreign relations, however, was China. I had thought for several years that I could detect small symptoms of strain in Russo-Chinese relations. But I used the word "detect" in the most literal sense. So carefully did Russia and China guard all details of their collaboration that it required the combined talents of Sherlock Holmes and, possibly, Mr. Moto, to find out anything at all. This in itself struck me as suspicious. If all was well why so much secrecy?

Obviously, the Sino-Russian alliance was the hard core of foreign policy in both countries, particularly since it was in the Far East where the great tensions with the United States were concentrated. Everyone knew that Russia and China were obligated to come to each other's aid in case of major war. But what were the limits? Why did China intervene openly in Korea while Russia sedulously avoided formal military commitment? Of course they were allied in their support of North Korea but the blood was Chinese.

Assuming that the two powers had no military differences (although the enormous military establishment I saw at Chita, on the Mongolian frontier, and at Khabarvosk, on the Manchurian border, and the delay in Soviet evacuation of Port Arthur might be subject to another interpretation), was everything going smoothly in the political and economic fields?

I did not believe so and my opinion was not changed by the new batch of agreements announced in October, 1954, when Khrushchev and other Moscow higher-ups went out to Peiping. These agreements, in all probability, were negotiated when the Chinese Foreign Minister Chou En-lai was in Moscow at the close of the Geneva conference.

Molotov gave a reception for Chou on that occasion at Spiridonovka Palace. It was the last Soviet function which I attended before leaving Russia and one of the most revealing so far as the mystery of relations between the two powers was concerned.

Chou indulged in some very pointed remarks. He was obviously in a mood of great self-satisfaction and confidence. He did not behave like a man who felt in any way beholden to his Russian hosts. He was polite to Molotov and respectful to Malenkov but quite sharp to most of the other Russians present.

It was a public occasion and foreign diplomats were sitting at the same table with Chou and the Russians. Foreign correspondents, myself included, stood at the open door of the dining room, ears cocked.

During most of the evening Chou elected to speak English and it was this language which he used for his most biting sallies. He directed them toward Mikoyan and Kaganovich, who did not speak English. However, he said he had no apologies since neither of them had bothered to learn Chinese. Chou told Mikoyan that considering how many dealings he had had with the Chinese it was about time he learned their language. He, Chou, had learned a good deal of Russian. He spoke a few sentences to show he spoke the truth and then asked Mikoyan, in English, what he proposed to do. Mikoyan said Chinese was very difficult. No harder than Russian, snapped Chou. If Mikoyan would kindly come around to the Chinese Embassy at ten o'clock the next morning he, Chou, would see that he got his first lesson.

When Kaganovich tried to intervene Chou choked him off, saying testily: "There's no excuse for you people."

I felt sure Chou was reflecting China's bitterness at the parsimony and cheap bargaining displayed by Russia in economic negotiations. I remembered, and I was sure neither the Russians nor Chinese had forgotten, a snub administered in this very Spiridonovka Palace not more than eighteen months before to a group of Chinese trade negotiators. At a Russian reception the Chinese had been excluded from the inner dining room where Chou was being feted and relegated to an outside room where a very junior Russian diplomat greeted them and then vanished even before the toasts began.

Another fact which had long made me suspicious about the true state of Sino-Russian relations was the persistent and long-continued absences of the Chinese Ambassador from Moscow. With such protocol-conscious people as the Chinese and the Russians this could only be a sign of coolness.

And Molotov himself seemed to be a little nervous about relations. When the British Labourite delegation passed through Moscow en route to China he expressed hope it did not propose to try to improve Chinese-British relations at the expense of Sino-Russian relations. Not the kind of remark a statesman who was fully confident of his ally would make.

For all the fuss and noise Moscow had made about getting Communist China into the United Nations, giving it great-power recognition, etc., I had always thought that Russia actually felt much more comfortable about the Chinese when Moscow was handling all their relations with the outside world.

Russians, possibly for psychological reasons, never seem to feel very secure in alliances based on equality. They demonstrated this by their suspiciousness in their wartime relations with Britain and the United States. The Moscow-Peiping relationship was a great-power relation and that put an immediate strain on the Soviet.

However, so long as the hard line of our policy operated to keep the two big Communist powers joined in mutual defense all these considerations seemed to me purely academic.

I had felt before Korea (and in this I think Admiral Kirk concurred) that the United States could damage or strain Russo-Chinese relations by a shrewd foreign policy in the Far East, predicated under the proper conditions on recognition of the Peiping regime. Communist aggression in Korea, of course, wrecked this chance.

But as I watched the lightning play of emotions on Chou's face that evening in Spiridonovka Palace I wondered if the time might not be coming again when we should think about this possibility. I knew very well that the architects of American foreign policy at the time refused even to consider such an approach. But I also knew that these architects held no monopoly on diplomatic wisdom or intuition and I knew many diplomats, non-British as well as British, who disagreed with the State Department.

I hadn't learned anything at Spiridonovka about the secret military clauses in the Sino-Russian treaty and I still didn't know why China fought in Korea while Russia stayed out, although I could guess. But I was now sure of one thing. My suspicion about lack of ease in relations between the two countries and their basic conflicts, rooted in factors of geography, spheres of influenue and psychology, had some foundation.

If at the beginning of 1954 I felt we should move slowly in any question involving Russia until we were more certain of the stability of the ruling junta, by summer I felt our policy was dragging badly behind the evolution of Russia's new line. That is to say that our attitude of inflexibility seemed to serve the Russian purpose better than our own.

For it was in the diplomatic field that the Soviet "new look" was achieving its greatest success. Russia was concentrating on our two chief allies, Britain and France, and partly by Soviet skill and partly by American ineptness, she was making gains.

The big card with the British was trade—trade with Russia and trade with China. The Russians were capitalizing on the natural British resentment at being economically dependent upon us. I would not mean to suggest the British might trade their relationship with the U.S.A. for one with the U.S.S.R. but the Russians had alienated more British sentiment than we realized.

The Russians dangled big trade orders before British manufacturers, closing enough to keep interest alive while constantly pressing for the sale of items barred under American-sponsored trade restrictions. This built up pressure for relaxation of the bans and resentment at the United States for preventing the English from earning good profits on deals with Russia.

And British good will was solicited through the encouragement of a steady stream of delegations and visits. Not a week went by without British guests in the Hotel National. They were well treated. So were British diplomats. When two underlings of the British Embassy got drunk and beat up half a dozen Soviet policemen they were permitted quietly to leave Russia without charges and without publicity. But when two American Embassy wives got into trouble about snapping some pictures *Pravda* turned it into a *bolshoi skandal!*

The soft technique was also used with the French. An agreement for exchange of students between the Sorbonne and Moscow University. A joint air service between Paris and Moscow, via Prague. Absence of editorial attacks when the showing of the Bolshoi ballet was banned at the Paris Opera. Release of a French priest from the Vorkuta labor camp. Permission to a famous French photographer to take pictures at will throughout Russia.

These little favors were part of a general policy which Molotov embarked on as soon as he took over the Foreign Office after Stalin's death. He decided to re-establish certain norms of Russian diplomatic behavior and that Russia would stop the calculated program of antagonism which Stalin had insisted upon.

He removed the large detachment of secret police who had been

assigned to harass the Yugoslav chargé d'affaires and promised the
chargé that relations between the two countries would be normalized,
as they were. He called for resumption of diplomatic relations with
Israel, broken as an offshoot of the Doctors' Plot. He agreed to give
visas to nationals of a number of embassies who had been virtual
prisoners in Moscow—an Englishman who had not left the British
Embassy for nearly five years, several old French ladies, the son of
the former Chilean Ambassador and his Russian wife, six Russian
wives of American citizens, etc.

When Stalin died both the United States and Britain were under
ultimatums to move from their embassy buildings close to the
Kremlin—the United States from Mokhovaya Street and the British
from the Sofiskaya Embankment. Within a week an apologetic
Foreign Office man phoned both embassies and told them they need
not move, unless they wished. The British welcomed the reprieve
and stayed put. The Americans, either to show pique or simply because of bureaucratic ineptitude (moving plans were far advanced),
insisted on hauling the Stars and Stripes down from the building
where it had waved in the eyes of the Kremlin for twenty years. It
now flies from a building in which Soviet stars were imbedded by
the Russians in the exterior décor on the Sadovaya Circle, a mile
and a half away. The new building may have been better in some
way unknown to me, but it is my contention that we had something to gain and nothing to lose in taking advantage of this Russian gesture. By a calculated policy of small favors and courteous
conversation the Russians for the first time in decades were winning
favorable comment among Western Europeans. Along with the
favors went a gentle patter of talk about Europe for the Europeans.
Anti-American but merely echoing what many Europeans said
themselves. No Marxian overtones. No Party admonitions. All
soundly based on the most effective of sales principles—telling the
customer what he wants to hear.

But beyond the soft talk with Europeans the Russians privately
hinted that ultimately they wanted to arrive at the big show—negotiations between Russia and the United States. When I heard suggestions like this I inevitably thought about Kennan and his analysis of
the situation.

For I could not doubt that in one respect Russia's new rulers shared a belief which Stalin strongly held. That was that in the world today there were only two really first-rank powers, Russia and the United States.

I had no doubt that the new managers of Russia felt that under suitable conditions these two powers could insure each other peace and prosperity by mutually agreeing to respect each other's interests—at least for a time.

I had no doubt, also, that the new regime was willing to go farther to reach an agreement than the late Generalissimo. But the words which troubled me in that sentence were "at least for a time."

For in any such agreement Russia's rulers and only Russia's rulers would know how fast the minutes were ticking off on the clock by which they were measuring the period which they had in mind when they said "at least for a time."

It was like that phrase which *Pravda* so often used about "coexistence" of communism and capitalism "for a long time." How long was a "long time"?

It depended so much on the men who were doing the measuring. Suppose it were the Zhukov group of the Army. They impressed me as conservative men, not likely to be hasty in their judgment. Like Army men almost everywhere they tended to be professionals —career soldiers rather than politicians or party doctrinaires. So long as these marshals who had led the Soviet Army in World War II remained at the top I thought Army policy would act as a brake against adventures.

But how many years would they stay on top? And what about the younger men coming up, the ones who had been captains and majors in the war, the ones who might have had no way of knowing the falsity of the propaganda which said that Russia smashed Hitler alone and unaided?

What happened when these men got control and had the right to set Russian military forces into motion?

Each year the X in the formula "X minus Stalin" grew more formidable.

Each year four million more metric tons of steel.

Each year four million more Russian souls.

And the rates were rising.

Russian steel production had risen from a fifth of ours to a fourth, from a fourth to a third. In another year it would be close to half our rate. Most of that rise had occurred during my own years in Russia. And in battle effectiveness I well knew that a pound of Russian steel was worth three of ours because Russia still lived in a wooden age and we depended on tin cans and automobiles.

Russia had 225,000,000 people. We had 160,000,000. Not to forget 600,000,000 Chinese whom we kept locked in her arms. But, our armchair strategists said, we have the A-bomb. We have the H-bomb. We have rockets and goodness knows what other new-fangled contraptions.

Somehow the talk about our A-bomb and H-bomb stockpiles had never seemed conclusive to me. Not unless we were going to stage an "atomic Pearl Harbor" on the Russians and I could not conceive of any American sinking to such infamy.

While I presumed that our science and technology would manage to keep a step ahead of the Russians I was not one to minimize Soviet ability to concentrate her energies. In my years in the Soviet I certainly never had stumbled on any nuclear bomb secrets but the application of common or garden-variety sense had enabled me to make certain deductions.

I felt fairly certain a great nuclear plant, probably for the production of hydrogen bombs, was being built in Eastern Siberia, near the Angara River not far from Irkutsk. I had not managed to get a glimpse of the huge Angara River hydroelectric plant when I flew over that area but I could see no other purpose to which such enormous quantities of energy might be devoted in that remote area.

From a variety of small clues it seemed probable that another nuclear works was located in the vicinity of Novosibirsk on the River Ob and that a new, larger installation was being constructed in that region.

Russia's speed in creating A- and H-bombs might have surprised some Western politicians, but I could honestly say it had not surprised me in the least nor did I think it had surprised anyone who had taken the trouble to familiarize himself with the facts of Russia's physical and nuclear research and theory. Russia had long been a leader in this field and if you took account of the aid which she got from German scientists plus espionage information from the West the results were fully expectable.

And several times a year in Moscow I had had occasion to witness demonstrations of Russian ability to match steps with us in another vital technical field—the field of jet aircraft.

Backed by military resources of the quality and scope of Russia's nuclear weapons and her jet aircraft I could well understand the self-confident approach which the new Russian Government had adopted toward foreign relations. Her military power was enormous and it was even more effective now that a certain concentration had been effected as a result of the partial liquidation of the peripheral belligerent areas in the Far East, of the fighting in Korea and Indo-China.

Not that the new Russian leaders were fooling themselves any longer about the real nature of nuclear warfare. Stalin had acted as though atom bombs were a kind of new trench mortar, uncomfortable but indecisive. One of the first things Malenkov did was to dispel that notion. He frankly told the Russians that atomic war meant the destruction of the whole world, not just of capitalism as Stalin had said. He accepted the judgment of thinking men everywhere on this question. If the Soviet still made no move to train its citizenry in atomic defense at least it quietly and without fanfare brought to completion the world's greatest underground A-bomb shelter, deep tunnels under central Moscow. Ostensibly they were additions to the subway system.

Where then were the Russian weaknesses?

They existed and I thought I could put my finger on most of them. So could almost anyone who had been in Russia for a few years. And the Russians, of course, had known about them for so long that sometimes they even forgot their existence.

The weaknesses of Russia, as I saw them, were the product of two things—Russian history and Communist methods. They were rooted deeply in Russian and Communist inhumanity to their fellow men. Too much of industry, too much of agriculture had been coercive too long.

By now I had seen a good many of the horrors of Russian life—

Siberia, convict labor, the grim life of the exiles in Central Asia, the poverty and deprivations of Russian rural life, the stench and drunkenness of the cities. I knew the hatred and the apathy of the minority groups toward Moscow and toward the Great Russians.

The foundation of no regime was firm when it was erected over such bottomless pits of inhumanity, dark sinks of evil. Yet Stalin had made it run. He had brought it through a fearsome war—at a fearsome price. He had done it with the knout. For generations Russian rulers, in the end, had solved every problem with the knout.

But now Stalin was no longer there. The formula was "X minus Stalin." And if X (in this case the Russian material potential), as I thought, was greater than it had been in the formula "X plus Stalin" still the sum total was smaller because the junta was not as great as Stalin. But one could not count on the junta remaining passive and inactive. In fact, we had every indication to the contrary. For these men were showing a striking flexibility and adaptability in their handling of domestic as well as foreign problems.

They were consciously and deliberately seeking to add to their strength by facing up to some of the harshest and least pleasant realities of the Stalin epoch and at many points, as I had seen, they had broken sharply, dramatically and decisively with the sterile and rigid precepts of the Generalissimo. The break was as sweeping in some respects as Lenin's substitution of NEP, his famous New Economic Policy, for the earlier system of war communism.

True, the Siberia I had seen was little changed, but something was stirring in the vast prison system. I had heard of more than a few rumblings in the labor camps, the most notable of which was the demonstration and strike carried out in the Vorkuta camps up in the Pechora coal region in the summer of 1953.

The Vorkuta camps, about fifty in number, were one of the three most remote areas for concentrating political and criminal prisoners. The others were the Yakutsk region, which I visited, and, farthest east, Magadan on the Sea of Okhotsk.

A demonstration had broken out in Vorkuta in July, 1953, apparently on receipt of news of the arrest of Beriya. The strike started among a group of prisoners who had been transferred to Vorkuta from the Karaganda prison coal fields as punishment for bad conduct. Some two hundred prisoners and guards were killed in the Vorkuta rioting, but an eyewitness who reached Moscow denied reports of large-scale executions. He said some ringleaders were shipped out, probably to Magadan.

The demonstration obviously stirred Moscow and a large investigatory commission headed by a General Derevyenko was sent to the scene and carried out an inquiry in which prisoners testified freely and complaints were aired.

Some of the worst features of prison life had been remedied, such as the mixing of political prisoners with depraved criminals who ran the camps with the complicity of the MVD guards. Other ameliorative measures followed. Prisoners were now allowed to write to relatives and receive mail. Wives might visit husbands for two weeks once a year and during the visit couples might stay together in special transient barracks. Prisoners were given permission to send money to their families. And working norms were revised so that they could earn more money.

I heard talk in Moscow that further steps might be taken—that young political prisoners who had been under seventeen when they were sent to camp might be released. And it was known that large numbers of persons sentenced to ten-year terms at the end of the war on charges of collaboration with the Nazis (prisoners of war and persons who remained in German-occupied areas) were due to be released in 1955.

A delegation of left-wing British lawyers headed by D. N. Pritt came to Moscow and was permitted to make some firsthand inquiries into the prisons, the first such inspection in many years.

Something seemed to be stirring all right, that was certain, although I was completely convinced that so long as the basic system remained, so long as the Soviet maintained a huge industrial establishment, run by police officers and dependent upon a constant supply of prisoners for labor, nothing fundamental would be changed. For the fault lay in the system, not in the way the system functioned. To be sure, the police were guilty of cruelty. To be sure, the guards were thieves and grafters. To be sure, the camps were inhumanely run. You could change the guards and improve the camps. But just so long as the police needed labor hands for their mines in Karaganda, their timber establishments in the north and their factories in the east—for just that period of time there was going to be a constant incentive to find new "political offenders"; to declare new classes of citizens "politically unreliable"; to find fresh cadres of field and factory hands to feed the insatiable maw of Siberia and Asia. Slave traders always found good excuses to stay in business.

I did not know to what extent the junta appreciated this circumstance, but so far the small ways and means about which I heard rumors were all based on amelioration. Not on basic reform.

Of course, Russia might only be in the first stage of something more fundamental and far-reaching than I sensed. Perhaps the junta was going further in its domestic program. But, if that was so, the Russians themselves seemed to be somewhat skeptical. They seemed to me to be somewhat less than impressed with the new look. While they spoke a bit more easily and freely and while I sensed a lightening of the mood of the street crowds, no Russian was falling all over himself to acquire new foreign friends. Wait-and-see still seemed to predominate.

After twenty-five years of Stalin terror, it was, I thought, going to take considerable time to convince the Russians that it was even safe to take the new Government at its word.

I sensed a certain apathy toward the changes the government proposed. If the visit of the Comédie-Française had stimulated the enthusiasm of Moscow's intelligentsia the call of the Party propagandists for freer discussions had had little result and the attacks on Pomerentzev, Zoshchenko and Pasternak had caused the writers and artists to draw in their necks again.

The atmosphere reminded me of that which greeted the reforms of Czar Alexander II, who came to the throne in 1855 after the death of the tyrannical Nicholas I and brought an end to serfdom. Cowed by twenty-five years of oppression by Nicholas, the Russian public of the mid-nineteenth century was supine in its acceptance of Alexander's reforms.

Much the same seemed to be true today—and for the same reason.

On the other hand, little things which cost Moscow nothing were bringing in big rewards of foreign good will. I had often heard it said that Moscow deserved no credit for stopping doing things which no decent or civilized country should ever have done in the first place.

None the less, when her new rulers liberalized their visa policy and began to admit a few token groups of American students at the very time when the United States refused visas to some Soviet students because they were Communists, *Pravda* didn't have to write an editorial about an American iron curtain. Our British and French friends made the point themselves.

But setting aside these surface factors, what was important and what would always be important was the Russian people. When I had been in America I had often been asked about the people, particularly by persons who felt there must be large groups in Russia eager and ready to revolt and throw off their chains. I had never felt I could give much encouragement to such ideas and now having seen MVD-land with my own eyes I did not believe that anything of consequence might be expected from the victims of the police.

Only rarely had I met an individual like the German lad in Stalinabad whose spirit and energy sufficiently survived the hardships of his life so that he managed to keep from sinking into the abyss of apathy and resignation which was the usual result of life in the labor camps or in forced residence in the East.

The ordinary Russian, sent to the East, turned to vodka rather than thoughts of revolution or revenge and with Slav fatalism sank quietly and dully into the morass of gray life as I had seen in Yakutsk.

No. I did not think much was to be expected in that direction and I felt we had an unfortunate tendency toward self-deception and wishful thinking about the possibilities for resistance under a dictatorship. Neither the will to act nor the possibility to act was as likely as we tended to believe. I could remember too well the false hopes which were pinned on the anti-Hitlerite Germans. Just as soon as Hitler marched they would rise in his rear and tear him down. Well, we had seen the results of that kind of dreamy thinking. The only elements who ever did rise against the German dictator were a handful of idealistic but confused and inept products of the Prussian General Staff. The great masses of "liberal" Germans, the famous Socialist millions, the Communist millions—where had they gone? Into Hitler's battalions, goose-stepping and heiling with the best of them.

So, in case of war, the Russian masses would go marching away just as they always had done so long as they believed and their Government was able to convince them that the war was not of its making, that it was a war of defense. That Mother Russia had been attacked. That point seemed vital to me. I did not believe the present Government at least for some years would be able to launch a war beyond Russia's frontiers except under conditions which would enable them to present it to their own people as a war of defense.

In that case the masses would march. As they had against Napoleon. Against the Kaiser. Against Hitler.

It would be difficult, I felt, for Russia's new rulers to disguise aggressive war in a defensive camouflage—especially if the West could avoid playing into their propagandists' hands. Difficult but not, perhaps, impossible. Was there any present incentive for them to go to war? Not too much. Not so long as those four million tons of steel and those four million new men and women came rolling in each year. Not so long as the stockpiles of A-bombs and H-bombs grew larger and larger and the fleets of jet aircraft bigger and more powerful.

They felt, I was certain, that time was working on their side.

Not, I thought, that they had the slightest moral compunction against war or against attacking the United States. For Russia's new rulers, like the dictator whom they replaced, were Communists. I did not believe for one minute that in ultimate goals they differed from Stalin and I felt confident that they were just as cynical as he was about getting what they wanted.

They had not, in all probability, hesitated at murder in order to come to power. They would not, certainly, hesitate at war to stay in power.

But while they had no objection in principle to war, they also believed, in accordance with their doctrine, that the victory of their side was inevitable. They were going to win whether there was war or not. Capitalism was doomed. Communism was the wave of the future. Unlike Lenin and his cohorts of forty years before these were not fiery revolutionists. They were middle-aged products of Communist schooling. They were practical men. When they talked about "peaceful coexistence" and the "competition of the two systems" they talked in the comfortable tones of the directors of a great corporation which was somewhat younger and newer than its principal rival. They did not believe they had to buy out or set about to destroy their rival because they were sure the natural hardening of corporate arteries would do the job for them. Much easier and simpler just to plug along and let the capitalist old fogies sink into bankruptcy.

Meantime, they did what they could to help the "decaying" process.

I was convinced that the Communists were totally mistaken in their analysis of the world's economic and social history. I felt that capitalism in the years since Marx promulgated his famous theory had demonstrated time and again that his basic postulates were faulty.

I had never been alarmed or frightened at the possibility that communism might be able to displace capitalism in any kind of competition.

But there was another aspect about Russia which concerned me much more seriously. I felt that Russia's expansionist, aggressive tendencies arose not alone out of her communism, which well might prove to be only a phase of her existence, but out of something much, much deeper.

Looking at history it seemed to me that since the time of Ivan, for nearly four hundred years, Russia had been growing and growing. There were setbacks, to be sure. But if you measured history in fifty-year segments you could see Russia getting bigger and bigger and stronger and stronger.

The nineteenth century had been one long struggle between England and Russia in which an armistice only was signed when Germany arose as a third world force, an even more aggressive and expansionist power.

It looked to me like the twentieth century and, perhaps, the twenty-first could well be one long struggle between the United

States, which had inherited England's role, and Russia. In many ways, of course, the Communists were more formidable opponents than the Romanovs, but perhaps we were more formidable than Victorian England.

While I supposed that my viewpoint would be rather depressing to easy-minded persons who were forever hunting for capsule solutions of foreign problems (not realizing that history is a stream and not a millpond and that the "solution" of a foreign problem merely creates new problems), I did not think it was founded in pessimism at all.

Because if my analysis was correct it did not preclude settlements of outstanding questions between the United States and Russia, from time to time—realistic settlements of the type which Kennan had envisaged, the kind made by two estranged people who must go on living under the same roof or perish.

It meant, to be sure, that we would go on living in a world where there was a threat of war. But in what way did that differ from the past? It certainly meant that we must at all times maintain a certain superiority of forces over the great colossus of Eurasia but surely our free-enterprise system was more than capable of this. We must maintain our position of strength, regardless of whether we talked with Russia, for to be second best in a nuclear world was unthinkable folly. And certainly we must maintain our system of allies and alliances to help counterbalance the enormous mass weight of Russia, and it seemed equally certain that we should exercise enough Yankee common sense and prudence to try to apply a little honey as well as vinegar to the critical joints in the great Communist machine—and devote a special kind of attention to the link between Russia and China, of course. And some of the other links as well.

People who thought that the threat of war could be banished from our lives were surely the greatest idealists of all time. Never in man's history had it been banished and who were we so overweening in our pride to think we had the key to Paradise?

Nor did I lean toward the gloom-mongers, the "let's drop the A-bomb now" school of unprincipled piracy. They were nothing but world criminals. England and Russia had survived a hundred years of rivalry and tension at times just as acute as any between Russia and the United States and, with the exception of the Crimean War, had never come to blows. Why couldn't we do as well?

Certainly the nineteenth century was an uneasy century, although, looking back at it, we think of it as a golden era.

No. I was not returning to the United States after nearly six years in Russia as a pessimist. Nor as an optimist. But, I hoped, as something of a realist. The world was not approaching Utopia but it was not coming to an end, either. If we based ourselves on realism and practicality, we would survive as had the generations before us.

We had new and formidable opponents in Russia. They were using new tactics and they had scored some gains. Specifically in creating a climate of opinion in Western Europe somewhat more favorable to them and somewhat less favorable to the United States.

Their tactics were different. More flexible and therefore more dangerous. Their manners were more pleasant and their words more polite. But we must never forget that they had the same goal as Stalin. We had not done so well against Russia's new alienation techniques. We had been slow to admit there even was a change.

But we had inexhaustible reserves and I had no doubt about our eventual victory.

There was only one memory which concerned me seriously as I boarded the Aeroflot plane at Vnukovo Field on a sunshiny morning in September, 1954, and left Russia for the last time. I had had no good-bys to say to Russians for although I had come to know many people I had made no Russian friends during five long years.

But one person lingered in my mind. This was the architect whom I had met in Leningrad on that winter's night so long ago, the man who was looking for a new "truth" and who found only propaganda on the American broadcast. Here was a man who long since had learned that there were worse things on earth than death. If now he and men like him could only learn that there were better things in life, then the stockpiles of A-bombs would not cast such long shadows.

I hoped that if ever he should tune in on the Voice of America again he would hear the real voice of the real America. The voice of freedom. Of liberty. And justice for all. One nation indivisible . . .

Index

Set in Caledonia
Format by D. F. Bradley
Manufactured by The Haddon Craftsmen, Inc.
Published by Harper & Brothers, New York

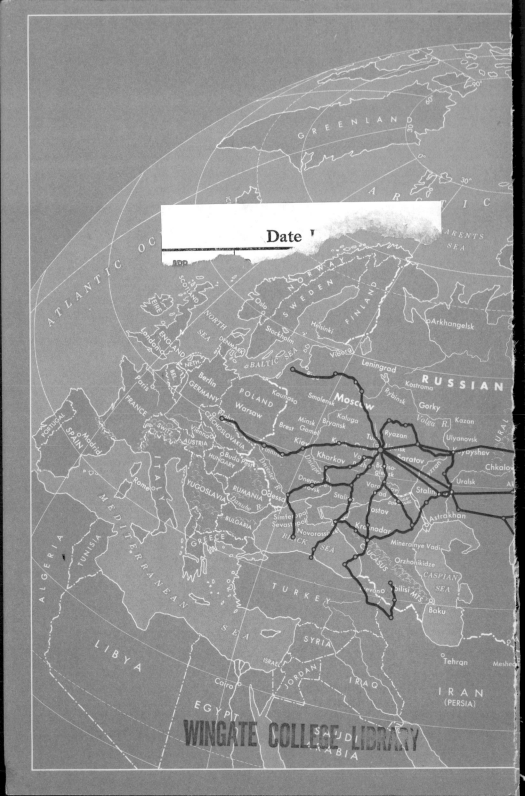